AT DEATH'S DOOR . . .

Susan, wrapped in her worn brown terry cloth robe, peered through the leaded glass panels on the front doors.

"Who's there?" she called.

"Deputy McGowen," he shouted. "I've got a felony warrant for your arrest. Open the door."

Susan grabbed the telephone and dialed 9-1-1.

"What's your emergency?" the operated answered.

"Yes, there's . . . at my door," she said, her voice angry and frightened. "I've filed several complaints with him for sexual harassment and I need some help *immediately*."

"Who is at your door?"

"This is a deputy who thinks he owns the world," Susan answered. "My name is Susan White and he's threatened . . ."

Outside, McGowen pounded again on the heavy wood doors. "Open the door or we'll kick it in," he threatened.

Back on the telephone the operator said, "We're going to get someone in route."

"They just broke in!" Susan screamed to the 9-1-1 operator.

McGowen sprinted into the darkened house, his pistol drawn. . . .

A WARRANT TO KILL

A TRUE STORY OF OBSESSION, LIES AND A KILLER COP

KATHRYN CASEY

AVON BOOKS
An Imprint of HarperCollins*Publishers*

A WARRANT TO KILL is a journalistic account of the actual murder investigation of Kent McGowen for the 1992 killing of Susan White in Houston, Texas. The events recounted in this book are true, although some of the names have been changed and identifying characteristics altered to safeguard the privacy of these individuals. The personalities, events, actions, and conversations portrayed in this book have been constructed using court documents, including trial transcripts, extensive interviews, letters, personal papers, research, and press accounts. Quoted testimony has been taken verbatim from trial and pre-trial transcripts and other sworn statements.

AVON BOOKS
An Imprint of HarperCollins*Publishers*
10 East 53rd Street
New York, New York 10022-5299

First Avon Books paperback printing: October 2000

Avon Trademark Reg. U.S. Pat. Off. and in Other Countries, Marca Registrada, Hecho en U.S.A.
HarperCollins® is a trademark of HarperCollins Publishers Inc.

Printed in the U.S.A.

WCD 10 9 8 7 6 5 4 3 2 1

To my family

Acknowledgments

As with any project of this scope, there are many to thank. First, all those who shared their experiences with Kent McGowen and Susan White so freely with me. Many of you are mentioned by name in the book; others are not. You know who you are. Second, my able readers who critiqued the original manuscript: Jane Farrell, Andrea Gross, and Ken Hammond; for her support, Claire Cassidy; my agent, Philip Spitzer; my editor at Avon Books, Sarah Durand; my information guru, Jim Loosen, at JAL Data Services in Seattle; Katie Guillory for her secretarial assistance; private investigator Rob Kimmons; reporter Steve McVicker; and the many capable and honorable members of Houston's law enforcement community I met and interviewed. While this is a book about a bad cop, please remember, such officers are an oddity, not the rule.

I'd also like to thank my editors at *Ladies' Home Journal*: Myrna Blyth, Susan Crandell, Pamela Guthrie O'Brien, and Shana Aborn. It's through my long relationship with each of you and the magazine that I'm able to maintain the freedom to take on such projects.

Author's Note

In an attempt to safeguard the privacy of some individuals, the author has changed their names and altered minor, identifying characteristics; such instances include Sherri Brandt, Pete Rodriguez, Sara Williams, Gary Roberts, Maggie, Alan Jefferies, Beetle, Karen, and the hairdresser, Paul.

All the difficult questions of government relate to the means of restraining those in whose hands are lodged the powers necessary for the protection of all from making bad use of it.

James Mill
(1773–1836)

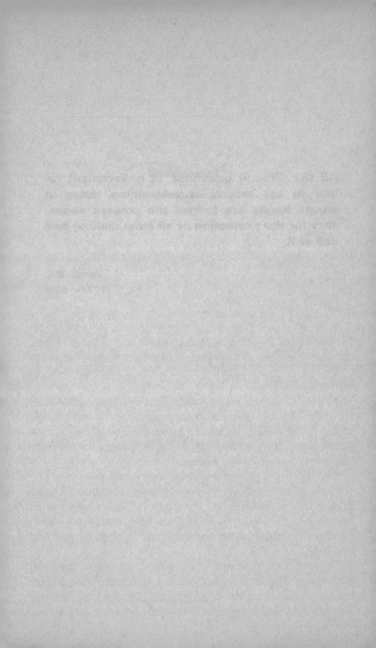

Prologue

—————

"There's a guy here you need to talk to," Alan Jefferies, the piano player, whispered, motioning across the room toward a large, lumbering man seated, arms crossed, at a pianoside stool.

On this, like so many other Friday nights, my husband and I sat in our customary places, on corner stools at the bar, listening to music at Resa's, the back room at Jim & Resa Kelly's Del Frisco's Steakhouse, not far from our suburban Houston home.

"Why?" I asked, only mildly interested.

"His name is Ray Valentine, and he dated Susan White, that woman killed by a cop in Olde Oaks," Alan explained. "They were in here a few weeks ago with another couple, a captain at the sheriff's department and his wife."

I'd read an article on White's death in one of the local papers the day after it happened. Little more than a footnote, the headline read: "Woman Accused of Making Threats Slain by Deputies." According to the article, Susan White had pulled a gun on a deputy serving a warrant for her arrest, and he'd shot in self-defense. I'd noticed it only because the woman lived not far from me. While sad, this particular tragedy didn't appear any more interesting than the plethora of others that cried out from local newspapers. In fact, both the *Houston Chronicle* and the *Houston Post* buried their brief accounts on inside pages.

When I hesitated, Alan, whose break was over, brushed back his thinning dark blond hair and shot me an exasperated look. "A lot of people are saying there's something fishy with this whole thing. Ray says she knew the cop who killed her, that she was afraid of him," he said, turning to walk back to the piano. When I said nothing, he concluded, "He says the cop had been harassing her."

I sighed, openly skeptical. It wasn't unusual for friends, neighbors, anyone who knew me as a writer, to pitch their latest "great story." Rarely did such "hot" tips pan out. Still, Alan and I were friends, and he had a good sense about people. From his perch behind the grand piano, he was ground zero for gossip, and he seemed particularly interested in the death of Susan White, a woman who had frequented Resa's earlier in the summer. This was the second time in a week that he'd mentioned her killing.

"At least talk to him," Alan urged.

Reluctantly, I uprooted myself from the wooden barstool and followed Alan, weaving my way through the maze of diners at candlelit tables, toward the piano. A waitress bustled past, brandishing a platter of raw steaks and a milky-white lobster tail. "This is our New York Strip," she remarked, launching into the merits of tenderloin and extolling the generous weight of the lobster to a group of apparent first-timers.

The place was busy, a not unusual condition.

Over the past decade, Houston's sprawl had traveled

north, resulting in typical suburbia: walled-in subdivisions that each day funneled tens of thousands of white-collar commuters onto freeways that led to the city's skyscrapered downtown. Most residents chose the area for the soaring pine trees, the quiet neighborhoods, and the price tag on a home, a third of those in Houston's close-in suburbs, like River Oaks and Memorial.

Kelly's Del Frisco's was a rarity in an area pocked with characterless chain eateries—a privately owned restaurant with a loyal following, notable enough to actually draw patrons from inside the city. Resa's, the dark-wooded, brick-and-forest-green piano bar my husband and I favored, was the restaurant's secret. With its private entrance, even some regular patrons didn't know it existed. While dinner in the main restaurant veered toward the sedate, on nights when everything clicked at Resa's, the scene resembled a congenial party with a highly diverse crowd. It was the latter I found fascinating—the chance to observe people in a confined space, lubricated by the pouring of generous drinks. From the bar, I eavesdropped on marriage proposals and divorces, business mergers and bankruptcies.

When I approached the piano on this Friday night, I noticed a few familiar faces, including a local romance writer of some repute, an oil-tool manufacturer who drove a white Rolls-Royce, and a saleswoman known for her collection of flamboyant hats. Nodding at the others, I did as Alan asked and introduced myself to Ray Valentine, a man of substantial girth, his bald head wearing a monkish fringe of dark brown hair, his unbuttoned shirt displaying a wide gold coin suspended on a heavy gold chain.

"Alan tells me you believe Susan White knew this deputy, the one who killed her," I said.

"Damn right she knew Kent McGowen. She was scared to death of him. I sat right there with her," he said, the words slurring together as he pointed at a nearby table with a beefy finger. "A month before she died, she told a friend of mine, a captain in the sheriff's department, that he was harassing her, that she was afraid if she didn't do what he wanted, he'd hurt her or her son."

"What did he want?" I asked.

"Sex," Valentine growled.

Inspecting what little remained of his drink, he raised his glass toward the waitress, then turned back to me. I noticed his eyes were moist, whether from emotion or the bar's smoky ambiance, I couldn't tell.

"You know, I didn't believe her," he said, frowning. "I thought she was being hysterical, just flat silly. I didn't think a deputy sheriff, a cop . . . She got so pissed when I didn't believe her. I told her to shut up about it. That she was imagining it."

Valentine fell silent. Around us, people laughed, couples danced, Alan, resettled behind the black-lacquer grand piano, trilled the keys then launched into a melancholy rendering of that piano-bar standard "Unforgettable," his smooth, clear voice amplified to ring over the clamor of the crowd.

"You know one of the last things Susan White said to me?" Ray Valentine challenged, his hand trembling as he swirled his glass of melting ice. He took a quick swig and turned again to me, his rheumy brown eyes focusing intently on mine. "She said, 'One day you'll believe me, but by then I'll be dead, and it'll be because Kent McGowen killed me.' "

My husband and I left Resa's that night and I was haunted by the remorse in the eyes of the man I had just met. Yet Ray Valentine was a stranger in a bar, a brief encounter. I tucked his business card in my purse and promised myself I would phone him in a few days at work, when he was sober.

Despite my initial hesitation, I'd spend more than two years investigating Susan White, Kent McGowen, and the circumstances that led to her killing. In the end, their story became an examination of power, how easily it is granted and how helpless the vulnerable become in its grasp. What I learned would forever change the way I viewed those entrusted with it, especially the deputy who patrolled my neighborhood, the officer behind me as I drove down the quiet suburban streets surrounding my home.

Eventually the key to what really happened that steamy Houston night in August 1992 became clear. Like most cases, it became a search for the truth, a need to know who—if anyone—could be believed.

PART ONE

Susan White

1

August 25, 1992

"Shots fired, one down," a thin voice crackled over the police-band radio at 12:30 on a muggy Houston night. Immediately the call went out, as it always does when a cop shoots a civilian. Ambulances, squad cars, a crime-scene unit, Internal Affairs investigators, and representatives from the district attorney's office all converged in the quiet neighborhood of expensive brick homes amid towering pines bordered by manicured lawns.

By the time Assistant D.A.s Don Smyth and Edward Porter arrived, Susan White, a forty-two-year-old former mortgage broker, was being barreled through the night in the back of an ambulance, one paramedic pounding on her chest as another forced oxygen into her lungs.

Outside, in the backseat of a squad car, White's son, Jason, watched. Seventeen, but small for his age, he'd awakened to the shrill scream of the burglar alarm. Moments later, the pop of gunfire and two uniformed deputies rousted him from bed and pulled him down the stairs and past his mother's darkened bedroom, where another deputy stood above the outline of her thin body covered by a bloody sheet. Despite the summer heat, the boy shivered, his eyes saucer-wide.

Smyth, a wiry man with a ruddy complexion, glanced at the boy, then cornered the detective in charge. "Who's the shooter?" he asked.

The detective pointed to a uniformed deputy in his late twenties who stood jawing with a cache of others. "Kent McGowen," the detective said. "He was with two other deputies, serving a retaliation warrant. She'd threatened a police informant. The deputies told her they had a warrant, but the woman wouldn't open up. They broke down the door. She pulled a gun. McGowen shot her."

It all seemed simple enough, but . . . "Retaliation?" Smyth repeated. Something didn't smell right. He eyed the house and figured it was worth a quarter million, easy. Retaliation, making verbal threats against a police informant, was a third-rate felony, with a bond of $2,000. Where was the urgency? The woman wasn't a flight risk. Why would they break down a door in the high-rent district in the middle of the night to serve a warrant on a trash-heap charge like retaliation?

Smyth pulled Porter to the side. "Cover it like a blanket," he whispered.

Porter nodded and Smyth guessed his gut was acting up, too. They were a team. Smyth was chief of the D.A.'s Civil Rights unit. Porter worked under him. It was department policy: When a cop shot a civilian, someone from Civil Rights made the scene. They'd done a lot of these investigations together, too many, and too often in the middle of the night.

While Porter, a balding man with a round face and brown eyes that appeared perpetually skeptical behind half-moon glasses, interviewed witnesses, Smyth analyzed the scene. On a pad he sketched the layout of the house, noting the back door splintered off its hinges and a black shoe print where someone had kicked it in. He found no signs of a struggle in the kitchen or the den.

In the living room, Smyth noted blood smears on the plush pale gray carpeting and torn, bloody gauze discarded in the adrenaline-pumping flush of attempting to save a life. *Is she dead or alive?* the prosecutor wondered.

Smyth made his way past the crime-scene officers into the bedroom. It was a jumble: clothes strewn on the floor; scribbled-on yellow legal pads piled on the desk; a half-empty Burger King drink cup sweating on the headboard; black-and-white photos scattered on the dresser—modeling-type photos of an attractive, tall, blond, athletic woman in her early forties. He noted the name printed across the bottom—SUSAN WHITE—the shooting victim.

Next Smyth inspected the waterbed, awash in blood; a fine, deep crimson spray fanned the wall behind it. White must have been in bed when McGowen pulled the trigger, sending a bullet careening through her profile. Another sliced through her chest. A third shattered her right arm.

Moments later, Smyth met on the front lawn with Porter, McGowen, and an attorney supplied by the policemen's union.

"Is he willing to tell us what happened?" Smyth asked. He sensed the young cop wanted to talk. He'd been pacing the front lawn, recounting his story for nearly everyone on the scene. Twice Smyth ordered the other deputies to contain McGowen. "Put him in a squad car and tell him to shut up," he'd cautioned. He wanted McGowen quiet, thinking about what had happened, collecting his thoughts.

"He's ready," McGowen's attorney answered.

Smyth had conducted hundreds of walk-throughs in his nearly a decade of investigating cops. But this time he looked at Kent McGowen and did something he'd never done before: He pulled out a tape recorder and switched it on. His instincts whispered, *Cross every* t, *dot every* i.

The walk-through began at the front door, McGowen detailing for Smyth, Porter, and the others how he'd knocked and ordered the woman to open up. The woman was a major turd, he charged. Her son was involved with big-time gun dealers who trafficked in automatic weapons. McGowen had arrested the kid two nights earlier, using a C.I., a confidential informant. It was the C.I. White had threatened to kill.

"We needed to get her off the street," McGowen said, nodding confidently at Smyth and the others. They were, after all, part of the same club—law enforcement, the good guys. This Susan White, he disdainfully implied, was one of *them*, one of the *bad* guys.

Like so much else about the scene, the jowly young deputy's demeanor rang wrong to Smyth. McGowen grinned, bragging, relishing his story, as if he'd saved a school bus full of kids or captured the head of an international drug cartel. Suddenly, McGowen said something that propelled Smyth's curiosity into overdrive: Susan White called 911 when the deputies kicked down her door.

What kind of a criminal calls the cops for help? Smyth wondered.

Just then word came over the radio: Susan White was DOA, dead on arrival at the emergency room. *No reason to dispatch anyone to the hospital,* Smyth decided when he heard the news. *She won't be talking, except . . .*

After the walk-through, Smyth made a hasty exit for his car, pausing only to confer with Porter on the street.

"I'm going downtown," he said with a knowing glance. "I'm going to get that tape."

Porter understood Smyth's urgency. The 911 dispatchers were housed in the county jail, the sheriff's department domain. It would be easy for anyone to erase Susan White's call. Smyth couldn't let that happen. He needed to know what White had said moments before McGowen pulled the trigger. If his instincts were right, the tape could be important; it could be evidence of murder.

2

E.L. Doctorow once said: "Writing a novel is like driving a car at night. You can see only as far as your headlights, but you can make the whole trip that way."

Real life is more mysterious. Though we labor for our futures, in truth we have control only so long as chance and fate allow us that illusion. We make our plans at the mercy of our physiology, our environment, and the wills of others. We drive in the dark without headlights, not knowing if the road is washed out ahead, just past the next bend.

That final summer, 1992, was the valley of Susan White's life. All she held dear dissolved around her, like beams of light once a lamp is extinguished. What thoughts flashed through her mind that final night while she was alone and frightened? Her life had begun with such promise. Who could have predicted it would end with her cowering in the darkness as three bullets rang from the barrel of a 10-mm police special?

* * *

She was born Susan Diane Harrison on October 8, 1949, the third daughter and fourth child of O.L. and William (W.A.) Harrison's five children. Her parents had met in grade school in Winnsboro, a one-stop-sign town southeast of Monroe in northern Louisiana. They married in 1939, the year W.A. returned from a prewar stint in the Army. Earl was the first of the children, followed by Gloria, Kay, Susan, and, finally, Sandra.

"I remember when Susie was a baby she almost died of pneumonia," oldest sister Gloria explains, her soft Louisiana accent rolling smoothly off her tongue. "Wheeeee, it was scary. Momma and me, we didn't know if she'd make it."

The Harrisons were simple, proud people, Baptists and sharecroppers, who worked the cotton fields, often resettling from farm to farm. As would be expected, they eked out a hardscrabble existence, but, their children insist, a happy one.

"Momma loved her kids. If there was a shortage of food, we would eat and Momma wouldn't," Gloria maintains. "We didn't have a lot of possessions, but we always had a lot of love."

Even as age claimed their youth, the Harrisons made a handsome couple. W.A. stood nearly six feet, hair brushed to the side, his face rugged and worn, his body stooped yet strong. Before the passing decades settled her bones, O.L. was five-foot-eight, a gregarious and athletic woman with a natural elegance who loved playing basketball with her children.

Of all the children, Susan seemed special. A happy child, as a toddler she danced and cooed each time she heard "Good night, Irene," or Hank Williams singing, "Why don't you love me like you used to do?" on the radio. "There was always a little bit of something about Susie that sparkled," her father recalls.

All the girls inherited their parents' tall stature. In addition, Susan inherited her mother's slim figure, fine features, and blue eyes, and O.L. doted on her, twisting her soft, dark blond hair around her fingers to form a tumble of curls. When Susan was two, the family moved to nearby Bastrop, where W.A. secured a better-paying city job, sweeping streets. O.L. continued working the cotton fields with Gloria and Earl until she was able to hire on at the Bastrop paper mill. The family rented a home in town, their fortunes bettering.

Still, their possessions were meager. At night, all four girls slept in the same bed, a crowded if comforting accommodation. When Susan awoke with a charley horse, there was always a Harrison sister willing to massage her muscles until the cramping subsided. And when a group of bullies chased Sandra on the playground, it was Susan who threatened them with the flat side of a board unless they left her baby sister alone.

Although tight-knit, the Harrison sisters weren't immune to girlish rivalries or sibling one-upmanship. The family labeled it "picking at" one another. "We'd get into hair pulling and Susie had the hardest head, she just wouldn't let go," recalls her second sister, Kay. "Even then, she just was so darn determined."

Long summer afternoons were spent playing Mother May I, Kick the Can, and Red Light, saving milk-bottle tops to get a discounted ticket at the local movie house, or staging a beauty pageant with cousins and friends, the most often recounted of which included a guest appearance by "Miss Arizona"—W.A. dressed in one of O.L.'s Sunday dresses.

"Daddy made a right pretty girl," laughs Sandra. "I think we even let him win."

Yet as close as they were, Susan always seemed somehow apart, different. While the others were content with their place in the world, from an early age Susan felt frustrated. When they lived in a two-bedroom shotgun house outside Bastrop, she was the sister who took a spoon to the backyard, breaking into the hard brown dirt, plunging again and again, determined to dig a swimming pool like the ones rich folks had in their backyards. She gave up only when her hand ached from the effort.

"I always settled for what was happening right now. Susie was the one who wanted more out of life," Kay recalls sadly, as if this need of her younger sister's lay at the root of the tragedy that awaited her. "Susie never seemed satisfied with things as they were. She always had dreams of someplace better."

When Susan entered her teenage years in 1962, the country was in the throes of a revolution, the *Leave It to Beaver* era of the fifties dissolving in the consciousness-raising sixties. The Beatles unseated Elvis and thinness became the national obsession, Twiggy its idol. The Harrison girls were no exception as they scrupulously dieted, then riled each other with taunts about who was the slimmest.

At eighteen, oldest sister Gloria married Al Hamilton, a solid family man and former soldier from Wisconsin who worked in management at a paper mill. He began the family's migration to Baker, an hour's drive northwest of New Orleans. Kay married a few years later and followed Gloria and Al south.

By then the Harrisons and their two youngest daughters, Susan and Sandra, lived in Monroe, where W.A. worked for a local carbon company. Susan attended Neville High School. She was a good student with an infectious laugh and the type of outgoing personality that fostered quick friendships. She'd moved up in social circles, her friends the daughters of the mayor and the school principal. She attended dances for what O.L. describes as "nice young people" at the local recreation center, and though her dream of having one in her back-yard never materialized, she signed on as a lifeguard at the neighborhood pool. Then, suddenly, Susan changed. To Gloria, it was "normal teenage rebellion." The good student had little time for studies, instead hanging out with a crowd of whom her parents disapproved. There were arguments, family tensions, and for a short time Susan left to live with Gloria and Al.

Finally, in her senior year of high school, the phone rang at the Harrisons' house. The principal informed O.L. that Susan had run off to elope with her boyfriend. "Daddy got in the car and drove to Arkansas to get her," Gloria recounts. "Momma and Daddy didn't approve of the boy, and when he got her home, Susie was still single, and mad."

By the late sixties, campuses across the country were rife with protest against the U.S. role in the Vietnam War. Yet the Harrison household held to more traditional values of patriotism, and in 1967, six months after her high school graduation, Susan joined the Navy. It was for adventure, she told her sisters, to see the world. Her official photo shows an attractive young woman posed in her blue-and-white uniform, her hair dyed dark and cut short, her blue eyes ringed in the thick, smoky-black liner of the day, her cheekbones high. Yet after a year in Baltimore and San Diego training as a Navy dental assistant, she was again unhappy and restless. She asked for and was given a discharge. "The Navy just wasn't for Susie," says Gloria. "She couldn't take the discipline, and she wanted to come home."

The sister who had been so eager to leave returned to Louisiana, this time to the Baton Rouge area, where she settled near her two married sisters, Gloria and Kay. Susan used her Navy training to get a dental assistant's job while she studied at a local beauty school. One night while trimming Gloria's hair, she accidentally clipped her ear. "I told Susie maybe cosmetology wasn't for her," Gloria says, chuckling softly at the memory.

That same year, a pattern emerged that would haunt Susan throughout life: She fell in love—hopelessly, desperately—only to have the man at the center of her obsession leave her.

"Susie always fell hard," remembers Kay. "I think it's because in her heart she was a real romantic."

In February 1969, a nineteen-year-old Susan Harrison wrote a parting letter to the first man to break her heart: "It's funny how I thought things would never change. But they're bound to, just as the falling rain . . . I never realized how much I really love you. I pray to God above that he'll take care of you and that someday, my darling, you'll love me too. I'll always love you, Susie."

Much of the pain that awaited Susan Harrison would stem from her obsession with being loved. Despite her wide smile, her casual flirtatiousness, her warm manner, there was an unhappiness in Susan that she would spend her life trying to cure.

"I think Susie had so much inside of her it was confusing," Gloria murmurs. "It was like, Susan tried so many different things, but she never found what she was looking for."

It was the cusp of the seventies. The Senate repealed the Gulf of Tonkin Resolution, Nixon withdrew U.S. troops from Vietnam; the Beatles split, leaving John and Yoko to stage love-ins; the women's movement demanded equal pay for equal work and every woman's right to control her own destiny. Across the country, women's ambitions broadened, including Susan's. She eagerly took Gloria's advice and left beauty school behind and enrolled at Louisiana State University in Baton Rouge, where she studied psychology and business. She bleached her hair to her childhood blond and let it grow long and straight. She wore bell-bottoms, skintight T-shirts, ankle-length, flowing skirts, and sandals with platform soles and shared a small apartment near the university with a roommate. Anything seemed possible.

It was in this era of rebellion and challenge that a mutual friend introduced her to Leonard Joseph "L.J." Aguillard, the son of a sugarcane family from Rosedale, a small town across the Mississippi River from Baton Rouge. For years Susan had insisted she wanted a man like Gloria's Al, solid and family-centered, but L.J., a muscular heavy-equipment operator who'd served six years in the Marines, was Al's antithesis—a long-haired, post-hippie-era hippie.

"I blame L.J. for what happened to Susan," Gloria says, expressing a sentiment shared by her sisters and parents. "Meeting him was the worst thing that could have happened to her. She had such potential . . . He turned her world upside down."

"It was those times," counters L.J., seated in the kitchen of the small, one-story home he once shared with Susan, his face craggy and browned from years of working in the Louisiana sun. "Everybody was into pot and partying. Susan and I got together. It was like she grabbed onto me and didn't want to let go. It was an intense, a violent, relationship. Truth is, she brought out the worst in me."

The Harrisons weren't in favor of Susan's new beau. He was one of the French-descended Catholics who populated much of southern Louisiana. Years later, they would maintain it was L.J. who introduced Susan to drugs and alcohol. He'd charge that by the time they said their first hellos, Susan had done her own experimentation with drugs. "For me it was pot," a mature and reformed L.J. explains. "In those days, everyone was doing it. But Susie liked prescription drugs, downers, Quaaludes, and Valium. She'd go from doctor to doctor to get them. Then she'd get so far down she'd take uppers—diet pills—to get out of bed in the morning. The pills made her as unpredictable as a tornado, with a temper to match."

Whoever began the arguments, L.J. finished them. He sent Susan to the hospital before they even married. That night, L.J. had plans with friends, and she wanted him to stay home. When he refused, she smashed his most beloved possession, his stereo, on the floor, shattering it into hundreds of pieces.

"I backhanded her and knocked her onto the bed," L.J. remembers, grimacing at the memory. "I didn't think I'd hurt her, but later that night I got a call saying she was in the hospital. I broke her jaw in three places. When I saw her, she kept apologizing. 'I didn't mean to break your stereo. I didn't mean it.' "

Still, despite the violence, Susan was determined to have him. Although by most standards the Aguillards would be considered middle-class, Susan seemed fascinated by his family's land, the two-hundred-plus acres of sugarcane fields they owned in Rosedale. For a girl who grew up the daughter of sharecroppers, it must have seemed like Scarlett O'Hara's Tara. And no one, not even L.J., doubted that she truly loved him—in her own way.

Over her family's objections, on November 11, 1972, Susan and L.J. married in a simple ceremony in the backyard of her sister Kay's home. The local newspaper, the *State Times*, gave their union a heady write-up on the society page:

The bridal gown was of satapeau on princess lines. The high neckline and the A-line skirt were ruffled . . . Her floor-length mantilla was held by a juliet cap and she carried a bouquet of rosebuds.

[The bridesmaids wore] paste green peau de soie with

matching headpieces and they carried bouquets of pink
rosebuds.   .

"His folks came and they were well off," Gloria recalls. "The women wore big hats and long dresses and
big, chunky shoes. Susie always liked to be with the
well-off people."

In the photo that accompanied the article, Susan was
reed-thin. She fingered the edge of her veil, and her bridal bouquet hung like an afterthought at her side. Her
smile was shy and there was a hint of expectation on her
lips. It was a fairy-tale wedding, the kind a young
woman from modest beginnings dreams of.

At first, it appeared that Susan had found all she
needed. At her insistence, they moved from her Baton
Rouge apartment into the small, one-bedroom cinder-
block house his family owned on an acre lot cut from
the sugarcane fields. Down the road lived L.J.'s parents
and cousins. The two gnarled and thick live oaks in the
front yard had been planted by his father on the day L.J.
was born. In summer, when the cane grew high on three
sides, the house was little more than an island in a sea
of sugarcane.

Yet to Susan, it meant everything. At her ten-year
high school reunion, she bragged to classmates that she
lived on her husband's sugarcane plantation, making it
sound like a great estate.

"All of these people we didn't know," L.J. remembers.
"I told her, 'Now don't go telling those people lies.' "

Although reality fell far short of her fantasies, Susan
seemed happy. In 1975, they had a child, a son they
named Jason. In celebration, L.J. planted a live oak behind the house and Susan called the child her "beautiful
baby."

But the calm wasn't destined to last.

It was after the baby's birth that the arguments—and
the violence—escalated. "It was Susie's craziness and

those pills," a weary L.J. says. "She'd just go nuts."

He recalled the weekend she wanted him to stay home instead of going hunting with friends. Furious, she buried his shotguns barrel-deep in the mud in the front yard, like wood and metal sculptures attesting to her anger. When he arrived home, she ran for cover, locking herself in his pickup truck. Seething, L.J. shattered the truck window and pulled her out by her hair. Still determined as he drove away, Susan followed him in her own car until it stalled wheel-deep in mud on a dirt road.

L.J. just kept on driving.

"When I got back on Sunday, she acted like nothing happened," L.J. recalls, shaking his head in disbelief at the memory. "It was always like that."

But the arguments persisted. One New Year's Eve in the mid-seventies, Susan called from a hospital emergency room. When Gloria arrived she found her younger sister bruised and crying. After another argument, L.J. admitted Susan to a psychiatric hospital. "A nurse called me and I went to get her," Gloria says. "The nurse said that she could tell there was nothing wrong with Susie, that she didn't belong there."

An older and calmer L.J. Aguillard, a man much like the solid family man Susan had always said she'd wanted, labels the relationship pure craziness. He was the one who, seven years into the marriage, wanted an end to it. "I did her wrong and she did me wrong," he concludes. "We just didn't mix any more than oil and water. And Jason, he was in the middle of all of it."

Through it all, her sisters say, Susan held out hope the marriage would miraculously turn happy; then, in a final act of betrayal, L.J. fell in love with another woman. "I don't know that she ever got over him," whispers Kay sadly. "She always wondered why it didn't work. I said, 'Go on with life, don't worry about him.' But she did worry."

Susan fought the divorce until the very end. "She contested everything," says L.J., frowning. "Everything with Susie became a war."

L.J. married again, a petite, dark-haired schoolteacher named Nancy. This time the marriage lasted. "I know the Harrisons blame L.J., but it wasn't his fault. In all the years we've been married, he's never raised a hand to me," Nancy maintains. "L.J.'s really a gentle man."

Although Susan and L.J.'s marriage ended, in many ways the battlefront merely shifted, and Jason became the prize. At first, the boy remained with Susan, but when Jason was six, L.J. filed for custody. In courtroom after courtroom, Susan's and L.J.'s attorneys filed motions claiming the other was unfit or unable to raise their son. "Susan would get a judge in Baton Rouge to give her custody; then L.J. would file in Iberville Parish, where his family lived, and the judge there would decide in his favor," says Gloria. "Jason was like a Ping-Pong ball bouncing back and forth between the two of them."

As the eighties began, Susan enrolled in a licensed practical-nurse program at Louisiana Technical College, a vocational school in Baton Rouge. She still dreamed of finishing college and talked of wanting to someday be an attorney or a psychologist, but she told friends she needed a profession more quickly attainable, one she could use to pay her bills and impress the judge with her stability as she continued the fight for Jason's custody. Driven by a deep, frantic fear of failure, Susan plowed through nursing school with fierce determination. A straight-A student, she became class president.

After graduation, Susan settled into single life, working as a nurse in a geriatrics home not far from Gloria and Al's house. Jason visited on weekends, and she clearly idolized him. She bragged about his grades and his fine, handsome features. From early on, she treated her son as if he were beyond reproach. She never disciplined him. When he grew unruly, Susan made excuses, reminding Gloria and the others what a difficult childhood Jason had, torn between two warring parents, never having a stable home.

"Jason's all I got out of that marriage," she said often. "He's all I got for all that heartache."

Yet it was obvious to those around him that Jason was a troubled child. "From second grade on, we'd get notes from the teachers," Nancy, L.J.'s wife, recalls. "Jason would hit other children at school, call them names, act out. We had him tested, sent him to specialist after specialist. They diagnosed behavioral and emotional problems. But when we tried to talk to Susan about it, she became defiant. She said that the only thing that was wrong with Jason was that he was a very gifted child."

Then, in 1982, a Louisiana court awarded L.J. permanent custody of seven-year-old Jason. Susan was despondent. Once she even kidnapped Jason while he shopped with L.J.'s mother at the grocery store and whisked him away to Monroe, where her parents then lived. "I had to take my custody papers, call the sheriff, and go get him," says L.J., still irritated by the memory. "When I found her, she had Jason hidden, wrapped up in a blanket in the backseat of the car."

At thirty-two years old, Susan seemed keenly aware of the disappointing turn her life had taken. Her marriage had failed and her son was rarely with her. "Susan was never the same," remembers Gloria. "She had an incredible drive to succeed, to do better with her life. But now she knew she could fail."

Perhaps Susan blamed herself for the breakup of her marriage, reasoning that she hadn't been perfect enough. After the divorce, the pills dominated her life. She went to doctors, her pockets loaded with weights to make her appear heavier on the scales. She begged for diet pills and tranquilizers. It was Gloria who stepped in to save her. Frightened by Susan's emotional swings and the drugged gaze in her eyes, she checked her into a rehab hospital.

When doctors released her a month later, a bright-eyed and grateful Susan thanked Gloria and swore she was cured, done with drugs forever. "It's over," she said. "I don't need them. I'm all right now."

For a while, she was.

"There must have been some escape in the pills," Gloria speculates. "I don't think Susan ever took the drugs when things were going good. I think she took them to forget."

Yet Susie was still Susie—warm and personable, the kind of woman who easily attracted friends. She loved a good joke and was known to tell them often. And she relished the excitement of flirting with a new conquest. Whether the man was older than her father or young enough to be her son, Susan Harrison Aguillard had a way about her that turned a conversation into a teasing, sexually charged encounter. As she aged, she grew more attractive, tall, blond, with a too-wide smile that kept her from being conventionally pretty. Friends said she looked like the comedian-actress Teri Garr. Because of her husky voice—the result of smoking three packs of cigarettes a day—she maintained that when Hollywood made the story of her life, she wanted whisky-voiced Kathleen Turner to play the part.

Not long after her first marriage ended, Susan wed again, briefly, to a man who worked in a Baton Rouge industrial plant. The marriage lasted less than a year, but they parted friends.

Single again, she rented a small apartment not far from Gloria's home. Jason was rarely there. Susan talked often of her disappointment, and that she dreamed of one day having her son with her and of being married to a man of means, a man who loved her.

At a party in her apartment complex in the mid-eighties, Susan met such a man, and she told her friends that he was just what she'd waited for. Ron White was handsome, smart; an engineer, he made a good salary. And he appeared to be captivated by her.

"Susie fell hard for him," Gloria remembers. "Al and I never felt right about him. He was the kind of guy who didn't look you in the eye. But when they were together, Ron hung on Susie like he was crazy about her. In the beginning, I thought things would be all right, that Susie's life had finally straightened out."

3

Why do men and women so often replace one bad marriage with another? Is it simply human nature to crave familiar pain, unconsciously reasoning, *Better the misery I know*? Or is it a way of fulfilling the preordained designs of fate, as if, before our births, God drew a personal life line for each of us, His all-knowing hand writing, "Destined to be disappointed in love," in red across a healthy sampling of pages in His holy ledger?

Could it be an eternal optimism, this belief that despite a history of unsuccessful relationships, this time, this *one* time, love would surely bring happiness?

"Susie talked about Ron's success," remembers Sandra. "I thought he was strange, a little quiet. But Susie liked him, and as long as she was happy and he wasn't hurting her, that was enough for me."

Ron White had a thick crop of salt-and-pepper hair, his fortysomething face ruggedly attractive. Seven years older than Susan and with two grown children, he flashed a wry smile and had a manner of focusing on a woman so intently that it seemed no one else mattered. He drove a Porsche and worked for Texaco as a project manager, overseeing plant installations.

To his credit, Ron White was honest with Susan. He told her early on that he was married, in the midst of a divorce from his second wife.

"Doesn't Ron remind you of Al?" Susan dreamily asked Gloria one afternoon.

"I don't know," Gloria said, unwilling to voice her misgivings.

White lived in Houston, but when he met Susan, he was supervising the building of a new plant in Baton Rouge. She introduced him to her family, and they spent every available moment together after they both finished work for the day and on the weekends when he didn't return home to Houston. Before long, Susan labeled him the answer to her prayers, the man who would finally make up for her past pain. Ron understood how she felt about Jason, she said, that he was her son and that she wanted him with her.

Less than a year later, as White cleaned up the loose ends on his Baton Rouge assignment, Susan made plans to move to Houston with him. "I'm really in love with him," she told her mother. "We want to be together."

"I knew she was hoping they'd get married," says Sandra.

Yet one more failure awaited Susan in Baton Rouge. Just before she left, she was arrested for forging a prescription for amphetamines and Valium. Ron and Gloria checked her into another hospital, and she went before a judge, swearing she was cured of her addictions. He gave her probation but stripped her of her nurse's license.

On moving day, Susan had little to pack. She'd accumulated few possessions in her thirty-five years.

When she loaded up her old car for the six-hour drive to Houston, it included only clothing and personal items, a rolltop desk, and one antique table. But to Susan, it didn't seem to matter.

"She was happy as a lark," remembers Sandra. It was a new start. Susan was leaving not only Louisiana behind but the failure and unrealized dreams that haunted her there.

It was in Houston's far northern suburbs that Susan and Ron rented a two-bedroom apartment on Wunderlich Road as they waited for his divorce to become final. Houstonians know it as the FM 1960 area, after its main thoroughfare.

Decades earlier, this northern rim of Houston had been called Jackrabbit Run—its wild, thick pine forests deemed by inside-the-loop Houstonians as fit for only frogs, lizards, rabbits, and armadillos. But by the time Susan and Ron arrived, much of the forest had toppled in favor of roads, strip centers, and fashionable, walled-in subdivisions of two-story brick houses on small yards, many surrounding pristine golf courses and ostentatious country clubs. Families dominated the culture. Saturdays were traditionally spent cheering at Little League and soccer fields. A row of churches lined Klein Church Road, and restaurants stocked an abundance of high chairs.

Susan settled in and adjusted easily to her new life with Ron. In the beginning it must have been all she'd hoped for. They took a romantic, two-week business trip to Scotland and England, where they roomed in ancient castles and dined in posh restaurants, lingering to snap a photo, arm in arm, in front of Loch Ness. They splurged on furniture, matching Rolex watches, all the things Susan wanted but could never before afford. It wasn't unusual to find her flooring Ron's Porsche on quiet, suburban side streets. "I bet she drove ninety miles per hour, minimum," laughs Sandra. "She was on top of the world."

For the first time in her life, Susan belonged to a country club, Northgate Forest. It boasted a swimming pool, tennis courts, and a clubhouse with three-story windows that framed the verdant thirty-six-hole golf course and the half-a-million-dollar-and-up estates that surrounded it. Susan, already a good tennis player, took up Ron's game of golf.

To Susan, Northgate was a symbol of her newfound wealth, her entrance into the upper classes. But her past left her unprepared for the social mores she'd encounter. "She just wasn't country-club material," says one member. "When she'd sign up for the ladies' league, no one wanted to golf with her. We formed teams and the loser, whoever had an empty slot, got stuck with Susan. She was loud, laughed too much, and she would say anything that came into her head. She told you more than you wanted to know about her personal life. She *really* wasn't country-club material."

In early 1986, Ron's divorce became final and they applied for a marriage license. Perhaps she sensed he was reluctant to legalize their relationship, or maybe it was just an example of her playful nature, but on March 29, as he rounded the curve at the fifteenth hole, she had a justice of the peace waiting. In shorts and golf shirts, a clutch of lace pinned to her visor, Susan and Ron repeated their vows. Afterward, they toasted with champagne, his golfing buddies made an arch of clubs for the newlyweds to walk under, and then Ron left to finish his round.

"Ron looked surprised," remembers Sandra, the maid of honor and the only family member to attend. "But he went along with it. I guess he was happy about it. With Ron you never could tell."

Two months later, in early June, Ron and Susan drew

up a postnuptial agreement in which Susan conceded she had no claim to his property, principally his retirement and employee stock accounts, certificates of deposit, and money markets. The document included future earnings and stipulated that in the event of one of their deaths, their separate possessions would be passed on to their individual children. Of course, the agreement also protected Susan's property, but then, she had little to speak of.

Still, Susan appeared happy, and, their friends say, so did Ron. Unencumbered by children or other demands, with Ron's money to foot the bills, they partied with friends and played golf at the country club. Susan became a not-uncommon sight in her bikini at the club pool, where she tanned her body a deep chestnut and gossiped with young mothers who brought their children to swim. At night, she and Ron frequented the restaurants up and down FM 1960, occasionally stopping in to listen to the music and eat dinner at Resa's, the piano bar attached to Del Frisco's. They rarely mingled with the high-rolling crowd of aging baby boomers who frequented the restaurant. "When Susan was with Ron, they basically kept to themselves," remembers one friend. "They didn't need anyone else."

Then something happened that changed everything, something neither Susan nor Ron could have anticipated—L.J. sent twelve-year-old Jason to Houston to live with his mother.

"Nancy and I couldn't handle Jason anymore, not that I didn't want him," L.J. insists. "He was always in trouble, at school and at home. He was uncontrollable. We'd done all we could, counselors, everything. Jason said he wanted to live with his momma and Susan said, 'Give me Jason.' One day I just said, 'Fine, if that's what y'all want, go ahead.'"

Susan couldn't believe her good fortune. She'd tried unsuccessfully for five years to have custody of her son, and suddenly L.J. handed the boy to her. She crowed to her friends and family about her happiness. Things couldn't have worked out better, as far as Susan was concerned.

The apartment suddenly too small, the newlyweds bought a tan brick, two-story house on Valley Bend in Oak Creek Village, a quiet, twenty-five-year-old subdivision, and she enrolled Jason at the neighborhood middle school.

To Susan, her son seemed perfect. He was small for his age, slightly built, with a thick shock of medium brown hair, finely shaped, handsome features, and a warm olive complexion that resembled his father's.

"I just can't believe my luck," she told one friend. "My beautiful baby has come home to me."

Oak Creek Village, the subdivision where the Whites settled, was white-collar and conservative. Most families voted Republican, attended church on Sundays, and assumed their children would go to college. Neighbors knew each other well enough to nod to as they took their evening walks, but only a smattering formed close friendships, instead abiding by Robert Frost's "Good fences make good neighbors."

As in much of middle America, lives were orderly. Husbands and wives kissed each other good-bye in the morning before driving off in their late-model cars, mainly Japanese and American-made sedans, to their respective offices. Children waited at the corner for the yellow school bus marked Spring Independent School District. In late afternoon, the same bus brought them home. Status equaled the bottom line on one's bank accounts, the size of one's house, the stickers on one's cars, and the talents of one's children, whether realized on the soccer field or in the classroom.

In this world, Susan White was as miscast as Dolly Parton portraying June Cleaver.

While her conservative neighbors clipped coupons for weekly trips to the local grocery stores, Susan, suddenly with a positive checkbook balance, phoned in orders to the convenience store a mile from her house. The prices were inflated, the selection limited, yet it offered what Susan deemed a great advantage, home delivery—for an additional fee.

"We were all flabbergasted," clucks one neighbor. "Couldn't she get in the car and drive to Kroger?"

While others jogged for their health, Susan chain-smoked, a cigarette continually dangling between her long, thin fingers. Ron White tended to keep to himself, but Susan, who often said she'd never met a stranger who didn't become a friend, disdained the cordial-but-distant doctrine. It wasn't unusual for her to corner a neighbor who was out to pick up the mail, or to rap on a door asking to borrow bread for Jason's lunch. More often than not, she was attired, not in the typical suburban uniform of khaki slacks and cotton shirt, but in a too-tight T-shirt and shorts cut high enough to showcase her legs.

As her neighbors exchanged chin-wags about the odd new woman on the block, Susan appeared unaware of her growing notoriety. She crowed to Gloria about the friends she'd made in Houston, emphasizing how nicely they all treated her. Yet perhaps in the quiet moments when alone, not worried about impressing family or friends, Susan felt very differently, the daughter of sharecroppers adrift in an upper-middle-class world.

The only neighbors to truly befriend Susan were Tom and Lorene Roy, a retired petroleum engineer and his wife, who lived directly across the street. The Roys' house, a white two-story with wrought-iron trim, recalled their Louisiana roots, a shared heritage that made them believe they'd found a kindred soul in Susan.

"At first, she struck me as a real upright lady. She had this husky voice and a Louisiana accent," recalls Tom Roy, a large man who favors worn coveralls for the endless puttering he indulges in around the house. "When she was really dressed up, she looked gorgeous. But I believe it would be fair to say that she threw it around a little bit, too. She was looking for attention. Ron? I think he wanted to give her that attention, but he was never able to find the way to do it."

When Tom Roy happened upon Susan in the front yard or getting in or out of the car in the driveway, they teased each other, laughing good-naturedly.

"You and me are going to go upstairs someday," Roy said with a quick wink.

"I'm going to tell your wife," Susan answered with a coy smile.

"Go ahead," he challenged, knowing his wife understood he was just "cutting up like an old man will do."

Most women in the neighborhood worked, and Susan was no exception. She'd lost her nurse's license after the forged-prescription incident in Baton Rouge, so with the help of Jean Morris, the agent who sold them the Valley Bend house, Susan enrolled in real-estate school and signed on with a nearby Century 21 office. In her mustard-colored blazer, she showed houses and took prospective buyers on house-hunting expeditions. She was relatively good at it, and working brought in the commissions she now needed to pay for Jason's expenses.

If the neighborhood women shunned her company, Jean and others at the office became her new friends. After work they stopped for drinks and talked over the happenings of the day. Spread among her marriage, work, the country club, and friends, Susan's days were hectic, and now that she had Jason, she wasn't quite sure what to do with him. In the best of circumstances, adjusting an adolescent to a new state, city, and home with a mother he'd rarely seen and a stepfather he barely knew would have been difficult. With a mother distracted by the demands of a new marriage, the situation spelled disaster.

Acutely aware of her dilemma, Susan told friends she felt like she was in the middle of a tug-of-war, pulled in one direction by Ron, who wanted to live the life he'd been accustomed to, and in another by Jason, who needed his mother. It soon became obvious that it was Ron who had won the contest. "I can't let this ruin my marriage," Susan told one co-worker. "I've got to put Ron first."

"It wasn't that she ignored me," Jason insists, maintaining he understood the conflict in his mother's life. "She did all she could, took me places, she wanted us all to be a family. But me and Ron, we just never got along. It just didn't work."

As a result, it was Jason whom neighbors gossiped about over shopping carts at the local grocery store, or standing in line waiting for a teller at the bank. He was alone, often late into the night, they said. One neighbor noticed the boy walking the darkened streets well after midnight. Tom Roy sometimes found the twelve-year-old sitting alone, smoking a cigarette on the curb at 4:30 when he and Lorene took their morning walk.

"It was a sad situation. I think Susan meant well, but she just didn't have much time for the boy," Roy says. "Sometimes we'd bring him home and feed him. We took him shopping with us, tried to help out. He always had this dog with him, a mutt, part golden retriever. He took that dog everywhere, like it was his only friend. Then the dog died and he was all alone."

When the Roys and others approached him on the street, Jason responded politely, peppering the conversation with "yes, ma'am" and "no, sir." Yet the boy made few friends in his new neighborhood; instead, he took to playing with children half his age, a situation that prompted more gossip.

"We all pretty much felt sorry for Jason. He seemed lonely. He told all of us his father didn't want him anymore, he had a new wife and son," recalls Kim Millikan, who lived with her family next door. "We thought the boy was redeemable, but then, after many incidents, we decided he wasn't."

The incidents are still legend on Valley Bend, like the time he convinced their then preschool daughters to dig tunnels, burying themselves under a pile of soil delivered for the garden. "By the time we realized what was going on, one of them could have died," remembers Kim. "Jason was a real Eddie Haskell kind of kid. He'd say, 'You make the best cookies'; then he'd get my daughters to do something they shouldn't."

Occasionally one neighbor or another made his way to the Whites' house to voice a complaint. It rarely resulted in satisfaction for the complaining party.

"If Ron answered the door, he'd just say, 'You need to talk to Susan,'" says Kim. "If Susan was there, she'd get this blank look on her face and then deny that Jason could have done anything wrong. You could tell Susan loved the boy, but she couldn't see he was in trouble. She always defended him. Nothing was ever his fault. It was always 'Poor Jason. Poor Jason.'"

Susan eased her conscience by making sure Jason never wanted for anything. She bought him new clothes, a bike, and, say neighbors, padded his adolescent palms with cash. "We'd take him to the mall and Jason would have twenty-dollar bills stuffed in his wallet, once more than a hundred dollars," remembers Tom Roy. "I'd say, 'Jason, where do you get all that money?' He alleged that his grandmother had sent it to him, but we knew that wasn't true. It came from Susan."

It was the "jewelry incident" that convinced the neighbors Jason was "beyond redemption." One afternoon a neighborhood woman returned from work to discover her home ransacked and her husband's gold chain missing. Her five-year-old daughter and her housekeeper said Jason had pushed his way into the house and rifled through the drawers. Irate, the woman stormed down the block to the Whites' house and knocked on the door. Jason answered, wearing the chain around his neck. Furious, she yanked it off. Despite the woman's having the evidence in hand, she had to be mistaken, Susan maintained.

"Jason would never do anything like that," she insisted.

As time passed, the White house became a magnet for disenfranchised neighborhood teens, mostly boys who wore baggy pants, enormous T-shirts, one earring, and backward baseball hats. The older ones drove dilapidated cars, the radios blaring. "The boys were always into something. Susan and Ron were always at work. Those kids would stand up on the roof, calling out obscenities at the little ones in the neighborhood," remembers Roy. "They took a can of hair spray and fired it into a lit match, causing an explosion. They egged folks walking down the street. Once a shed burned down, and neighbors figured Jason and his pals probably did it. Typical teenage stuff, but worse."

Friends say that Ron, too, found his stepson a constant irritant, and Jason made it clear he returned his disdain. They had heated arguments over everything from Jason's friends to the way he kept his room. Jason retaliated, including one day spiking Ron's coffee with antifreeze.

"He didn't really drink it," said Gloria, whom Susan later told about the incident. "But Ron was absolutely furious. He chased Jason all over the house."

"I never much wanted to be around Ron," Jason says. "He kept his distance and so did I. He was an old man. All he wanted to do was golf and eat out at restaurants.

I asked her, 'Why'd you marry him?' My mom said she loved him and he could afford to make a home for us."

Jason's problems weren't confined to his relationship with the neighbors and his stepfather. As in Louisiana, they spilled over into school, where he disrupted his classes and pulled pranks that made him as common a topic of conversation in the teachers' lounge as on Valley Bend.

Susan spent afternoon after afternoon arguing with counselors and teachers. Although she gave him little of her time, she was fiercely loyal to her son. As always, she denied Jason could be guilty of any of the accusations leveled against him. When counselors talked of emotional and behavioral problems and suggested discipline and counseling, Susan, as unconcerned as if they'd mentioned an occasional tardiness for classes, replied that she didn't believe in pushing the boy.

"He's just going through a stage," she maintained at parent-teacher conferences. "You'll see. It's just teenage-boy stuff."

Before long, and over Susan's angry protests, Jason was transferred to the Wunsche School, the district's last resort for kids with physical, mental, emotional, or behavioral problems. "When counseling and regular school don't work, they're sent to Wunsche," explains one former teacher. "Jason was there for emotional and behavioral reasons. He may have been fifteen, but emotionally he hadn't matured. He was physically small for his age and he still acted like a little kid. He had bad judgment, and he was a follower. If one of his friends told Jason to rob a bank, he'd do it, without even asking why."

Once Jason was enrolled in Wunsche, his separation from the neighborhood became complete. While other children waited for school buses on the corner, a smaller bus equipped with a wheelchair ramp to accommodate the school's special population pulled up in front of the White household early each morning. Jason was nearly always late, and Calvin Edgin, the driver, grew used to seeing Susan, still dressed in her worn brown terry-cloth robe, wave to him from the front door.

"Jason'll be there in a minute," she'd shout.

Moments later, she'd reappear with a Styrofoam cup of coffee for Edgin. "She was really friendly, always up," he says. "And she was always talking about Jason and how he was really such a good boy. She said people just didn't understand him and all he'd been through."

Edgin listened sympathetically, but he knew another Jason, a teenage troublemaker who made fun of the boy with cerebral palsy who rode the bus.

"You could see Jason going downhill. He hung around with some rough-looking characters. They'd be waiting for him when we drove up after school. I can't remember how many times I saw Susan coming up to school," he says. "When I did, I knew Jason was in trouble, again."

When Susan's family visited, she told them none of her son's problems, instead putting on a things-couldn't-be-better facade. She bragged about Jason's grades and acted as if everything were fine at home, as if no tension existed. For the first time, she was able to splurge on her family, and she did so with abandon. She sent her parents on a trip to the West Coast to visit her uncle, their first plane ride. She bought her mother clothes. When O.L. refused them, Susan insisted, often hiding sweaters or jewelry in her mother's suitcase. "Once, when we were all visiting, Susie announced, 'Today, we're all going to get a new pair of shoes,' " remembers Kay. "She took us shopping and bought a pair for each of us. Susie was just that way. She used to say, 'I'm just like my daddy, I've got money stashed away and nobody knows I've got it.' "

Her sisters would later judge it was in 1989 that they

first realized everything wasn't ideal in Susan's new marriage. At the time, Ron worked in Port Arthur, Texas, on an extended assignment, overseeing the building of a new plant, just as he had in Baton Rouge years earlier when he and Susan met. Neighbors remember Susan felt uncomfortable about being at home alone. "I can't say how many times she called the police, claiming someone was trying to break in," recalls Tom Roy. "If they weren't there over something Jason had done, they were there because she got scared in the middle of the night."

Then, one weekend when Ron made the trip home, Susan found photographs in his pocket, photographs of another woman. "It devastated her," says Sandra. "Ron called her day and night for weeks after that. He begged, 'Tell Susan that I love her.' I'd said, 'Susie, just give him another chance. If you love him, the two of you can work it out.' "

It was the third marriage for each of them, and perhaps Ron was as frightened as Susan at the prospect of yet another failure. Or perhaps he truly loved her. Whatever the reason, that fall, Ron White capitulated about many things, including rescinding the postnuptial agreement that had barred Susan from ever claiming any of his assets, and writing a new will, in which he listed Jason as one of his heirs.

Shortly thereafter, Ron White left his high-salary job at Texaco and signed on with a small, oil-contracting concern. Susan told friends it was an opportunity so potentially lucrative, he couldn't refuse to accept the offer. They moved to Korea in the fall of 1989, just as Susan celebrated her fortieth birthday, for what was supposed to be a one-year assignment. Millikan and others on Valley Bend sighed in relief, grateful that, at least for a while, Jason would no longer interrupt their quiet neighborhood. But just a few months later, they returned. "It was like, thank God he's gone, and then Jason was back again," remembers Millikan. "None of us could believe it."

Susan's sisters were never quite sure why Susan, Ron, and Jason returned from overseas so much sooner than expected, except that Susan had detested Korea and fallen ill. Once back in Houston, Ron again looked for a new job. Susan introduced him to a former real-estate client, a highly placed executive with Brown & Root, the engineering and construction giant. The company had an opening, and Ron secured a slot as a project manager.

In the summer of 1991, Susan left real estate and signed on as a broker with First Union, a small, three-broker office that specialized in mortgage loans.

This might have been the best time of Susan's life. With money rolling in, she splurged on a white BMW convertible with leather seats. She became a common sight barreling through the streets of Oak Creek, the BMW's top down, her long blond hair whipping in the breeze, her skin burnished to a dark tan from visits to a nearby tanning salon. She and Ron sold the Valley Bend house and bought a brand-new one on Amber Forest, in a tony section of Olde Oaks, a more prestigious subdivision that butted up to Oak Creek Village on the east.

The house was a two-story, rose-colored brick fortress, on a street populated by upper-level managers and professional couples and their families. It had leaded-glass windows in the stately double front doors, a marble-floored entry, a game room and a gym, a black marble floor-to-ceiling fireplace in the living room, and a cedar-shingle roof that glistened silver in the harsh Houston sun. Despite her decidedly nontraditional nature, Susan decorated like an Ethan Allen brochure: a deep-shine polished Chippendale dining room set, a cherry bedroom suite with a four-poster bed under an oil painting of an ancient sailing ship tossed on an angry sea. Copper pots hung over a kitchen counter, and rows of crystal goblets lined the china cabinet.

"She wanted more than she had on Valley Bend," says Millikan. "And we were glad to be rid of the problems with Jason on the street. The only thing I heard in the neighborhood was people wishing they'd moved farther away."

Susan had come a long way from the shotgun houses of her youth. "The house I grew up in would fit in our living room," she bragged to one friend. "I always knew that someday I'd have a house like this one."

That Thanksgiving, Susan's parents, Sandra, and Kay came to visit. "It was a wonderful time," says Sandra. "Susan was so excited about the house, about everything. I don't ever remember seeing her so happy."

They used Susan's new video camera to record the event. In the tape, she traveled through the house narrating in her gravelly voice; at one point, in a scene that would later smack of high irony, she playfully chased a reclusive Ron.

"You hiding from me?" she quipped.

Never much of a cook, Susan ordered a prepared turkey dinner with all the fixings from a local grocery store. Yet before they had time to claim it, a boom reverberated through the neighborhood, shaking the house. They rushed outside to find the home directly next door engulfed in flames.

O.L. called 911, but by the time a fire truck arrived, there was little left to do but wet down the cedar-shingle roofs on the surrounding houses to keep the fire from spreading. Susan watched in horror as greedy flames devoured her neighbor's home, tears streaming down her cheeks. "She sobbed like a baby," remembers Kay. "She was so afraid that the fire would jump over to her house and they'd lose all their beautiful things."

The fire never did reach Susan's beloved home, but something else happened that day, something Susan didn't even notice at the time, something that would prove more deadly to the world she'd so carefully constructed.

"I think it was a while after the fire," Kay muses. "The phone rang, and I saw Ron pick it up. He gave me kind of a funny look and turned away. He whispered real soft, like he didn't want me to hear, and all I could think was, *Oh, no. Not a girlfriend.*"

4

Life doesn't happen in earth-shattering events or great revelations. It builds in moments, fleeting thoughts, and forgotten deeds; in a series of installments, each separate yet connected. Mysteriously, minor decisions become life-shaping; a mere acquaintance alters destiny. Life is a kaleidoscope, its pieces tumbling haphazardly, forming one pattern that merges seamlessly into another, until a twist of the bezel casts an unanticipated design, an unforeseen possibility, a final resolution.

In early 1992, Susan White's world shifted, undetectably at first, then at such speed that it sent her reeling.

A nineteen-year-old drifter with dark hair and earnest eyes, Michael Todd Shaffer moved into her life that winter, gradually, innocuously. Shaffer would later discount the part he played in Susan White's death, but as providence would have it, he became one of the central elements necessary to seal her fate.

*   *   *

"It was just talk," he maintains. "We were just a bunch of punks trying to act bad."

Jason met Shaffer in 1991, through mutual friends, and they quickly became as thick as brothers. He was a sullen young man, two years older than Jason. Like Jason's, his childhood was marked by uncertainty and trauma. When he was eight, his parents separated, and of their three sons, Michael took the breakup the hardest. "He was the youngest and he had the toughest time adjusting," reports Shaffer's mother, Jeannie Jaques. "He was a great kid, but by adolescence we were having one crisis after the other with him. He just shrugged things off, never accepted any responsibility."

Michael dropped out of school at fifteen and moved to Houston, where he took on a nomadic lifestyle, at times living in run-down rented houses with his two older brothers, Bobby and Myron, both auto mechanics. Other times, he migrated among the homes of his latest best friends. He cultivated connections with cars and money, with kids who lived in big houses. By the summer of 1991, Michael drifted in and out of the Whites' house on Valley Bend, staying with Jason whenever it was convenient. Susan liked him. He was older than Jason and, she judged, therefore more solid. "She'd ask me to keep an eye on Jason," Shaffer recalls. "She'd say she didn't worry about him when we were together. When Jason was with me, he didn't have a curfew."

It is possible Susan didn't know, distracted as she was by the ups and downs of her marriage. Or maybe it was easier not to know. But during those late nights when her son caroused with Shaffer, they did more than pop wheelies in Michael's old white Pinto in the deserted cemetery near the house, trip neighbors' car alarms, or slam golf balls into the Dumpster parked in the front yard of the burned-out house next door.

When Susan and Ron were out of the way and Jason and Michael had the run of the house, word spread, cars lined the street, every light shone into the night like a beacon calling to bored or displaced teenagers looking for a few hours of a good time. Loud music, louder laughter. Some brought liquor raided from their parents' cabinets; others bought six-packs at the local convenience store from clerks who looked the other way. A few supplied drugs.

"Jason and Mike liked to brag about being bad and they did what the crowd did," says one of the throng of teenagers who hung out together that year. "We were almost always high on something, mostly pot or acid. It was a blast. Nobody talked much about anything past the next weekend."

As on Valley Bend, the patience of the neighbors on Amber Forest wore thin. On weekends, calls flooded the Cypresswood substation, the sheriff's department nearby headquarters. "There's another party at 3407 Amber Forest," one neighbor or another would complain. "Nobody can sleep."

A squad car responded, but before it arrived, neighbors watched in frustration as lights flickered off and all became quiet, teenagers disappearing from the house like ants abandoning an injured hill.

In January 1992, Michael Shaffer moved into the Whites' home on Amber Forest, settling his few possessions into a vacant second-floor bedroom. His girlfriend, Amy, an airy fifteen-year-old with long blond hair and wide-set blue eyes, an unwed mother of an infant son, became a regular. She and Jason were old friends. They rode the Wunsche bus together to school in the mornings.

"Jason was easy to make friends with. He thought everybody was fine. He even tried to pick me up when I was pregnant," she relates with a childish giggle. "I was, like, 'You're crazy.' He'd walk up to girls and say, 'Hey, baby, what's up?' "

It would be months before Michael Shaffer's role in

the events leading to Susan White's death would become clear. Yet, looking back, his mother would remember her youngest son's childhood and speculate on why he so readily capitulated to a cop and betrayed his best friend: "In the final divorce decree, his dad got the house, but I was fighting him. He got a court order, forcing me to vacate the property. I refused. It was my house and I wasn't leaving. But the police pulled up in a squad car and threw our stuff on the curb. I screamed at them and they handcuffed me and dragged me off to jail. I'll never forget the look on Mike's face. He'd watched the whole thing. He was just a little kid, and he looked like he was in shock. After that, Michael was always uncomfortable around cops, really anyone in authority. You could just see it in his eyes. Whenever he talked to a cop, he just froze up, went back into his little-boy world. He was scared to death of them."

Just weeks after Mike Shaffer took up residence in Susan's world, a brown envelope arrived at her office at First Union Mortgage, marked "Personal" and postmarked January 28, 1992. Inside, someone had tucked seventeen photos of her husband's car in a hotel parking lot and a letter typed all in caps:

DEAR SUSAN:

ENCLOSED ARE SOME PICTURES TAKEN LAST WEEK OF RON'S CAR AND [SHERRI'S] CAR PARKED AT THE HILTON ON THE KATY FREEWAY . . . IN CASE YOU DON'T KNOW IT RON IS PLANNING TO FILE FOR DIVORCE SO HIM AND SHERRI CAN BE MARRIED. THEY ARE PLANNING TO GO TO SAUDI ARABIA TOGETHER. RON IS SHOWING UP AT THE OFFICE EARLY SO THAT HE CAN BE ALONE WITH HER FOR MORNING COFFEE. SHE RECENTLY ASKED HER HUSBAND FOR A DIVORCE, BUT

HER HUSBAND DOESN'T KNOW ABOUT RON . . . THIS OFFICE ROMANCE HAS BEEN GOING ON SINCE OCTOBER. THE NIGHT YOU SHOWED UP AT THE RESTAURANT, YOU JUST MISSED THEM TOGETHER. THE REASON SHE AND RON WERE THERE WAS FOR RON TO MEET HER SISTER AND MOTHER. DON'T YOU THINK THAT IS A PRETTY SERIOUS RELATIONSHIP?

THE AVENGER

"Susan literally screamed," remembers one co-worker. "I didn't know what could have happened. She ran out of her office, threw the letter on my desk, and started shaking and crying. She kept saying over and over, 'I can't believe he's doing this to me. I can't believe he's doing this to me.' After that, she spent hours staring at the letter and the photos."

Ron's office romance had begun the previous October. "He was the typical flirt, very charming," says Sherri Brandt, tall, auburn-haired, ten years younger than Susan, and the mother of a young daughter. "I resisted and resisted. Finally, I guess it was a month or so after we met, I gave in."

Giving in meant lunchtime liaisons at the Hilton, stolen hours when their respective spouses believed they were at work. To Sherri, Ron was an ardent suitor. He brought flowers, catered to her. "He was still living with Susan, but he'd call me all the time," she recalls. "He'd check on me constantly, driving by my house and, after I moved out, my apartment. People at the office picked up on it pretty quickly. And once the gossip starts, it's like cancer. It spreads."

Friends say Susan confronted Ron about the affair and he denied it, blaming the letter on someone's overactive imagination. But from that day on, Susan became a different person. Looking back on her life, she must have viewed Ron's possible infidelity as her final betrayal, the last in a series of deceptions perpetrated by those she loved. Her first marriage had ended in disappointment and violence. Again she'd staked her future on a man who turned his back on her. *Why me?* she must have wondered. *Why is this happening to me?*

"Susan became obsessed with finding out whether or not Ron was telling the truth and what the other woman was like," says Cindy Doerre, one of her co-workers at First Union. "She became obsessed with getting Ron back."

The marriage teetering, Ron left in mid-February to visit his stepmother and father in South Carolina. The older man had heart problems. With Ron's whereabouts temporarily accounted for, Susan reconsidered her husband's claim of innocence. Unconvinced, she turned investigator, running the license number of the truck in the Avenger's photos on a computer available to the public at the Texas Department of Motor Vehicles. The name that popped up was "Sherri Brandt," just as the letter had indicated. Distraught, Susan burst into Ron's office at Brown & Root at five one evening. In a frenzy, she confronted Sherri, slapped her, and threatened her with a soda bottle.

"Susan lost it," recounts Sherri. "She was shrieking, calling me names, 'a fucking bitch.' I grabbed my car keys and made a break for the door."

Susan called Sandra in Baton Rouge, confiding in her about the letter and what she'd discovered. "I can't believe he did this to me," she kept insisting, her voice thick with emotion. "When we went to his company Christmas party, everyone there knew—everyone but me."

This time, Ron didn't call begging Sandra to intervene to save his marriage. Instead, when he returned from South Carolina after Valentine's Day, he ignored a dozen red roses Susan had bought and was displaying on the coffee table, hoping to make him jealous. "Susie said he didn't even react," says Sandra. "He acted like they weren't even there."

However, Susan did receive one Valentine, a card covered with flowers that read, "To Mom, from the both of us," signed by Jason and Mike. "I felt sorry for her. She was going through hell and she was really cool," remembers Shaffer. "She talked to me like I was an adult, and I liked that. She told me her problems, and I guess I was one of the few who listened."

Adding to Susan's woes were Jason's continuing brushes with trouble. In January, showing off, he had picked a fight with a teenager twice his size. As they tangled on the ground, a crowd of friends urged them on, until Michael Shaffer saw blood streaming from Jason's face. Shaffer and others wrestled the two apart, and Jason ended up in the emergency room, Susan hovering over him.

"My beautiful baby," she had cried. "What have they done to my beautiful baby?"

In the fray, Jason's adversary had bitten off a patch of skin from the tip of his nose, leaving a jagged cut that required stitches.

A police officer was assigned to the case, but no charges were ever filed. Yet for months after, the investigating deputy grew used to picking up his phone and hearing Susan White's raspy Louisiana drawl.

"She wanted to talk about the kid," he recalls. "It was like I was her friend, someone she could confide in. She was worried about him. She wanted me to tell her what to do, but when I said she had to lay down the law for the kid, get him away from the bad element he was hanging with, she'd just hem and haw."

That spring, Susan White's life slowly fractured and cracked, then crumbled beneath her. Soon it became commonplace for Shaffer to find her in the kitchen or the den when he returned late after a night with friends.

In one hand she held a glass of white wine, in the other a cigarette, trancelike, watching thin puffs of smoke evaporate around her. Forty-two years old, nearing the end of her third marriage, she cut a solitary figure.

At such moments, Ron, undoubtedly, filled her thoughts.

Once she was angry enough to greet him at the door with a broom. "She swung it at him and hit him in the head," says Shaffer. Another time, she threw his clothes onto the front lawn and insisted he leave.

Before long, she was begging him to stay.

During that spring, Ron continued to insist he didn't want a divorce. Still, Susan began a crusade to discover if he was, in fact, unfaithful. Like two cops staking out a suspect, Susan and Jean Morris, the real-estate friend who'd sold them the house on Valley Bend and who'd helped get her into the business, spent night after night waiting silently in the parking lot at Ron's office, watching as one after another of his co-workers left for home. When he appeared in his Porsche, they eased out behind him, tailing him through the heavy Houston traffic, eager to see if he drove directly home or to the small apartment Sherri had rented after she'd left her husband, saying simply that she needed space to assess the marriage.

"We never saw him do anything," recalls Jean, a quiet woman with a thin, nasal voice, who favors high heels and business suits with slim skirts. "We never really caught him doing anything."

Yet Susan was far from convinced. Theorizing that the letter could be Ron's awkward way of manipulating her into a divorce, in late March she hired a handwriting expert to determine if either Ron or Sherri had written her address on the envelope in which the Avenger's letter arrived. As examples of their handwriting, she supplied the expert with a note Ron had written, plus eleven pink phone-message slips from the office, messages Sherri had taken.

"Susie wanted to know if Ron was helping Sherri do this to her," says Jean. "She was convinced the letter didn't come from a third party."

When the report came back, it concluded that it was Sherri who had written the address on the envelope. "It is my opinion as a certified graphologist that the writer of exemplars 1–11 [the phone messages] also wrote the suspect questioned document [the Avenger's envelope]."

Years later, Sherri would deny that she was responsible for the letter and photos: "Susan thought I sent them, but I didn't. I believe a couple of girls—very vindictive—who knew about Ron and me did it."

In the midst of so much turmoil, Susan asked for and was given a psychological disability leave from First Union Mortgage, based on the finding from a psychiatrist who said she suffered from depression. He prescribed lithium, which seemed to take the edge off her sadness. She packed up the few things she'd moved into the office and told Cindy Doerre that someday she'd be back—after she and Ron had worked things out.

But to Doerre, Susan didn't look well. "She wasn't the same person, not happy-go-lucky, the person who didn't let little things bother her. She told me to watch out for men, that none of them were to be trusted. Sometimes she just rambled on about how I shouldn't trust anyone."

It was Jason who again threw his mother's life into further chaos that spring. For months Susan had ignored him as she'd tried to piece her marriage together. Calvin Edgin, the school-bus driver, grew used to pulling up in front of the White house, only to have Jason inform him that he wouldn't be going to school that day. "I hated to leave him behind, but I had to," remembers Edgin. "I couldn't force him to go."

When he did climb on board, Jason was a constant irritant, teasing the other students, especially the handicapped kids. He'd bring a bowl of cereal on the bus or a massive black boom box he cranked up until rap music pounded the van's frame. With his pierced earlobe and its small gold hoop earring, a baseball cap pulled solidly over his forehead, Jason resembled a cross between a bewildered third grader and a street thug, juvenile yet frightening.

Then, on the morning of Tuesday, April 7, Edgin pulled to the curb in front of the Amber Forest house and Jason ran toward him. Edgin hit the air brakes, the door popped open, and he found himself staring into the barrel of a gun, Jason laughing maniacally behind it.

"Jason, what're you doing?" the driver demanded. "Are you going to school today?"

"No," Jason said, "I'm not."

"Then you'd better get off the bus."

As if nothing unusual were taking place, Jason obeyed. "Okay," he answered before simply walking away.

Edgin sped off. At school, he turned the case over to an investigator. Jason was charged with reckless conduct, a misdemeanor.

Yet Susan still refused to believe her son was responsible.

Years before Paducah, Kentucky, Littleton, Colorado, and the late-nineties outbreak of school-yard violence that bloodied playgrounds across the nation, Susan, oblivious to the danger, shifted the blame to the bus driver. "We've always been so nice to Calvin," she told a friend. "How could he do this? I thought he liked Jason."

To the attorney she hired to represent Jason, she argued against any punishment for her son, describing the gun as nearly a toy, a BB gun. Her protestations, however, weren't enough to stop the wheels of justice from bearing down on the teenager, as a court hearing was set for July.

After Jason's arrest, Susan called Gloria complaining that he was being treated unfairly. "It wasn't even a real gun," she repeated, writing off the entire incident as just another example of boys being boys. "He was just fooling around."

Gloria, who for too long had felt Susan didn't give Jason the discipline he needed, cautioned her sister that not taking Jason's actions seriously would prove a mistake. "You've got to sit on him some," she said. "You've got to get that kid under control."

Furious, Susan defended Jason. "You just don't understand!" she told Gloria, seething.

Despite the problems at home, Susan soon left for South Carolina to care for Ron's father while his stepmother underwent a minor operation. Her luck took another bad turn there, as a head cold she'd left Houston with developed pneumonia-type symptoms. Doctors diagnosed Legionnaires' disease.

She ended up in a hospital, part of it with a tube in her chest for a collapsed lung. Dr. Ronald Littlefield, the cardiologist in charge of her care, had seen only a handful of Legionnaires' cases in his career. He was never sure how Susan had contracted it—in the office, at home, or maybe even on the airplane. Susan fought high fevers and a dry, shattered cough; she was disoriented and had difficulty breathing.

In mid-April, Ron called Sandra and asked her to come to Houston. "He told me about Susan being in the hospital in South Carolina and how he had to go up there to get her. He wanted someone to stay with Jason." A fourth-grade teacher, Sandra had the week off, so she and O.L. drove to Houston to help out. It was a long week for them. The strange house in the big city made them both nervous. Every night there were reports on the television news about murders and rapes. At the time, a string of criminals roamed the better neighborhoods of the city. "Home-invasion robbers," reporters labeled them. Dressed as police officers, they flashed badges and ordered their victims to open the door. Once inside, they bound and gagged their helpless prey, then robbed them.

Jason's actions that week didn't ease their fears. Twice the seventeen-year-old sneaked out at night, propping up pillows and covering them with a blanket to fool them into believing he was in bed. A phone call from a teenage girl in the middle of the night sent Sandra in search of Jason. "She said he'd walked off with her money," says Sandra. "I told the girl he was in bed, but when I got up there, Jason was gone."

Sandra waited for her nephew when he climbed through an unlocked window just before daybreak the following morning. "Jason was real calm about it," she remembers. "He actually laughed."

His aunt, however, didn't find it funny when she discovered he was palming brass knuckles.

"What do you need those for?" Sandra asked.

"For protection," he said, as if it were the most reasonable explanation in the world coming from a teenager who lived in a quiet, affluent suburb.

Sandra confiscated the weapon, but a short time later, she found Jason staring out the front window, as if fearing someone had followed him.

By the time Ron returned with Susan on Saturday, April 18, the day before Easter, Sandra and O.L. were eager to escape Jason's pranks and the big city and head home. Susan appeared thin and pale, but in good spirits. As

Ron unpacked the car, she rattled on about his parents, the hospital, and the drive back. Suddenly the phone rang. Susan answered only to hear the line click off. Glaring at Ron, she hit the Call Return code on the phone, *69. It rang.

Sherri Brandt answered.

"Susan looked like she'd been slapped," says Sandra.

The atmosphere in the house on Amber Forest remained tense that spring. Ron moved in and out during a series of splits and reconciliations. Distraught, with time on her hands now that she wasn't working, Susan—accompanied by Jean—followed him to Sherri's apartment, taking pictures as he arrived and left. One such afternoon, she banged on the door as they hovered in the dark. When Sherri finally opened the door sometime later, she discovered a note from Susan. *He's not serious about you,* it read. *He'll do to you what he's doing to me.*

Other times, the phone rang at Sherri's apartment or at the office. "It's Susan," a voice on the other end said. "I just thought we should talk." Sherri slammed down the receiver, rattled by the phone call and wondering what would happen next.

"Susan was desperate. She was fighting to save her marriage," says Jean Morris. "She wanted Ron. She loved Ron."

Near the end of May, Susan was hospitalized again, a recurrence of the Legionnaires' disease that had plagued her earlier. Her doctor checked her into Houston Northwest Hospital, where he inserted a main intravenous line into her chest to pump in antibiotics and fluids. Through it all, Susan sat alone, day after day. Finally, she asked her doctor to call Ron. "Tell him I'm really sick and that he needs to come and see me," she begged.

The doctor did as his patient requested, but Ron

didn't respond the way Susan had hoped. Instead he called Sandra.

"Susan's in the hospital," he said. "You need to come take care of her. I'm washing my hands of her, Jason, of the whole thing."

A frightened Sandra called the hospital.

"I'm all right," Susan told her sister. "I'm getting better. I didn't mean to scare you or Momma. I just wanted Ron to worry about me."

By the end of May 1992, Susan White's life had entered a nether land; everything she'd held dear slipped through her fingers. She was forty-two years old, her health failing her. Jason, "her beautiful baby," fluttered in and out of trouble. Even Gloria, the big sister she'd always admired, said he was headed down a path that could only lead to further unhappiness. Ron, her husband, the man who'd rescued her from a life of near poverty, didn't want her anymore. He was finished with her. What had he told Sandra? "I'm washing my hands of her."

Searching for something to hold onto, Susan grasped for help wherever she could. She joined the Baptist church near her home. After one service, she paused to talk to the pastor, who gave her a book on Jesus' love.

At night she called Sandra, recounting her problems, her disappointments. Yet when Sandra urged Susan to move home to Louisiana, Susan, perhaps embarrassed by yet another failure, said no. "I've got friends here. Jason has friends here," she insisted. "Houston is our home."

"It's such a big city," Sandra said. "Are you safe there?"

"I've got friends in the police department," Susan assured her. "They'll look out for me."

Later, when Susan lay dead, slain by a deputy sheriff,

Sandra would look back and wonder whom Susan had been talking about.

Could it have been McGowen, the deputy who killed her?

Ron would later tell Sandra something else, that one night before he moved out late that spring, he awoke to find Susan gone. He drove through the quiet streets of Olde Oaks until he found her BMW parked near the country club, its lights off, and next to a deputy sheriff's car with someone inside. Their windows were rolled down and they were talking. Ron turned around and drove home.

Others would remember how Susan had stopped deputies' cars as they patrolled her neighborhood, offering the uniformed officers a cup of her dark Louisiana coffee with chicory and explaining that her husband had left her and that she was now a single mother, alone in the world.

"Mrs. White asked me to look out for her and Jason," recalls one such deputy she cornered during his regular patrol through Olde Oaks. "She said she was scared being alone in that big house at night. I didn't think anything special about it. She just seemed like a woman who was having a rough time."

Did Susan stop McGowen, perhaps with a similar request?

It was in April that Joseph Kent McGowen was first assigned to patrol Olde Oaks. In May, Susan stood outside Resa's piano bar talking to Alan Jefferies, while he sipped a clear glass of white wine on his break and lazily watched the occasional car slip by through the Houston night.

In Ron's absence, Susan had begun frequenting the club, often coming alone, claiming a stool at the piano, drinking splits of champagne, and striking up conversations with anyone who would listen.

"She was a needy kind of person," Jefferies recalls. "She kind of clung to whoever she could. She'd dominate the conversation. She always wanted me to sing a James Taylor song, 'I've seen fire and I've seen rain.'"

Usually, Susan left Resa's alone, but occasionally she'd strike up a conversation with a man and they'd leave together. After one such night, she confided in Jean that she'd accompanied a stranger home and awoke the next morning in his bed. "I told her she was crazy, the world was different than when she'd been single before," Jean says. "It wasn't safe to pick up a man at a bar. There were too many diseases, too many crazies out there."

Yet on this particular night, the night she stood outside the restaurant talking to Jefferies, Resa's had been quiet, and Susan was alone.

"You know why I like that James Taylor song?" she asked Jefferies as she lingered on the sidewalk, in front of a jovial mural of a bevy of the bar's regulars.

"Why?" he answered.

"Because it's about me," she claimed.

When Jefferies raised his eyebrows skeptically, she continued.

"I'm the Suzanne in it," she said, chuckling. "James Taylor and I were in a drug rehab together once, years ago, in my wilder days."

Jefferies laughed along with her. He felt sure she'd made the story up. A lot of people, after a few drinks, tried to impress him. He didn't mind. Then, as Susan turned to go, he cautioned her, "You've had a bit to drink; you'd better be careful driving."

"Oh, it's okay," she answered, flashing her broad smile. "I'm friends with all the deputies in the neighborhood. There's a new one on at night. Mac. He looks out for me. He'll make sure I get home."

With that, Susan spun on her heels and headed into the darkened parking lot, toward the white BMW.

Later, Jefferies would remember Susan's words: "There's a new one on at night. Mac. He looks out for me."

Mac? McGowen?

McGowen fit the description; he worked nights and had been transferred in only weeks earlier.

If it was Kent McGowen, Susan White didn't yet understand whom she'd befriended. In his uniform, his navy blue shirt meticulously pressed, his badge shining, he must have appeared responsible and strong, someone she could trust. How could she have known that, though just in his late twenties, Kent McGowen had amassed a checkered past in law enforcement, that he'd jumped from one police agency to another under a cloud of suspicion? How could she know what lay ahead, or how powerless she would be to stop it?

PART TWO

Joseph Kent McGowen

5

"Most people don't understand about cops, about how really vulnerable they are to a bad one," a veteran detective explains one afternoon over a BLT in a Denny's restaurant. A hulking bulldog of a man, he devours half the sandwich in a determined bite, dropping bits of lettuce slathered in mayo onto the plate.

"People think they have power, that if they're in the right they'll be able to prove it. The truth is, eventually they probably will," he says, shrugging noncommittally and licking an errant crumb of bacon from his thumb. "Eventually they'll hire a lawyer and get in front of a jury. But in the meantime, if a cop has it out for you and if he doesn't much care about breaking a few rules or telling a few lies . . . well, you're in deep shit. I mean deep shit. Because I can get in my car right now. I can pull over the next car I see. I can walk up to that car and order the person inside to get out. I can slap a pair of handcuffs on him and run him downtown. I can make up a charge, speeding, running a stop sign, resisting arrest, and book him. And who's the D.A. and judge going to believe? A cop or some Joe off the street?

"The majority of cops would never do that. They don't get off on harassing people. For them it's a job, a way to put food on their tables, maybe help people out a little if they're lucky. But it's the other cops, the ones not in it for the weekly paycheck or to do the occasional good turn. For those cops it's the rush they get from wearing the badge, carrying the gun, talking the talk, living the life. To them, being a cop is more important than love or hate or sex, more intoxicating than booze."

Susan White was fifteen when Joseph Kenton McGowen was born in Midland, Texas, on April 3, 1965. His father, Bill McGowen, a nervous yet imposing man with a proud bearing, worked for an oil company. Kent was his first child, but the third for his wife, Carolyn, a stocky woman with a helmet of dark hair, who had two sons from a previous marriage. It was a difficult pregnancy, Carolyn forced to spend the last two months in bed. "Kent was the most beautiful baby," recalls his father. "The most beautiful, the most ideal little boy."

A year later, the McGowens' only daughter, Melissa, was born.

From Midland the family relocated to Shreveport, Louisiana, then to Conroe, Texas, a small town north of Houston, when Kent reached the fifth grade. In 1972, Bill McGowen struck out on his own as an independent oilman. "I consulted for different people," says McGowen. "I built and sold my own companies."

A risky business, it offered great rewards to the successful, especially by the late seventies and early eighties, when the price of a barrel of oil catapulted to $38. Houston enjoyed an unprecedented boom. The four-star restaurant at La Colombe d'Or, a small hotel in the city's trendy Montrose section, offered the oilman's lunch,

seven courses for that day's price of a barrel of crude.
Oil was king and the McGowens prospered.

Still, theirs was a volatile union. Friends characterize
the McGowens as strong-willed, dominant personalities
who sometimes clashed. In the eighties, they split, di-
vorcing for four years, only to later remarry. "But we
always loved each other," says Bill earnestly, furrowing
his heavy brow for emphasis. "We were always a family."

Yet from the time Kent was a young boy, a dark cloud
hung over the McGowen household—the suicide of
Kent's uncle, Bill McGowen's brother. "Bill never really
got over it," says one family friend. "He always fretted
about why it happened and what could have prevented
it. He always worried that Kent would do the same
thing."

Those who knew the family say from the beginning
the ties between Bill McGowen and Kent, his only bio-
logical son, were strong. "Bill believes Kent walks on
water," maintains a friend. "No matter what he does, he
believes Kent is justified."

When Bill McGowen talks of a young, school-age
Kent, that admiration is palpable: "If you could say perfect, I guess Kent was. He never gave us any trouble. He
was studious, interested in hunting and fishing, average,
no—above-average intelligence, very very intelligent.
Kent was born an anointed baby."

Anointed as in chosen by God. The McGowens were
born-again Christians, believing in the laying on of
hands and speaking in tongues, in a literal interpretation
of the Bible. "When Kent was a police officer, people
would stop him in the street," Bill McGowen contends.
"They'd say, 'I can see Jesus in you.' Kent was an exceptional police officer, an exceptional young man."

Yet others describe a very different Kent McGowen:
a troubled teenager with a fascination for guns; a controlling and manipulative young man who displayed no

compunction about twisting the truth to fit his own purposes; a man drawn to violence, especially toward women.

"I met Kent while he was in high school, when he and Michelle began dating," recalls Pam Jones, Michelle's sister. "He seemed really nice at first; then everything went wild."

Kent met Michelle Morgan when she was sixteen years old, in drivers' education classes at Robert E. Lee High School in Houston. At the time, the McGowens owned a fashionable town house in the Galleria area, a decidedly urban neighborhood of glittery stores and restaurants and expensive condos and homes.

Michelle was a year ahead of Kent in school and six months older. The youngest of three sisters, she's described by friends as a quiet, shy girl with long dark hair and a ready smile.

Classmates describe Kent as a loner of sorts. He was small for his age, his dark hair often falling over his eyes. What his classmates recalled most was the way he flaunted his family's wealth, like the day he drove his birthday present—a shiny, new, black Jeep—into the school parking lot after Easter break. Whenever the opportunity arose, Kent bragged of a trust fund he claimed his parents had set aside for him, boasting one day he'd be rich, never having to work. Over the years, his estimate of its value mushroomed from hundreds of thousands to millions of dollars. As time passed and the money didn't come his way, the age at which he claimed he would gain control of that vast sum also increased, from twenty-one to twenty-five to thirty and beyond.

"He was a big talker . . . he made it sound like he was living the glamorous life," says Pam. "Michelle liked that, but at the same time, she would have been satisfied with the vine-covered cottage, kids, and a yard. The original Mommy-Daddy set."

Later, Bill McGowen would shake his head in denial that Kent could ever be a problem, blaming any teenage changes in his son on his relationship with Michelle. "We never had any trouble until they started dating," he maintains.

Perhaps the most telling explanation of Kent's future relationships with women came from someone who grew to know him well over the years. "Kent idolized his father; he wanted to be like him, to make a lot of money," she says. "I've always felt it had something to do with his parents' divorce, but ever since I've known him, Kent has acted like he hated women."

Throughout high school, Kent's relationship with Michelle took on a pattern of love and disdain. At times he was affectionate and thoughtful, leaving small notes professing his devotion to her. At other times he became violently angry.

"I guess the first time Kent threatened suicide that I know of was at sixteen," says Pam. "Michelle was going out with girlfriends and Kent showed up at our house. He had a knife in his hand and he threatened to use it on himself. My ex-husband took the knife away. It was so odd. He didn't want Michelle, but he didn't want anyone else to have her. Even going out with girlfriends made him jealous."

Kent blamed the Morgan family, especially Michelle's parents, for their arguments, charging that they plotted to keep them apart. During a split, Kent sent Michelle bitter letters, letters in which he called her family "devil worshipers."

Over the years, Pam saw many examples of Kent McGowen's fits of anger. He'd sometimes arrive at her house with his Jeep crowded with guns and rifles. On more than one occasion after an argument with Michelle, Kent stood on the front lawn holding a knife to his throat or a gun to his head. It ended with Pam's husband taking the knife or gun away, and a frightened Michelle agreeing to take Kent back.

"Every time they would break up over some terrible fight, we would think, *God, please let this be the end*," recalls Pam.

It was at a Halloween costume party at Pam's house, in the early years of their relationship, that someone snapped a photo of the young couple. In it Kent McGowen, dressed in camouflage fatigues and cap, an ammunition belt slung across his hips, cradles her ample waist. Michelle, her body wrapped around Kent, her hand confidently resting on her left hip, wears a black leotard and stockings, a bow tie at the neck, with slender white ears jutting upward, anchored to her softly curled brown hair.

Kent and Michelle: hunter and rabbit.

In 1982, his junior year, Kent dropped out of high school, to the great consternation of his father. Bill McGowen, a University of Texas grad who'd hoped Kent would follow in his footsteps, would later blame Robert E. Lee High School and its teachers for his son's disinterest. "The teachers weren't teaching," he charges. "They were more interested in getting through the day. Kent was tight with Michelle and she'd already graduated. And we took his Jeep away and he kind of rebelled. Maybe he was just bored in school."

Others say Kent never really had an interest in school. "He had no desire to go to college," says a friend. "All he ever wanted to be from the get-go was a cop. He was in love with the idea of that badge."

During the fall, he enlisted in the U.S. Air Force. Yet even in the service, Kent allowed his fascination with law enforcement to rule his choices. In January 1983, he began basic training at Lackland Air Force Base in San

Antonio, followed by classes leading to certification as a security specialist.

Back in Houston, the Morgan family initially hoped Kent's absence would end his relationship with Michelle. They'd grown frightened of Kent and the influence he had over her. But on April 9, 1983, the two eighteen-year-olds married. Rather than as a happy occasion, the Morgan family viewed the ceremony as a reason to grieve.

"Right before she went down the aisle, Michelle turned to me and said, 'This is a mistake,' " says Pam. "We told her she shouldn't go through with it, but she went ahead and married him. No one can understand what it's like trying to get away from Kent."

After the wedding, Kent and Michelle left for Malmstrom Air Force Base in Great Falls, Montana, where Kent joined the 342nd Missile Squadron as a nuclear security specialist. The following month, he completed a correspondence course through Lyndon Baines Johnson High School in Austin, Texas, to earn a high school diploma. Bill McGowen flew to Montana that spring and stayed at the small apartment the newlyweds had rented not far from the base. When he discovered they were sleeping on a mattress on the floor, he had a brand-new bed delivered.

Yet those early days of the marriage offered little comfort or security. Kent spent most of his day at the base, working, and Michelle was left alone. When he returned, he'd sometimes fly into jealous rages. After one such argument, just months after the wedding, Michelle called her mother, who mailed her a one-way ticket home to Houston. Michelle fled one afternoon while Kent was at work.

"We thought it was finally over," says Pam. "This time for good."

At home, Michelle moved in with her parents and, on July 1, filed for a divorce to end her three-month marriage. Yet a few weeks later, Kent appeared at the Morgans' front door, crying. Not long after, Michelle's mother returned from work and found a note: "I've gone to Montana. I've just got to try one more time." The next thing the Morgans heard, Michelle was pregnant.

Kent and Michelle would eventually have four children together. "Each one was conceived during a reconciliation," says Pam. "They went back and forth and back and forth."

By the fall, Kent had soured on the Air Force. Some say he disliked being away from home; others, that he found it difficult to follow orders. Poring over volumes of military programs, Kent analyzed the system and discovered the Palace Chase Program, an obscure procedure intended to allow soon-to-be-released personnel to leave early by volunteering to continue on in the Air National Guard.

Although three years remained on his enlistment, Kent applied and was accepted into the program, his only commitment to work one weekend a month at Ellington Air Force Base, a small, rarely used facility southeast of Houston. Just fourteen months after entering basic training, in March 1984, Kent and Michelle returned to Texas, leaving him free to pursue his dream.

Less than two months later, he applied at the Houston Police Department.

Law enforcement in Houston, as it is in much of Texas, is a maze of overlapping agencies. School districts, airports, transit authorities, hospitals—each employs its own police force, fully empowered to carry guns and make arrests. Constables, originally intended to serve civil warrants, and the sheriff's department, once little more than the authority that maintained the local jails, have also mushroomed over the decades into a complicated network of districts and precincts to patrol the fringes of the county, those areas that fall outside the city limits.

Of them all, in law enforcement circles, H.P.D. was considered *the* place to work.

"The department's big enough for advancement," explains one ex-cop. "Plus, the pay's better, the facilities are better, and you've got the backup departments like forensics, homicide, sex crimes, et cetera. For a cop, it's the top of the ladder. None of the other agencies measure up. Plus, it's the city, it's where all the action is."

From the beginning, H.P.D.'s siren call lured Kent.

Once he'd applied, a series of steps clicked into place that would lead, if successful, to the badge he so coveted. Physical and psychological testing, medical examinations. It was H.P.D.'s polygraph that, at least temporarily, thwarted his dream. During it, Kent admitted he'd smoked marijuana within the previous year, an automatic flag requiring his rejection, since a regulation at the time held that no applicant could have used any illegal drug within one year of employment. Kent was told to wait out the year before reapplying.

Ironically, another entry on the polygraph test went almost unnoticed. If considered, it might have indicated much of what Kent McGowen was really about and predicted what kind of a cop he would become. The remark that would be so telling noted that McGowen openly admitted being prejudiced against blacks, Hispanics, Asians, women—everyone but white men.

While marijuana use quickly ruled out Kent's immediate hiring at H.P.D., prejudice against the majority of people he would interact with on Houston's highly diverse streets was not considered important enough to disqualify him. The report dismissed the importance of McGowen's startling confession with the conclusion that "applicant stated he could work with any race or sex without letting prejudices interfere."

*   *   *

Once H.P.D. had rejected him for a year, Kent McGowen searched for alternate avenues to his goal of a career in law enforcement. He first applied to a handful of small departments, all of which turned him down. Not to be denied, he bypassed the traditional route of hiring on in a department before entering training. Instead, in July 1984, McGowen enrolled at the Criminal Justice Center at the University of Houston-Downtown, a kind of adult education program for would-be policemen.

That summer, Kent McGowen took courses in everything from firearms to the use of a baton, and completed the fourteen weeks and 560 hours of required training (little more than a third of the fifteen hundred hours demanded by the state for those wanting to become licensed hairdressers). In August, he became eligible for certification by T.C.L.E.O.S.E., the Texas Commission on Law Enforcement Officer Standards and Education.

The following January, 1985, Kent entered the ranks of licensed police officers, albeit in another roundabout fashion—as a reserve officer, an unpaid volunteer for the Waller County Sheriff's Department, the agency that oversaw the bucolic ranching community north of Houston that included Bill and Carolyn McGowen's sprawling new cattle ranch.

They called it the Deuteronomy 28 Ranch, a spread reminiscent of J.R.'s Southfork on *Dallas*. The name referred to a biblical verse in the Book of Deuteronomy, one that promises believers "blessed shall you be . . . shall be the offspring of your body . . . shall be your basket and your kneading bowl." For the enemies of God's chosen, it promised they will "be defeated before you."

In a setting befitting an oil tycoon, white picket fences and a stately, tree-shaded driveway led to the ranch's main house, where Bill and Carolyn lived, and the swimming pool, the tennis court. At night, lights shone softly into the towering trees.

To his new neighbors, Bill McGowen would occasionally hint that he had influence and access, including a friendship with then Vice President, soon to be President, George Bush, stemming from their shared beginnings in the Midland oil patch.

Meanwhile, the ranch took on the aura of a compound as Kent, Michelle, and their son, Joseph, moved into a mobile home on the property. A similar trailer housed Kent's cousin "Bubba," the son of Bill McGowen's deceased brother, and his family.

Bill McGowen soon bailed out of the oil business in favor of life as a gentleman rancher, giving his enterprise the grandiose title of McGowen Land and Cattle Company. By then the spiral had taken a downward turn, leaving the domestic oil industry in disarray and small independents like the McGowens drowning in a sea of cheap, imported oil.

For the most part, Kent worked on the ranch during the day, feeding the cattle and making repairs. A few nights a week, he patrolled as a reserve deputy with the Waller County Sheriff's Department, his real love. Deputies McGowen worked with there would later remember little about him. Some described him as a good or adequate officer, young and untested. Another would say that even then Kent McGowen appeared to have ambivalent reasons for wearing a badge. "Kent was looking for ladies," he'd say. "He used the badge more to impress women than to serve and protect the public."

In April, as the time when Kent would become eligible to reapply at H.P.D. drew near, an innocuous evening jog down a country road resulted in an injury that again postponed his dream. At 6 P.M. on April 14, 1985, twenty-seven-year-old Bubba and twenty-year-old Kent told their wives to hold dinner and went out for a run. The woman whose car bore down on them in the twilight never even put on her brakes as she barreled into Bubba head-on and deflected Kent into thick foliage on the side of the road. Bubba died; Kent broke his collarbone. When arrested, the driver claimed she thought her car had hit a mailbox.

Kent collected a settlement for his injuries and bought himself a Rolex diver's watch, stainless steel and gold with a navy blue face. It didn't quite measure up to the gold Rolex that Bill McGowen wore, but it was a start. Later, he would sometimes brag that H.P.D. had awarded him the watch as a commendation for police work well done, the heroic saving of a life. "I knew police departments don't give out Rolex watches," says Michelle's sister Pam. "But there was no sense in pushing it. When you disagreed with something Kent said, he just got more determined to convince you that it was true."

Later that summer, Kent McGowen again applied for an officer's position with the Houston Police Department. He listed his present employment as vice president of McGowen Land and Cattle Company, and for references he used an aunt and two friends of Michelle's mother, people who barely knew him. In September, the call came in; Kent McGowen had been accepted as a cadet in H.P.D.'s October 1985 academy class, number 132. He'd made it. It all lay before him: the badge, the gun, the busy city streets, the power.

A classmate at the academy who described himself as a friend of Kent's would later sum up what he saw in the young recruit: "He liked to talk about 'the job,' police work. He was a rebel—someone I was afraid to be. He didn't like foreigners, Asians, Hispanics, blacks, anyone who wasn't a fellow officer. He reminded me of Dirty Harry, the way he felt like it was up to him to right all the wrongs of the world. He lived and breathed law enforcement."

In March 1986, just before his twenty-first birthday,

Kent McGowen swore to "faithfully execute the duties of the office of regular officer of the City of Houston, Texas, and to the best of my ability preserve, protect, and defend the Constitution and laws of the United States, and this state and city." With that, he became one of the more than four thousand H.P.D. officers in the city charged with keeping peace and enforcing the laws.

"When you're the new kid at H.P.D., everyone gives you the benefit of the doubt," explains one veteran officer. "But officers, by nature and experience, are skeptical. We watch. If things don't look right, pretty soon we're comparing notes. Word gets around, like 'Watch out for so-and-so. He's not to be trusted.' Once that happens, a cop gets a jacket, a reputation. And that's something that stays with him for as long as he's at the department."

At H.P.D., Kent redesigned himself as Officer J.K. McGowen and for the first year appeared to be in the honeymoon phase of his employment. The officers who worked with him at the time remember nothing significantly noteworthy about the young, dark-haired, boyish-looking cop with the broad smile. His partner, Sergeant R. Montalvo, would later write a recommendation for Kent: "I worked with him on a professional basis in patrol for a little over a year . . . I know J.K. McGowen to be a fine, above standard police officer."

Yet others, including one officer he'd been through the academy with, would notice an aggressiveness in Kent and a penchant for living on the edge. "He wanted to do things his way, not necessarily the way things were supposed to be done, kind of a John Wayne type," remembers the officer.

At the time, Kent and Michelle were back together after a breakup, living in a rented house in Tomball, another of the small towns north of Houston. "It was strange. He didn't talk highly of his wife," remembers one officer. "But every time I talked to him, he was back with her. It was one of those on-again, off-again things."

Kent and Michelle's second child, Kenton Layne McGowen, had been born that February.

That summer, Kent and his partner, Montalvo, were commended for helping a volunteer officer. The man, who was policing a downtown festival on horseback, collapsed and fell, seriously injuring his spine. Kent and Montalvo gave him CPR, keeping him alive until the ambulance arrived.

In January 1987, another letter was placed in J.K. McGowen's file, a thank-you for assistance given a woman whose car was burglarized. Yet a month later, in February, McGowen's H.P.D. evaluation was less than stellar: two Very Goods and three Satisfactories. "That's not an endorsement, more like a shrug that the guy hasn't gotten in any serious trouble," maintains one sergeant. His August evaluation was a mirror of the first, and later that month, McGowen was transferred to the Westside Service Center, a substation in far west Houston. He was to work evenings, 3 P.M. to 11 P.M., in Neighborhood Services, a patrol division. It was at Westside that his fellow officers gave J.K. McGowen his first "jacket," a reputation as a braggart and a compulsive liar, as a man who disdained women, as someone not to be trusted.

"It was little stuff at first," says one Westside officer. "Kent was always bragging about his past, saying he'd spent four years in the Air Force, that he had a college diploma. We added up the years. [At twenty-two] there was no way he could have done all that."

"It was one of those things you tend to ignore," says another officer. "It's like, if they're not bothering you, you just figure it's bullshit and go on."

Yet as his time at Westside continued, other aspects

of Kent's personality came to light. His co-workers grew weary of the young officer bragging about his million-dollar trust fund—which he by then claimed he'd inherit at twenty-six—boasting that one day he wouldn't need a career at H.P.D., that while they might have to struggle, he'd be rich. Most troubling was the way McGowen took credit for himself that belonged to other officers. "We'd hear about a high-speed chase or a shoot-out in the district," remembers one officer. "By that night, Kent was claiming he'd been there, that he was the one who caught the bad guy. We knew it wasn't true. Usually we let it slide, but talk started up around the station that Kent McGowen didn't seem to know the difference between telling the truth and telling a lie."

Though still married and living with Michelle, Mc-Gowen spent little time at home those years at H.P.D. When the evening shift turned in its cars at 11 P.M., a handful of officers, stressed from eight hours patrolling Houston's hectic streets, headed to "choir practice"— clandestine meetings on deserted dead-end streets. They drank and told tales from the job. Kent relished the camaraderie, rubbing elbows with his fellow officers, an opportunity to brag about his "exploits" and his father's money.

After choir practice, instead of making the forty-minute drive home, Kent often bunked with one or another of his co-workers.

If law enforcement types are a subculture, the officers Kent hung out with were a subculture within a subculture, mainly rogue cops, christened "gypsy cops," who lived by their beepers. They camped out in apartments supplied free of rent in exchange for acting as "courtesy officers," unofficial security on an apartment complex's grounds. They came and went, rootless, often moving every six months to a year, their doors open to fellow cops who needed a place to bed down. Few of his co-workers knew Officer J.K. McGowen had a home, a wife, and two children.

Soon after arriving at Westside, Kent put in for a transfer to another division at the station, the one that patrolled Richmond Avenue, the city's densest concentration of clubs and singles' bars. It was to Houston what the West End was to Dallas, or Rush Street to Chicago. "McGowen wanted to cash in on the uniform, get himself some road runners, groupies," says a fellow officer. "The kind of women who are turned on by the uniform."

McGowen admitted as much to another officer, recounting his sexual exploits in the era of AIDS: "I want to be where the pussy is. All these women want me to wear condoms. I don't wear condoms. One finally forced me to wear a condom and it broke on her. So that was a joke on her."

When he saw a woman or women on the street or in a restaurant, his contempt for them shone even clearer. He was known to point to a woman waiting for a bus and announce, "She's a whore." When asked how he could tell, he'd maintain, "I just know." One night at a restaurant with a friend, he motioned toward three women in business suits enjoying a cocktail and laughing, possibly co-workers winding down after a rough day at the office. "Look at them," he sneered. "Tramps."

Not long after Kent joined Westside, he began dropping over unannounced at the house of Michelle's sister Pam, who lived within the district. There, he'd come up with war stories from the street, like the morning he crowed about arresting a man for speeding, throwing him over the hot hood of his car, then pulling him off, but not before the metal had blistered the skin on his palms. Sometimes he showed up with prisoners in the back of his squad car and declared, "I just want you to see what kind of scum I'm picking up in your neighborhood." Other times he brought along crime-scene photos of dead bodies at murder sites.

"Blood-and-guts horror stories," says Pam. "He was going to kill this person, he'd threaten Michelle. He'd threaten to kill himself. He just thrived on threats and mayhem."

Then he began showing up with women. "He would bring female officers with him that he was supposedly having affairs with," says Pam. "To my house, and he's married to my sister. When I'd tell Michelle, he'd convince her that I was the one lying. Kent had a way of talking, drawing things out of you, your deepest, darkest secrets. He'd come off as your best friend. Then turn around and use it against you."

To Pam's then husband, Mike, Kent gloated about new business ventures he planned. "He could never tell you much about it, but there was always some kind of a new business and it was always going to bring in big bucks, usually thirty thousand dollars a month," says Pam. "Once he said he was going to act as a middleman for a South American rancher who wanted to buy U.S. cattle. Another time he was going to be an expert hunting guide, flying all over the earth. Pretty soon the story changed and he was on to something else."

The marriage, as it had from the beginning, continued to be troubled. Michelle repeatedly confided in family members that Kent threatened to walk out on her, taking the children with him, using his parents' money as leverage, to hire lawyers who'd claim she was a bad mother.

When Kent and Michelle sought counseling through Bill and Carolyn's church, a charismatic Christian church, the minister, who usually tried to keep marriages together, took the unusual step of calling Michelle's mother. Without explaining, he simply advised her to get Michelle away from Kent. "The situation," he said, "is terribly dangerous."

"We tried," says Pam. "Mom talked to her. I talked to her. But it was hopeless."

At H.P.D., Kent McGowen's dramatic episodes were to become legendary. Some co-workers would later describe him as acting not unlike a mischievous child who never took responsibility for his actions, yet always wanted to be the center of attention. When a fellow officer or a supervisor crossed him, vindictiveness was added to Kent McGowen's growing jacket. "If he got pissed at you for something, he'd threaten to go to Internal Affairs on some trumped-up charge," says one co-worker. "Pretty soon a lot of us just tried to stay away from Kent."

His supervisors also grew weary of Officer J.K. McGowen. He was a malcontent, complaining bitterly about H.P.D. management and squawking when ordered to drive an older squad car. Often, when assigned to a car he didn't like, Kent grumbled at the sergeant, then returned moments later to say the car's mirror was broken and the car was unsafe. "I figured he broke the mirror so he didn't have to drive it," says one sergeant. As far as the supervisors at Westside were concerned, Kent McGowen was a thorn in their sides, more trouble than he was worth. "When you supervise people, you're expecting them to go out and be police officers," says another sergeant. "You're not expecting them to horse around, ask for districts where there are women, or, as McGowen referred to it, 'pussy.' "

The next year, 1988, the seeds of distrust McGowen had sown at H.P.D. grew. By the time he tendered his resignation, few of his fellow officers at Westside would be saddened by his departure. Kent McGowen was fated to carry his jacket with him until the day he finally walked out the door.

6

"There's a phase police officers go through," explains Greg Riede, Ph.D., head of H.P.D.'s psychology department. "It's called adolescence. It usually covers their first year or two. During this period, new officers develop an us-and-them mentality. 'Us' includes people in law enforcement; 'them' means everyone else. They live and breathe law enforcement. Their only friends are other officers. Everything they talk about pertains to 'the job.' But most officers—the good ones—pass through adolescence and mature. They see people as people again, good and bad. They no longer like to talk about what they do, simply because people react differently to them once they find out that they're police officers. So at their kids' softball games, they don't volunteer the information.

"There are some, however, who never make it through adolescence. They get stuck there. Their view of the world is skewed. They see anyone besides their fellow officers and their families as the enemy, and often themselves as the only ones who can right the wrongs.

When that happens, they react less carefully, they're more prone to be rigid. We try to weed those officers out. On the street, they can be dangerous."

Kent McGowen's real problems at H.P.D. began on April 21, 1988, with a ten-year-old boy he found walking the streets late at night. His mother, the youngster claimed, had thrown him out of the house. When the woman insisted that, rather than being abandoned, the boy—whom she described as a chronic runaway—had sneaked out, McGowen didn't believe her. He seemed to view himself as the boy's savior, going so far as to suggest he take the child home to live with Michelle and their children, an offer that recalled the plots of various TV police dramas, but one that violated H.P.D. policy.

The case was referred to Children's Protective Services, and Kent—if he had followed the rules—should have been out of it. But in the month that followed, he repeatedly interjected himself into the situation, infuriating the mother. Many of the officers at Westside remember McGowen being preoccupied with the case, talking about it constantly.

"McGowen was always the crusader," says an H.P.D. sergeant who ordered him to stay away from the youngster. "You could never tell him anything."

The mother finally filed a complaint with Kent's supervisors. When that didn't solve the problem, she retained a lawyer and threatened to file a restraining order, barring him from coming anywhere near her son. Only then did Kent McGowen back away.

Not everyone viewed McGowen's actions with cynicism. A woman who claimed to be the boy's guardian wrote a letter to H.P.D. a month later, "commending Officer McGowen for his caring attitude toward the boy." Also in May, Kent received a commendation from headquarters, which read, "Officer's average [arrests] for the month of April was 50 percent above the average total crime for officers in eighteen districts."

But by the summer, Kent McGowen, who never seemed able to remain above the fray for long, was again embroiled in controversy.

It actually began the previous December, when Officer Sara Williams, a tall, attractive, high-strung blonde, attended a birthday party for a fellow H.P.D. officer. Most everyone drank—many, including Williams, too much. "It was cops acting like high school kids," says one officer in attendance. "You tend to get caught up in it. Things can get a little crazy." A wild affair, it went well into the night, degenerating until, in the early-morning hours, a drunken officer unholstered his gun and discharged it toward the stars, the blast echoing through the night air. Someone called Internal Affairs.

It had been a rough night for Williams. Not only was she dazed from a bellyful of alcohol, but her boyfriend—another officer—had locked himself in the bathroom with another woman cop. When the investigating lieutenant made his way to her, Williams mouthed off. That earned her a fifteen-day suspension.

Williams' round of bad luck continued that spring as her boyfriend dumped her. "He was on a pedestal with the other guys at the station, and law enforcement is still a man's world," recalls an officer. "He was very attractive, very charismatic; he always had a beautiful woman at his elbow. When he dropped her, she was considered dead meat."

"Dead meat" sentenced Williams to isolation by her ex-boyfriend's horde of admirers. No longer did they drive by to check on her when she wrote a ticket or made an arrest. Her list of friends at the substation dwindled, along with a hefty portion of her self-respect. "Sara was an emotional wreck," says a friend.

It was in May that Kent McGowen stopped Williams and asked if he could talk with her about his troubles with the young boy. She agreed. "Most cops won't talk to other guys about emotional stuff," explains a woman officer. "It's not odd for them to seek out a female officer to confide in about stuff at home or anything kind of soft. They don't want to let down their guard. It's important to keep up the machismo."

At her apartment that night, McGowen told her about the ten-year-old he'd befriended and how the system got in the way.

"Sara was impressed that he was so caring about a little kid," says Williams' then-best friend. "She was lonely and tired of being ostracized by the others."

A few nights later, Kent and Sara, who was nine years older than McGowen, shared a quiet dinner and a few drinks. They finished the night in Williams' bed.

Afterward, Williams maintained their liaison was a lapse in judgment, and that from the beginning she felt a relationship with McGowen would be a mistake. Who tried to break it off with whom would later be the source of much argument. For her part, Williams contended she told McGowen early on that he was too young for her and she wasn't interested. McGowen insisted he was the one who dumped Williams, sneering at the memory of a woman he called "plain crazy."

For days their feud interrupted H.P.D.'s radio waves as they bumped each other through the night on their MDTs, the mobile data terminals in their squad cars.

The tension erupted later that summer when a group of Westside cops clustered at choir practice. Guns holstered, beer flowing, at the end of a dead-end street, they told war stories and ribbed each other, whispering gossip and belittling their bosses. McGowen had another woman on his arm. Sara brought an old boyfriend, also a cop.

Williams later told H.P.D. investigators that as the others partied, McGowen pulled her to the side and issued a threat: "He told me I was going to regret breaking off with him. He said he'd ruin my life."

In the early hours of the following morning, July 13, Williams showed up at Kent McGowen's apartment, according to her, in an effort to end the hostilities between them. As Williams described that night, Kent was furious, screaming at her about bringing her old boyfriend to choir practice. He ordered her to leave; she refused.

McGowen called the substation and a sergeant came to the scene and ordered Williams from the apartment.

Two days later, Kent McGowen filed a formal report. In it he portrayed Williams' behavior as "abnormal" and maintained that he'd observed her to act in "a hostile and irrational manner." Kent said Williams, not he, had monopolized the MDT, that she became "verbally abusive" toward him, and that she "threatened to blow out my squad car windows." That she warned, "That's it, motherfucker, you'll regret this."

He claimed that at choir practice she'd held a cocked, loaded gun to her head and threatened to commit suicide, that she'd stalked him, and that she'd shown up at his apartment that night begging him to make love to her. He described her as "intoxicated and belligerent."

Kent McGowen concluded: "Officer Williams has spoken to me several times about committing suicide. I truly believe she is fully capable of doing it. My only intent in writing this letter is to get her the help she needs, possibly saving her life and the life of another."

Other officers at the station would later say they didn't know whom to believe about the feud. They knew Sara Williams drank too much and described her as troubled, but Kent McGowen was well known for "covering his ass," and for "lying his way out of a situation."

"I figured it was a match made in hell," says one officer. "I didn't totally believe either side, but knowing Kent, my sympathies went to Sara."

Based on McGowen's complaint, H.P.D. suspended

Williams for forty-five days without pay and ordered her to attend psychiatric counseling. They also began an investigation into Kent McGowen's behavior. During the time she was off work, Kent's threat came true for Williams, who lived on the financial edge. Her car was repossessed, her credit ruined.

At the station, McGowen bragged he'd slept with Williams and she'd wanted more. Possibly he failed to notice his fellow officers' lack of amusement at his tale of sexual conquest. If he'd expected to be praised for his liaison with Williams, that didn't happen. Instead, after word spread that he'd filed a complaint on another officer, McGowen was blackballed. As had once happened to Williams, officers stopped checking by on his stops, and few talked to him. "You just don't file on another cop," explains one officer. "Not unless the guy's committed rape or worse. A snitch is the worst thing to have on your jacket."

In July 1988, H.P.D. again received a letter from a civilian commending Kent McGowen, this time for his handling of a car theft. But at the end of August, as his superiors continued to look into his role in the Sara Williams situation, Kent clashed with the substation's higher-ups again, remarkably over what should have been a routine call.

The incident took place on August 30, when Kent responded to the scene of a minor car accident. Moments later, an angry woman called Westside from a pay phone and asked for McGowen's superior, Sergeant C.J. Grysen. McGowen, she said, had refused to give a ticket to the other driver, a Mexican immigrant who spoke no English. The sergeant, an avuncular man with a quiet demeanor, rushed to the scene. After sizing up the situation, Grysen judged the woman was right; the driver who had hit her had rear-ended her at a stop sign. He also noticed that the man had been drinking and had no proof of insurance, as required by Texas law. Grysen pulled McGowen to the side.

"Why haven't you written the guy a ticket?" Grysen demanded.

"Conflicting statements," Kent replied.

"How do you even know?" Grysen queried, exasperated at the young cop's answer. "That guy doesn't speak English and you don't speak Spanish. Anyway, he's clearly in the wrong. Write him a ticket."

To Grysen's surprise, McGowen claimed, "We don't write tickets anymore."

Grysen figured Kent was referring to an order that had come down from H.P.D. headquarters discontinuing an unofficial quota of two tickets per day per officer. No one, though, had told the patrol squads not to write traffic tickets.

"Write it up," Grysen ordered.

To the sergeant's amazement, McGowen snapped, "I don't even have a ticket book with me. I haven't carried one in a year."

Furious, Grysen handed him his own ticket book.

"Well, I'm not going to write a ticket," an angry McGowen responded. "That bitch has a big mouth."

"Write it up or you're ordered back to the station and relieved of duty," Grysen insisted.

With that, McGowen took Grysen's book and wrote the man a ticket.

That December 20, as investigations into McGowen's actions at the accident scene and his confrontation with Williams continued, Kent tendered "with deep regret" his resignation at H.P.D., effective in three weeks, on January 9, 1989. As his reason for leaving, he cited "an opportunity and financial resources to further my education." He bragged to his fellow officers that his wealthy father had better plans for him than to waste his life as a cop, that he was sending him to vet school at Texas A&M, paying his tuition and his family's living expenses.

That same day, Lieutenant M. H. Luiz wrote a letter accepting McGowen's resignation. "I further recommend," he noted, "that should Officer McGowen apply for reinstatement with the department he be considered for employment."

Those who worked with McGowen and Luiz would later say that at the time the lieutenant wrote the letter, he'd supervised McGowen only months and not on a daily basis. "Luiz really hadn't had much to do with McGowen," said one sergeant.

Yet even with his parting in sight, Kent McGowen appeared unable or unwilling to stop bucking the station's routine. His last three weeks at H.P.D. were peppered with rancor. It began when McGowen asked Grysen if he could leave early. Still irritated about the traffic-accident incident, the sergeant refused.

An obviously steaming Kent McGowen left on patrol. For the rest of the night, whenever Grysen clicked on the radio to bump his squad by MDT, someone clicked out his message, much the same way Sara Williams maintained McGowen had done to her. Grysen assumed McGowen was responsible, but couldn't prove it.

A week or so later, Grysen overheard McGowen bragging to a rookie officer that he was going to run as few calls as possible and take as long as possible on each call for his last two weeks with the department. "I'm taking it easy," he said, launching into a laundry list of complaints about H.P.D. Not wanting McGowen to sour the young officer, Grysen refused his request to have the rookie ride along in his squad car during patrol.

That night, as before, each time Grysen transmitted on the MDT, someone clicked him out. Finally, the sergeant asked an officer to repeat an address, only to hear a mocking voice on his radio. "Duh," the officer said, as if Grysen were too stupid to get the information the first time.

Grysen recognized McGowen's voice.

When Kent returned to the station, Grysen threatened to write him up. McGowen snapped back, threatening to file a complaint with H.P.D.'s Internal Affairs Division, charging that Grysen drank on the job. "It was a lie," said an officer on duty that night. "But Kent knew it would force the sarge to defend himself, and that even when it was proved false, it would be on his record."

At his exit interview in early January, Kent McGowen maintained that he'd enjoyed his stint at H.P.D., but that there were problems at the agency, including a lack of leadership and career opportunities for young, aggressive officers like himself. The twenty-three-year-old turned in his badge and walked out the door, concluding his three years with H.P.D., a job that had once been his dream.

Three days later, on January 12, 1989, Sergeant C.J. Grysen had his opportunity to write an exit report and document his impressions of Officer J.K. McGowen. "Performance poor with a lack of maturity," he wrote. "A general bad attitude toward the department . . . In the time I supervised the employee, I did not observe any significant strengths worth noting . . . He has poor relationships with supervisors, brought on by his lack of orientation to authority. Though tolerated by some peers, he is not respected by others . . . He asks for special favors and threatened bogus I.A.D. complaints about supervisor that would become part of his permanent record . . . The employee talked about leaving as long as I knew him . . . When he gave notice, his actions turned from disrespectful to mutinous . . . The employee apparently enjoyed the excitement of police work, but was an arrogant malingering malcontent when placed under any form of supervision . . . He was a disruptive influence among peers, often giving advice where not requested or warranted."

Grysen then went on to detail incidents in which he maintained McGowen had shown bad judgment: the episode with the ten-year-old boy ("he showed a crusader arrogance in which he didn't care about what was the proper or correct way to handle a situation"), the conflict with Sara Williams, and his refusal to write a ticket and exchange information at an accident scene ("when the civilian had a justified complaint").

To the question *What type of divisional assignment do you feel the employee is best suited for?* Grysen wrote: "One in which he would work alone, with few responsibilities and no contact with the public."

Two days after Grysen completed his caustic exit report on McGowen, Lieutenant E.G. Huhn wrote another memo on McGowen. It read: "Negative information was received from all levels of supervisors and from co-workers associated with Mr. McGowen during his tenure as a police officer with this department."

Lieutenant Luiz, who just a month earlier had endorsed McGowen, called the young officer a "chronic complainer." Sergeant R.D. Hayes noted that McGowen was "not dependable, always wanted to ride where the women are." Two officers labeled McGowen "immature and conceited," and another said he would never ride with him, citing as his reason, "McGowen's too aggressive." More than one classified him as "dangerous."

Into McGowen's I.A.D. file, along with the exit report and supervisors' and co-workers' statements, was tucked his Internal Affairs record for his three years at H.P.D.: one complaint, sustained by I.A.D., detailing McGowen's actions on the MDT with Williams; another sustained complaint for not sharing information at the accident scene; and five unsustained complaints, including two alleging excessive force.

There was also a complaint from a ninety-year-old Nigerian woman who charged that Officer McGowen had called her "a fucking nigger."

A reasonable person might assume that such scathing assessments would finish Kent McGowen's career in law enforcement, that no agency would ever hire him again. Unfortunately, this would not prove to be the case. Like companies around the country who fear lawsuits, H.P.D., it would later appear, buried Kent McGowen's highly unfavorable evaluations in his I.A.D. file, leaving only Lieutenant Luiz's initial response to McGowen's resignation in his personnel file, the letter in which Luiz had recommended that McGowen should be eligible for rehire.

It would simply be the first of many missed opportunities to deprive Kent McGowen of a badge.

7

That spring semester, 1989, Kent McGowen enrolled in North Harris County College, a two-year institution, despite having bragged to his fellow H.P.D. officers that he was leaving the department to enroll at Texas A&M University. Kent had a long road to go before even becoming eligible for the latter school's veterinary program, one of the most prestigious in the country. He had only a handful of college credits and a high school diploma earned through a correspondence course. For someone with his academic record, the community-college system offered a second chance. If he performed well, he could become eligible for many of the state colleges, including A&M.

True to his word, Bill McGowen supported his son's family. He paid their bills, bought their food and clothing. In fact, Kent's father seemed pleased with the arrangement. "Bill never liked Kent's being a cop," says a friend. "He always thought Kent could do better."

Yet Bill McGowen's good intentions yielded little.

Kent's brief college career began in January with classes in a pre-veterinary program. He enrolled in five subjects: English Composition and Rhetoric I, Introduction to Algebra, Medical Terminology, Introduction to Veterinary Medicine and Nutrition and Feeding. But by March he'd withdrawn from the latter three. Of the fourteen credits McGowen attempted, he earned only six, an A in English and a C in algebra. "Kent lost interest in school," remembers one friend. "He couldn't wait to get back to being a cop."

"It couldn't have been more than two months after he quit," says another. "Kent had the bug back. He said he'd made the biggest mistake of his life leaving H.P.D."

Kent had another motivation for a quick return to the Blue Brotherhood: To maintain his license as an officer in the state of Texas, he needed his state certification, and state regulations stipulated that licenses of officers not commissioned by a sponsoring law enforcement agency for a period of six months or longer were automatically withdrawn. The day McGowen left H.P.D., a bureaucratic clock began ticking off the days until his state certificate would lapse. If he ever attempted to return to law enforcement, losing his license was a formidable roadblock, requiring him to retake tests, including the mandatory psychological examinations.

There was, however, one loophole, a way former officers often retained certification without a full-time job in law enforcement—volunteering as an unpaid reserve officer for a small city or town, as he had done four years earlier with Waller County. Most departments dependent on reserves were rural and without the tax dollars to hire paid officers.

It was a comedown for McGowen.

On the scale of prestige associated with law enforcement in Houston, H.P.D. represented the top, while reserve deputies hung onto the bottom rung. "Some reserve officers are hardworking, dedicated people," says one detective. "But some volunteer because they feel naked without a badge and a gun, the kind of guys who put themselves into a bad situation and then rely on the badge to get themselves out. Those are the ones no police officer can stand." Although a significant drop in prestige, a reserve position served Kent's purpose, allowing him to retain that all-important link with police work, his state certificate.

That spring, Kent McGowen walked into the Tomball Police Department and offered his services as a reserve officer to Leroy Michna, the acting chief of police. Until the mid-eighties, Tomball was a sleepy little burg an hour's drive north of downtown Houston. Its status changed as the city's building boom sprawled north. Strip centers, subdivisions, supermarkets, and traffic descended on the small community like ash from a rumbling volcano. Michna, a white-haired, fatherly man who'd retired after twenty-one years in juvenile sex crimes with H.P.D., needed to augment his forces without straining his budget. A certified officer with H.P.D. training, one willing to work free, was an ideal candidate.

When Michna asked, Kent told the acting chief he'd left H.P.D. to pursue his education. "I want to keep my hand in police work," a friendly McGowen explained.

After McGowen left, Leroy Michna studied the young man's application. Everything seemed in order. He then took the precaution of calling H.P.D. "All they told me was he'd worked there," Michna later complained. "And that he had a letter from a lieutenant saying if he wanted to come back, he should be considered for rehire." Yet before Michna could call McGowen, the phone rang in his Tomball office; an H.P.D. detective he'd known for decades wanted to talk.

"I understand Kent McGowen was in there looking for a reserve job," the detective said.

"Yup," Michna answered.

"Well, I want to tell you, that boy has no business

being a police officer," the caller warned. "If you're smart you won't give him a commission."

Michna hung up the phone, not sure of what to do. Then he remembered the H.P.D. letter saying, "should be considered for rehire."

"I figured there was maybe one guy mad at him," Michna sums up. "Of course, I later thought, *Boy, I wish I had listened*."

On May 12, 1989, Michna signed Kent on at Tomball P.D. as a reserve patrolman. Initially the veteran cop was pleased with his decision. Where other reserve officers worked a day or two a month, McGowen willingly took shifts of up to twenty-four hours a week. And at first, Michna's other officers admired Kent, impressed with his H.P.D. training. "He'd handle a domestic dispute and get the man and woman separated and cooled down," says Michna. "Everyone would say, 'How'd he do that?' I had to tell them, 'Hey, think about it. We get maybe twenty calls like this a year. At H.P.D., they handle them every night.'"

Yet that nascent respect quickly faded. Within a month of Kent McGowen's arrival, his fellow Tomball P.D. officers had compared notes on the young cop's stories, on the years he'd claimed to be in the Air Force and his education. As his H.P.D. peers had done three years earlier, they added up the numbers and came to the same conclusion: It was impossible for Kent, just twenty-four, to have done all the things he claimed. "Kent told fish stories," one officer says. "No doubt about it."

When it came to his departure from H.P.D., McGowen was unclear. Sometimes he maintained he'd quit to return to school; other times he complained about a supervisor who'd "railroaded" him. Officer Tina Anderson heard a third explanation: "Kent told me he'd just gotten burned out at H.P.D.," says Anderson, an energetic, matter-of-fact Tomball officer. "I'd been a cop since eighteen and my dad was a cop. Nobody gets burned out that fast. At three years, he should have been pissing vinegar."

Others grew perplexed by their new reserve officer's private life. At bars after work, Kent arrived with his arm around his girlfriend, Karen, a dark-haired woman in her early twenties who worked at a local department store and went to college part-time. But when Karen wasn't around, Kent talked of his wife and children. "He'd say it real natural, like, of course he had a wife," says Anderson.

Meanwhile, behind the scenes, McGowen's married life continued to operate like a roller coaster. After years of threatening, Michelle McGowen filed for divorce. On August 31, 1989, it became final. Kent was granted visitation with their three young children and ordered to pay $750 a month in child support. Yet it was far from the end of the relationship. Before long, Kent and Karen split, leading Kent, as usual, back to Michelle. Whether pulled by love or fear, she repeatedly took him back. Over the years they parted and reunited so many times, even her family was unable to keep track of their status.

Those who knew Kent say he never acknowledged the divorce, and that, as the years passed, he continued to refer to Michelle not as his ex-wife but as his wife— unless being divorced suited his purposes. "I never understood what was going on with him," says one friend. "Was he divorced or not? He'd call her 'my wife,' but he carried his divorce decree, folded, in his wallet. He used it in bars, whipped it out and showed whatever woman he was romancing that he was single."

Still, the character of their union didn't change. More than once over the coming years, Michelle McGowen called the police, insisting they remove Kent from apartments she'd rented. Once he'd slapped her so hard the sting left a raw bruise across her swollen face. Another time she complained to Pam that he'd held a gun to her head and threatened to shoot.

"It always turned out the same way. Michelle called and the squad car pulled up. But then they'd walk inside and see Kent and say, 'Oh, it's McGowen. We know him,' " says Pam. "They'd refuse to take Kent away. Michelle had to take the children and leave."

Despite continuing turmoil in his private life, that summer Kent had reason to be excited. A position opened up that could match a young officer's fantasy of police work. It echoed the plots of the nineties' most popular TV shows, *NYPD Blue* and *Law & Order*, where cops manipulated informants and cracked the big cases.

Kent McGowen's new position came to pass after a call to Leroy Michna from the captain in charge of the Harris County Organized Crime Unit, a force of officers donated by each of the communities within the county lines. He requested Tomball assign an officer to their drug task force. Michna considered his ranks. Not eager to part with a full-time, paid officer, Michna thought of McGowen. He was gung-ho, he had H.P.D. training. "I figured it would be a good match," Michna later explained. "No pay and he had to drive his own car, but they'd reimburse him for gas. But it wasn't long before things seemed really peculiar."

Twenty-three separate county law enforcement agencies worked with H.C.O.C., the county's organized crime unit, along with the Federal Bureau of Alcohol, Tobacco, and Firearms (ATF), and the FBI. Once assigned, McGowen was partnered with Detective Curtis Mills, a veteran officer with shaggy, prematurely gray hair. Mills was from Humble, Texas, a quaint old town surrounded by new subdivisions, just northeast of Houston. The detective was an anomaly in a city of migrants from other states and countries, a native Texan.

After settling in, Mills and McGowen learned of the task force's emphasis on street-level operations, where one undercover officer made buys from drug dealers and a second officer moved in to make the arrests. "The concept was to go from one buy-and-bust to the next to get the dealers off the streets," says Mills. "Most of the time we were on the phone, talking to confidential informants, C.I.s, setting up our next operation."

As usual, McGowen latched onto this new assignment with enthusiasm. He grew his dark hair long, along with a scruffy beard, and wore an earring, mimicking the stereotypical drug dealer. To Pam, Michelle's sister, he bragged about his new assignment. "He reveled in the fact that now he could kill some of the bad guys," she says. "Bikers and drug dealers. He thought it was really cool."

But before long, as in Houston and Tomball, rumors questioning McGowen's veracity circulated at H.C.O.C. Mills himself heard three versions of McGowen's resignation from H.P.D., including that he no longer needed to work because he was about to cash in on a multi-million-dollar trust fund from his rich parents.

"Most cops don't have a college degree, but they have an overload of horse sense, and we can usually figure somebody out pretty quickly. It wasn't long before we had his number," says Mills. "He also had a hang-up about women. He'd call them 'pussies' under his breath. If a secretary asked a question about his expense report, he'd grumble, 'That bitch must have a bad case of PMS.'"

Back in the police groove, McGowen told Mills he was considering applying for his old job at H.P.D. Although he'd often gloated about his three years with the agency, Mills sensed Kent wasn't sure he'd be welcomed as warmly as the prodigal son.

The two partners formed an uneasy alliance. For the

most part, Mills avoided working with him. Then, in midsummer, their lieutenant asked him to help the young officer with a big case, one that could yield a major drug player. "Kent's got an informant at a restaurant and he needs task-force money to make a buy," the lieutenant ordered. "You take care of it. I'll make sure you're reimbursed."

The funds in hand, a wary Mills walked into a restaurant and eyed McGowen with a twentysomething man in a booth. McGowen introduced the stranger as a narcotics officer from another jurisdiction. Then he began detailing his plan for the buy-and-bust.

"It wasn't long before the whole thing smelled," said Mills later. Rather than a clear-cut case of McGowen having reliable information from a C.I., enough for a judge to sign a search warrant, Mills sensed that the young cop had nothing concrete.

"McGowen was talking in riddles, and the guy he was with knew nothing about narcotics. I found out they didn't even have a search warrant," he reports. "They were planning a 'knock-and-talk,' where you bang on the door and talk your way into a house. In other words, he was trying to lead me to believe he had enough probable cause for a search warrant, but he didn't have one."

When McGowen's confidential informant, his C.I., arrived, Mills' chagrin multiplied. The woman, white, heavyset, in her mid-twenties, looked "like a mud fence after a hard rain," says Mills. He sized her up, judging she was nothing more than a small-time user, not a link to a major dealer.

"I can get you anything you want," the woman crowed to Mills.

"I want a supertanker of cocaine," replied Mills sarcastically. "Can you get me that?"

The woman, looking at him like he'd lost his mind, replied, "No."

"Well, now we've set some parameters," snapped Mills "What can you get?"

"I can buy you a few twenty-dollar rocks," she said somewhat sheepishly.

Frowning at the woman he now knew he'd judged correctly, he asked, "Have you got a C.I.'s number with the task force?"

The woman glanced quizzically at McGowen.

"Shit, McGowen," Mills growled. "What the hell?"

It appeared obvious to Mills that this bust was another example of Kent McGowen's active imagination and his penchant for exaggeration. The woman wasn't a registered informant, which meant paying her violated task-force rules, and at best she was a small hitter. If McGowen hadn't outright lied to him, Mills felt certain he'd purposely misled him.

Disgusted, Mills turned to McGowen. "All right, you want to put buffalo butt up in a room, that's fine. You want to give her spending money and buy her lunch, okay," he snarled at the younger officer. "But you're going to sign all the papers. I'm out of this deal. It stinks to high heaven and I want no part of it."

"I'm going to do this," a furious McGowen shot back. "I've got a great case, a big-time drug dealer."

Mills walked out, shaking his head.

"I never really knew of him making a drug case," Mills would say later. "Maybe he did, but I never heard about it. I left him totally alone after that."

About the same time that Mills wrote off McGowen at the H.C.O.C. task force, his fellow officers in Tomball were also seriously questioning their reserve officer's judgment. Bill Rather, a stocky, good-natured officer who worked nights, had little contact with McGowen until that August, when he was radioed to a scene to help the young cop serve a warrant. When Rather pulled up in front of an old house off Tomball's main drag, he immediately recognized the place as the home of Beetle, a confused, tattooed, eighteen-year-old drug addict who circulated through the Tomball area. "He was wired on dope most of the time," says Rather. "His eyes were glassy and he could have a bad attitude, but I'd never known the kid to be violent. The kid was all mouth. The only arrest he'd had was failing to sign a traffic ticket."

When Rather arrived, he greeted Kent. Then he noticed McGowen had brought a friend along to watch him in action. Rather, wondering what was up, took off his cap to scratch his head and asked, "Why are we here?"

"I've got a warrant for selling a controlled substance to serve on this turd," said McGowen. "He sold me cocaine."

"How much?" Rather asked. Beetle was well known to use drugs, but not to sell them.

"Not much," McGowen admitted. "But I've got a warrant. We're gonna take him in."

Then, to Rather's amazement, Kent and his friend dropped to their knees, then fell on their stomachs. A glint of determination in his eye, Kent focused the barrel of an AR-15, a semiautomatic assault-type rifle, at the front door. Rather shook his head. To him, the whole thing seemed crazy. "What was he going to do, bring out the bullhorn, order in the helicopters, on a little ol' delivery charge?" a still dubious Rather questions years later.

Perplexed by McGowen's "shenanigans," Rather simply walked up the front steps and rang the doorbell. Beetle's eightyish grandfather, a man so emaciated his ribs rippled the front of his torn T-shirt, answered.

"Beetle here?" Rather asked.

" 'Round back in the little house, Officer," the man said. He then chitchatted with Rather as he escorted him to a small cottage behind the old house. McGowen and friend followed, gun poised. When the elderly man opened the door, Beetle looked up from his bed, startled.

A girl beside him covered her nakedness with a stained bedsheet.

"Beetle, we've got a warrant on you," Rather said.

"Hell, on me?" he answered.

"Yeah, selling drugs."

"Goddamn, I knew that guy was a narc," Beetle said as he pulled his clothes on to follow Rather outside. "He had a goddamn Rolex on. What kind of druggie wears a Rolex?"

"Then why'd you sell to him?"

"I needed the money," Beetle admitted sheepishly.

Rather turned Beetle over to McGowen and left. For weeks after, whenever Rather thought of Beetle's arrest, he chuckled. "It was just silly taking an AR-15 to serve a warrant like that," he says, recounting the incident. "You'd have thought McGowen was coming down on a serial killer. The funny thing was, the next week at the station the other guys started ribbing me, saying McGowen's been talking 'bout how Rather didn't know how to serve a warrant."

At H.C.O.C., Mills didn't hear of the arrest. If he had, he, too, might have enjoyed a laugh at McGowen's expense, remembering how the young cop had flaunted his imminent crackdown of a "big-time drug dealer in the Tomball area."

Possibly sensing the gossip that swirled around him that August, Kent McGowen made a move to leave Tomball when he reapplied at H.P.D. The first official notice within H.P.D. of his action was a memo by Captain W.A. Young, dated September 9, 1989—just nine months after McGowen had tendered his resignation. "I have researched the records regarding the former Houston Police Department officer Joseph K. McGowen and recommend he not be considered for reemployment," it read. "His previous supervisor considered his performance to be poor and he is generally described as immature with a negative attitude." McGowen's application was forwarded through the bureaucracy.

In the meantime, Kent mounted a campaign to bolster his case for reemployment, collecting letters of recommendation from family, friends, supervisors, and coworkers. One came from the apartment manager where Kent was a courtesy officer, who called him "an asset." A former H.P.D. partner described Kent as "professional and dedicated." Chief Michna wrote, "Kent's work attitude was exemplary." Sergeant Larry Lakind, one of Kent's former supervisors at H.P.D., described McGowen as "professional, courteous, and thorough. I highly recommend J.K. McGowen as a police officer."

Michna would later speculate that his letter, undated, must have been written before gossip about McGowen flitted through the Tomball station. As Houston's sultry summer drew to a close, Michna maintained he knew better, that by then he'd heard accounts of McGowen's elaborate and often conflicting tales. McGowen's jacket at Tomball, it seemed, was quickly fashioned from the same cloth as the one he'd worn at H.P.D., woven from questionable judgment, dubious motives, an inclination to exaggerate, and—the main ingredient—skepticism regarding his honesty.

"I'd begun realizing that Kent McGowen said a lot of things that never came to pass," explains Michna. "I was wondering if the kid lived in a fantasy world. He was always talking about some big drug bust he was closing in on. The bad guys were always Colombians, a big cartel. I'd seen this in other officers. They get all entranced about making the big bust. It always had worldwide connections. I figured McGowen was one of those."

It was not entirely unexpected, then, when in mid-September, Michna received an angry call from the lieutenant supervising Kent at the organized crime unit. As Michna listened, the lieutenant complained that Mc-Gowen's H.C.O.C. expense forms didn't make sense.

"He couldn't have used all this gas," the irate lieutenant said. "Where the hell is this kid driving?"

"I'll get to the bottom of it," Michna promised.

Michna hung up the phone after making a mental note to discuss the gas issue with McGowen. He then reconsidered a call he'd received from Michelle Mc-Gowen. "She said they'd split, that he was having an affair and he was calling and threatening her," says Michna. "I didn't know what to think."

It wasn't long, however, before the lieutenant's irritation and Michelle's charges slipped in importance behind an even more pressing issue. Michna would soon come to the conclusion that the H.P.D. friend whose opinion he'd dismissed as an aberration had been right, and that Kent McGowen "had no business" in law enforcement.

"I guess it was late September," Michna recounts. "Kent called Dispatch about six o'clock in the evening and said someone was after him, threatening to kill him and his wife. The department swung into full alert. A threat to an officer we take seriously."

Quickly, deputies were dispatched to find Michelle McGowen and her children as another group hastened to protect Kent. Although he wasn't well liked, the Tomball station fell into an uproar, officers outraged that another officer's life and family had been threatened. But soon news filtered back to the station that the threat appeared a sham. When asked, Michelle McGowen knew nothing about Colombian drug lords coming after her, and the investigating officers judged McGowen's story as full of holes.

"Word came in that the report was 'a windy,' bogus,"

says Anderson. "We were all bummed out. We couldn't believe that any officer would do this to his fellow officers. It was like, *I don't believe this.*"

Michna beeped McGowen and ordered him into the station.

Seated across from the chief, McGowen told his story. He'd been out working on the ranch, he said, when someone bumped him on his beeper. Kent went to a phone and called the number. A man answered.

"I know where you live," he said. "And I know where your wife is."

Dumbfounded that anyone would use a beeper to leave a threat, Michna asked, "So who do you think is behind this?"

"I figure it's probably those Colombians I've been after," McGowen said proudly. "They must know I'm ready to make a big bust."

Michna then asked McGowen for the phone number on his beeper. Although the chief assumed the number would lead to a pay phone, it brought him to the door of a small oil-machinery company just off one of Houston's main arteries. Inside, the office appeared stamped out of the same mold as thousands of others: inexpensive framed prints of not-very-good paintings, scattered and dusty artificial plants, well-worn office furniture, a secretary, salesmen, and the owner in the only office with a window. Michna asked to talk to the boss, and the secretary escorted him to a pale man in a gray suit. After the chief explained why he'd come, the man looked tense but not surprised.

"Have you had anyone unauthorized coming in here and using your phones?" Michna asked.

"No," the man said, fidgeting with papers on his desk.

Michna's antennae flew up.

"Look, if you're involved in this in any way, you need to tell me. We're talking about a serious crime here," he said. "I don't know if you've ever been to jail, but you could be going to one."

The man claimed he knew nothing about either McGowen or the threat. A suspicious Michna threw down his business card and left. Early the next day, the same man called the Tomball station.

"Kent's father, Bill McGowen, doesn't want him in police work," the oil-tool man told Michna. "He asked me to do this. I know it's not right, but I did it."

"This is crazy," Michna muttered as he hung up the phone, then leafed through his records for Bill Mc-Gowen's number. On his way out of the station, the chief filled Kent in on the man's allegations and said he was en route to the ranch.

"It's true he doesn't want me in law enforcement, but I'm sure he didn't do it," Kent sputtered. "My daddy is a big shot. He's a friend of President Bush. He can call right into the White House."

"Well," said Michna, "I'm just going to ask him a few questions."

Within minutes, the gray-haired chief turned into the impressive driveway of the Deuteronomy 28 Ranch, where Bill greeted him, then invited him inside to meet Carolyn.

"So I hear you can call into the White House. You know Bush," Michna mentioned, hoping to break the ice.

"Who said that?" Bill challenged.

"Oh, nothing. Just a rumor, I guess," Michna replied. Then he launched into his reason for the visit: the previous day's threat and the allegations made by the man at the oil-tool company. He didn't have to wait for a response.

"The guy's lying," Bill McGowen blustered angrily. "That's nothing but a lie."

"The man has demons in him to make him lie," Carolyn shouted, her face blanching under her thick makeup. "This is the work of the devil."

Getting up to leave, an exasperated Michna replied, "Well, you're out of my realm of knowledge and authority."

Bill McGowen would later deny Michna's account of their meeting. "I have no idea where that came from," he says. But as the acting chief tells it, that afternoon's episode at the ranch set the stage for Kent's dismissal from Tomball.

At the station, Michna filled Kent in on the encounter with his parents. "Would your dad do this?" he asked again.

"It's possible," Kent allowed. "But I don't think so. I think it's a real threat."

"Well, Kent, the guy admitted it. As far as I'm concerned, the matter is closed."

The following day, a troubled Michna once again called McGowen into his office. He'd thought about the situation all night and decided he had no choice. McGowen had to go.

"I don't know what's going on in your life, but it's one of the sorriest messes I've ever seen," the older man said. "You're going to hit the front page and I'd be willing to bet it won't be for something good. I don't want it to read, 'Kent McGowen, Tomball police officer,' when it happens. I'm pulling your commission before this city gets embarrassed."

Furious, Kent argued that he'd thought over what had happened the day before and he was sure the threat was legitimate and that the Colombians were behind it.

"And why would they be coming after you?" Michna asked.

"Because I've got an informant and I'm going to make a big bust," he said. "I'm getting too close."

Michna looked at the young officer in disgust. "It's over, Kent. Turn in your badge."

*   *   *

A week after McGowen's departure from Tomball, Curtis Mills received a call from a Texas ranger asking about his former partner.

"I worked with him," Mills said. "What do you need to know?"

The ranger said that McGowen had filed a complaint claiming members of a Colombian drug cartel had threatened his life.

Mills roared with laughter.

"What's so funny?" the ranger demanded.

"We've got guys here who take tons of Colombian drugs off the streets and arrest Colombian nationals. The cartels don't take out contracts on them," Mills replied. "Why would somebody who, to my knowledge, has never brought in a stalk of marijuana have a drug lord wanting him dead?"

Two days after Michna pulled McGowen's commission in Tomball, a second memo on McGowen's request for reinstatement circulated at H.P.D. Dated October 3, 1989, it noted: "A review of his personnel file shows McGowen was never formally disciplined but records in Internal Affairs indicate he has received two sustained disciplinary complaints." Sergeant C. J. Grysen's exit report on McGowen was also reviewed, the one that called him "arrogant" and "mutinous."

The memo, addressed to H.P.D. chief Lee Brown, concluded, "It is recommended that Mr. McGowen's request for reinstatement be denied."

On October 13, Kent received the news and filed an immediate appeal. With his hope of a return to H.P.D. threatened, he penned apologies to the officers who'd questioned his competency. On November 14, an appeals board summoned him to appear before them.

At the meeting, McGowen reported that he had apologized to the officers who'd vetoed him and claimed they now welcomed him back. He denied ever having had any verbal conflicts with his supervisors. To back up his claims, he brought Charlie Hunt, an H.P.D. officer who'd known him since the academy. Yet with McGowen out of the room, Hunt testified that while the young man was "knowledgeable about the law and dedicated," he was also "more aggressive than myself—not to imply that he was too aggressive."

The appeals board voted. Kent McGowen's application was unanimously rejected.

A short time later, Leroy Michna received a call from Bill McGowen. As Michna later related the conversation, McGowen divulged his concerns like one father seeking the advice of another. During the conversation, Kent's father lamented his attempts to interfere with Kent's decision to be a cop. "I realize now that this is what he wants," Michna would later recall McGowen confiding. "It's made a lot of trouble for my family."

The veteran cop hung up, confused by Bill McGowen's call. But as the days passed, his office phone rang often, first with similar calls from Kent's father, then from Kent himself, who accused Michna of blackballing his reinstatement at H.P.D. and his applications at other agencies. "I keep getting jobs and then they suddenly don't take me," McGowen said. "I know you're behind this."

The last time Kent McGowen phoned Michna, the Tomball chief was at home. As before, McGowen angrily accused his former boss of interfering in his quest to regain a badge. Michna had reached the end of his patience. "Listen, Kent," he warned. "I'm not doing anything to you. You stop calling me, or I'm going to swear out a restraining order against you."

The calls stopped.

*   *   *

After repeated attempts to reverse the appeals board's decision, McGowen again threatened a lawsuit. Taking the investigation another step, the higher-ups dispatched Sergeant J.A. Leggio to Westside to talk to Grysen and others to see if they, in fact, wanted to withdraw their scathing evaluations of McGowen. Grysen adamantly refused. As Leggio made his way down the list of McGowen's other accusers, he found no one willing to change his unfavorable assessment, as Kent had claimed.

For a while, at least, it appeared H.P.D. had settled the matter. It's doubtful that they yet understood just how important a badge was to McGowen, or realized the measures he would employ to reclaim what had once been his. But in the meantime, Kent McGowen understood that H.P.D. amounted to merely one law enforcement agency in a parcel of Texas crowded with agencies. There were so many others to choose from.

8

That winter, Kent McGowen sauntered into the Precinct Four offices in far northwest Houston, Constable Dick Moore's fiefdom, with his T.C.L.E.O.S.E. certification intact. On February 6, 1990, he was issued a uniform and resurrected his law enforcement career as an unpaid reserve deputy.

It would be a brief tenure.

Precinct Four's home was the Cypresswood courthouse, an unremarkable tan brick, low-slung building. It also housed a branch of the county clerks' office, the local justice of the peace, and sheriff's deputies working out of that agency's substation and small, satellite jail. At the time, McGowen lived only six miles from his new headquarters, in a large wood-sided complex bordering FM 249, the main thoroughfare connecting Houston with Tomball.

The apartment was free, a benefit of McGowen's position as a courtesy officer, which required he be on call should a disturbance break out. Such arrangements worked well for leasing agents who, without becoming liable by claiming the complex had security, could assuage potential renters' concerns by mentioning that one or more police officers lived on the property.

Years later, Constable Dick Moore and the precinct's higher-ups would decline comment on Kent McGowen's stint with their office. They also refused to answer questions regarding the precinct's screening procedure for reserve applicants—specifically, how they failed to know about McGowen's actions at H.P.D. and Tomball.

The defining incident in Kent McGowen's brief stint at Precinct Four took place one month after he signed on: in the early morning of March 3, 1990, at approximately 2 A.M.

It was rodeo time in Houston, an annual, two-week span during which the city flaunted its cowboy roots. Houstonians steamed their Stetsons and shined their boots, and the city, which normally looks about as Old West as Los Angeles, welcomed trail riders from throughout the state, driving in on buckboards and horseback. Once advertised as the eighth wonder of the world, the Astrodome hosted bull riding, buck breaking, calf roping, pig races, and the like. Rodeo cowboys with saucer-sized silver belt buckles and country-and-western stars who belted out their latest releases claimed center stage.

That night after attending a rodeo, Daniel Newrones, a twenty-three-year-old computer repairman, drove home with a friend, Kelly Kieselhorst, a hairdresser. Willie Nelson had been the evening's headliner, grumbling out "Whiskey River" and other long-ago hits in his distinctive raspy tenor.

Forty minutes northwest of the city, Newrones, with

Kieselhorst beside him, swung his red Toyota pickup truck into the acres of parking at Virginia City, a cavernous country-and-western club on the far northwest side. At two o'clock, when the club's lights flickered and bartenders shouted their final call, Newrones and Kieselhorst agreed to join friends at a party at the apartments across the street, the same complex McGowen called home. Both would later maintain that although they'd been drinking, they weren't drunk when they followed a caravan of friends' cars through the complex gates.

What happened next was so startling that at first they weren't sure of what lay ahead. For as Newrones and Kieselhorst drove past a bank of apartments, their eyes focused on a dark figure charging from the shadows, a man in shorts and a Precinct Four windbreaker with a nickel-plated pistol pointed toward the night sky—Kent McGowen.

Frightened, Newrones pulled to the right to escape the armed man, but McGowen grabbed his shirt through the driver's-side window and pointed the pistol's barrel squarely at the center of Newrones' forehead. Kieselhorst screamed.

"You speed through here every weekend," McGowen shouted.

"You're crazy," Newrones answered. "We're looking for a friend. Get that gun out of my face. Who are you?"

"I'm a cop."

"I don't care who you are," Newrones shouted back. "This just ain't right!"

Furious, McGowen pulled back the pistol and slammed its barrel into the center of Newrones' forehead. As her friend shrieked with pain, Kieselhorst jumped from the car and fled to a nearby apartment, where two teenagers pulled her inside and dialed 911.

When a sheriff's department squad car arrived some two hours later, a weary Newrones argued with a young deputy who refused to write a report on the occurrence. "Once he found out McGowen was a cop, the guy wanted no part of it," says Kieselhorst. "By then Daniel had an ostrich egg sticking out from the center of his forehead, but the cop didn't even want to help."

The next morning, Newrones' father took photos of his son's injury and the two headed to Precinct Four headquarters, determined to make the deputy accountable for his attack. Once inside, they were referred to Precinct Four's Internal Affairs, where they filed a formal complaint against Reserve Deputy Joseph Kenton McGowen.

The following morning at 8:15, an officer assigned to investigate the incident read McGowen his rights. During the course of a statement, McGowen denied he was the complex's courtesy officer (precinct rules barred reserve deputies from acting as courtesy officers). He also described Newrones as intoxicated and said the young man hadn't appeared frightened that night, only angry. He claimed Newrones had squealed his tires and was driving dangerously.

The following day, the investigator walked into the office at McGowen's apartment complex and introduced himself to the manager. When questioned, the woman maintained she'd had no other complaints about McGowen, mentioning that he had lived on the property and acted as a courtesy officer for several months. Noting the courtesy-officer statement on his report, the investigator knew McGowen had told at least one lie. After reinterviewing Newrones and talking to Kieselhorst at the beauty shop where she worked, he filed his report.

Within weeks, the investigator's report, a memo from his boss, Chief J.R. Jones, and photos of Newrones, his forehead swollen and hideously bruised, landed on the desk of Constable Moore. The memo noted: "Deputy McGowen has been working apartment security even though he stated he was not. It is my recommendation that he be relieved of his commission with this department. The complainant [Daniel Newrones] should be referred to the civil rights division of the district attorney's office if he wishes to pursue criminal charges [against McGowen]. There is a possibility of a Class A Assault."

On March 27, less than two months after he was hired, Kent McGowen's commission was pulled by Precinct Four. Two days later, for some unexplained reason, possibly ego, McGowen wrote Moore a letter of resignation, stating, "I intend to seek full-time employment elsewhere." When Precinct Four's F-5 report—the withdrawal of commission—arrived at T.C.L.E.O.S.E., no mention was made of the incident that led to his termination.

A supervisor from Precinct Four contacted Daniel Newrones a short time later, after Kent McGowen's departure. "They told me he'd been fired," Newrones recounts. "I said, 'So he's not a police officer anymore?' and the man said, 'Yeah.' The guy said I could take my complaint to the D.A.'s office, but I figured there wasn't much reason to. All I wanted was for that guy to never be a cop again. And the man said I didn't have to worry, McGowen was gone. He wouldn't hurt anyone else.

"Of course," Newrones adds, his voice heavy with regret, "if I'd known then what I know now . . ."

9

Later, as Susan White's body lay in her grave and Kent McGowen's tainted career in law enforcement became public, many would ask questions. How was he able to circulate so easily from one agency to another? What glitch in the system allowed a bad cop to bury his past?

Few satisfactory answers emerged. Some of those who hired McGowen blamed H.P.D., charging that agency had buried all damaging information on McGowen in his Internal Affairs folder. One sergeant voiced a theory based on the infighting of competing departments drinking from the same trough—tax dollars. "When an agency calls to check on a guy, it's usually viewed as a joke," he explained. "No one tells anyone that a guy they're looking at hiring is an asshole, maybe even dangerous. They figure, hell, let them hire the jackass. No love lost."

*   *   *

Through the 1980s, Texas' penal system was in crisis. Under court order to relieve overcrowding in prisons, state prison board officials stayed in compliance through wholesale paroles and by refusing to accept regular transfers from county jails. While in the past, prisoners convicted and given substantial sentences were quickly shipped to a state prison, suddenly many languished their entire sentences in county jails. Not surprisingly, the number of inmates housed in jails across the state mushroomed.

In Houston, the Harris County Sheriff's Department ran the jail on Franklin Street, near the downtown criminal courthouse. With the state no longer accepting many prisoners, the inmate population swelled to a dangerous high. Prisoners slept on concrete floors, six confined to cells designed to house four. News reports labeled the situation a powder keg and a second federal lawsuit targeted the county. As a result, in the late eighties, plans were drawn, funding was voted, and construction began on a second jail, scheduled to open in the fall of 1990. As the time neared, the department faced a new crisis— how to hire 1,087 people to staff it with only eight background investigators.

"We were flooded with applications," one sergeant recalls. "We ended up hiring people we shouldn't have. They'd be working in the jail and some inmate would point at a jailer and say, 'Hey, that ain't that guy's name; ain't he so-and-so?' We found out we'd hired felons. It took years to weed them out."

As the hiring push began, Kent McGowen applied for a position in early July as a reserve deputy at the sheriff's Cypresswood substation, next door to his last— albeit brief—reserve position with Precinct Four. According to his application, he was then living with his parents on their ranch. He'd long since lost interest in college, and next to the request for "Present Employer," he listed Orion Investments, his father's latest cattle venture, describing himself as vice president. He claimed a whopping $10,000-a-month salary.

Sheriff's Reserve Deputy Bruce Paige, a lanky, bookkeeperish-looking man who spent his days working as a computer technician, was assigned to do the background check on McGowen. The department had no written policy guiding background investigations, so Paige treated the McGowen case like any other he'd handled over the previous five years, beginning with a routine criminal-history and driver's-license check. That done, he dropped in on H.P.D., armed with a signed release from McGowen, and asked to see their files on the young recruit. He was handed McGowen's personnel file—filled with commendations and Lieutenant Luiz's proclamation that if Officer J.K. McGowen reapplied he should be considered for rehire.

On the surface, Paige should have had a dilemma. He knew McGowen had been turned down by H.P.D.— McGowen himself had admitted as much on his application questionnaire. Next to "Have you ever been denied employment by an agency?" McGowen had written, "Yes . . . at H.P.D. due to slanderous allegations."

Inexplicably, Paige made no attempt to unravel the apparent contradiction. Although the release he carried gave him the right to all "confidential and personal files," he never requested McGowen's I.A.D. or recruiting files, the ones containing the paperwork on McGowen's unsuccessful attempts at rehire.

Instead of seeking out supervisors and peers from Kent's tenure at H.P.D., Tomball, and Precinct Four, Paige contacted only five people—the minimum number called for by department policy—all references McGowen listed on his application.

As to be expected, they gave glowing endorsements. Then, as his reserve application neared approval, Kent

McGowen changed his mind. Possibly aware of the hiring push, he reapplied, seeking a position as a full-time, regular, paid deputy.

Presumably this switch should have changed all the ground rules. Certainly McGowen's claims of earning $120,000 annually at Orion could have raised eyebrows. A deputy's salary amounted to a nearly $100,000-a-year cut in pay.

But even the red flag raised by his required preemployment polygraph was ignored. It stated, "inconsistencies in the applicant's employment history might require further investigation."

On October 4, 1990, twenty-five-year-old Joseph Kent McGowen signed a tentative employment agreement, joining his fourth agency in as many years, the Harris County Sheriff's Department. After fire and safety schools, and a course in basic jail procedures, he was assigned to work at the county's existing jail on Franklin.

The Franklin Street jail was connected by a tunnel to the criminal courthouse one block away. Its first floor housed Booking, where deputies and officers brought prisoners for processing. The second floor comprised a small medical facility; the third, the psychiatric floor. Women prisoners made up the fourth-floor's population. Floors five to eleven housed male prisoners, ranging from those caught driving without a license or insurance to multiple murderers.

Two distinct groups staffed the prison: civilian jailers, nicknamed "white-shirts" for their county-supplied cotton shirts and black, police-type pants; and "blue-shirts," deputy jailers who wore their official navy-shirted-and-tan-panted deputy's uniforms, badges, insignias, black patent-leather holsters, and all. With his T.C.L.E.O.S.E. certification still in force, McGowen became a blue-shirt. His job was to turn keys, working the

floors where inmates milled throughout the day with little to distract them. "He took inmates to meetings with
their lawyers and to the dentist," said a co-worker. "It
was baby-sitting for convicts." McGowen performed
well and soon earned a plum assignment as an instructor
for new recruits.

Overall, the jail wasn't a popular assignment. "The
days are boring. There's not much difference in working
in a jail than being in one," says one of McGowen's fellow blue-shirts. "The only exception is that you get to
go home at night. And it's dangerous. When every day's
just like the last, it's easy to drop your guard, which you
can't do when you're surrounded by murderers and
thieves."

Most sheriff's department applicants viewed a stint
staffing the jail as a necessary evil, a stopping point before being promoted to the streets. Work the jails for a
few years, new recruits were told, and then put in for a
transfer. The hope: a quick reassignment to one of the
department's substations that ringed the city, where they
were given a car and a gun, and a piece of the county
to patrol. "Blue-shirts consider a transfer out of the jail
to patrol a promotion, you get congratulated. There's a
waiting list to leave," says a sergeant.

Despite its undesirability, in hindsight Kent Mc-
Gowen's sojourn working behind bars would appear to
be the calmest of his career. There were the usual reac-
tions of distrust and irritation from his peers as he
bragged endlessly of his trust fund—then, by his estimate, up to $15 million—and his father's connections—
especially those he intimated led directly to the White
House. Others found his continual boasting about his
stellar law enforcement career and expansive experience
grating.

"He wasn't there for a month and he was talking
about how this was Mickey Mouse stuff," recalls Sergeant John Denholm, one of McGowen's supervisors. A

bulky man with squarish wire-rimmed glasses and blue eyes that appear to instantly digest information and make judgments, Denholm adds, "McGowen was always just about to get back in at H.P.D. 'I used to work undercover stuff. I'm just waiting to get back with the city,' he'd say."

Such bad-mouthing didn't sit well with Denholm, who planned to make a career with H.C.S.D. More than once, he called McGowen into his office for a tongue-lashing.

"You may have these new kids bullshitted, but I'm telling you right now, I don't want to hear this crap no more," Denholm growled at the young blue-shirt. "If you were such a hot shit you'd be back at H.P.D. You've got some kind of problem and we probably shouldn't have even hired you."

Another sergeant described McGowen in much the same words as Grysen's review, "failing in maturity and responsibility."

Only Sergeant Tom Pruess, McGowen's most immediate supervisor in the jail, would later praise him, calling McGowen an outstanding deputy with a knack for perceiving a situation. By that Pruess meant the way McGowen proved adept at cajoling inmates into admitting what really happened in situations like a fistfight in a cell. "Kent would lay out the scenario and talk to the prisoners until they filled in the holes," he says. "Kent loved police work. He lived, ate, slept it."

While working at the jail, McGowen met and befriended another blue-shirt, Deputy Ronald Wayne Acreman. Two years older than Kent, he, too, was a gypsy cop who, since first licensed in 1983, had worked for three different agencies. Acreman, a sandy-haired, muscular man who enjoyed displaying his physique and referring to himself as The Ultimate Police Machine, had joined H.C.S.D. in July, another of the stream of deputies hired to satisfy the appetite of the new jail. His fellow deputies called Acreman "highly aggressive," and gossip swirled around him, that he manhandled inmates.

Not long after McGowen and Acreman began hanging out together, Sergeant Denholm heard similar rumors, but this time about both his new deputies. "The word was that Acreman and McGowen were bullies with a badge," says Denholm. "They liked to take advantage of the inmates. They knew they could whip them and there wasn't much they could do. A convict's word against a cop is hard to prove."

Denholm would later admit he never actually caught either deputy abusing a prisoner. "But they were the guys, you'd see their names on complaints, you'd hear the talk," he concludes. "But there was nothing to act on. Deputies don't break the code, they don't tell on each other."

Before long, Acreman and McGowen bunked together in a stucco apartment complex surrounded by trees hung with Spanish moss, located on Wunderlich Road. That was where Acreman served as courtesy officer. Ironically, it was the very same apartment complex Ron and Susan White moved to when she first arrived in Houston, before Jason joined them and they purchased the house on Valley Bend. Though McGowen and Susan White wouldn't meet for another year, it was almost as if fate had already begun setting the stage for their final encounter.

"It's pretty unusual for H.P.D. not to rehire an officer, especially in the early nineties, when we were in a hiring boom," recalls an officer who worked in H.P.D. recruiting. "If the guy hasn't been gone long, it's almost automatic. After all, we've got a lot of training invested in an officer. We usually want them back."

In response to McGowen's new application that spring, H.P.D. investigators again made the rounds, delving into the young officer's past. Leroy Michna received one of the first inquiries. "They said somebody was pushing for this boy to be rehired," remembers Michna. "I told them about Kent's work in Tomball, including that Colombian mess. They walked away saying no way they were taking him back." Sergeant R.D. Hayes at H.P.D. talked in similar terms. "He was a squirrel," says Hayes. "He said things that you didn't want to hear as a supervisor."

Next, investigators talked to Sergeant Grysen at Westside, and he, too, reiterated his contempt for McGowen. "You take him back and he'll be trouble," Grysen warned, prophetically adding, "He's going to end up killing someone."

H.P.D. rejected McGowen's reapplication for a second time that April, but he still wasn't willing to accept defeat. Instead he threatened a lawsuit. So even with a file full of negative evaluations against him, H.P.D.'s personnel department dug deeper into McGowen's fitness to wear a badge, this time by referring him to Psychological Services to determine his emotional and mental health.

It was a risky proposition for McGowen, who had to sign a release allowing H.P.D. to notify T.C.L.E.O.S.E. of the psychological exam's results. Theoretically, if Kent McGowen failed, the agency could pull his state license in law enforcement. He might never be a cop again.

McGowen wanted H.P.D. He took that chance.

The tale of Kent McGowen's psychological testing began on May 6, when he met with H.P.D. psychologist Lisa Berg Garmezy, Ph.D., at her office in a high-rise north of downtown. First, McGowen completed a questionnaire on his history as an officer. In it he denied problems at any of his past departments and maintained he was eligible for rehire at all of them. When asked why he'd jumped from one to another, he stated he'd left Tomball for personal reasons—not mentioning that Chief Michna had pulled his commission—and that he'd parted company with Precinct Four not over the Daniel Newrones incident, but simply to apply at the sheriff's department. He characterized himself at H.P.D. as an exemplary officer with no sustained I.A.D. complaints.

Yet during the interview with Garmezy, Kent McGowen's carefully constructed veneer cracked. When questioned about Tomball, an incensed McGowen described his old boss, Michna, as "a crook," claiming he'd blackballed him with future employers. "I was not in control of the situation," he complained regarding his most recent H.P.D. rejection. "It was embarrassing . . . everyone recommends me."

Along with these mischaracterizations, McGowen told a blatant lie that afternoon, one easily discovered by reviewing the records. According to Garmezy's written account of the interview, McGowen bragged about his intelligence and that he so excelled in high school, he'd graduated two years early. The truth, readily apparent from his diploma in his T.C.L.E.O.S.E. file, showed that he'd graduated at the usual age, eighteen, and that was via a correspondence program.

When the conversation in Garmezy's office turned to women, Kent McGowen's well-known disdain for the opposite sex seeped through as he railed against Sara Williams, the officer he'd had the affair with at H.P.D., claiming she'd threatened him and once tried to shoot him. "She's a lunatic, crazy," he said. At one point, Kent even cursed one of his aunts, labeling her "a raging bitch."

When Garmezy turned the conversation to his present employer, the sheriff's department, and asked why he wished to leave, Kent McGowen's words echoed closely those he'd used just years earlier when he tendered his resignation to H.P.D. "It seems like no one is in control," he said. "And I want more money. I'm very good at my job."

Yet when Garmezy compared McGowen's version of his past with his H.P.D. employment records, the inconsistencies were glaring. Her evaluation concluded: "[Kent McGowen] is emotionally rigid leading to a lack of flexibility in his response style. . . . he may react poorly to citizens . . . . applicant's rigidity may also be manifested in difficulty seeing others' points of view or acknowledging his own errors. Applicant appeared to be concealing information in the interview and made inaccurate statements. If rehired, he might use similarly deceptive practices in policing."

Still, fearing McGowen's threatened lawsuit, H.P.D. took one additional step, referring him for a second evaluation to psychologist Lois Friedman, Ph.D., at Houston's Baylor College of Medicine.

After her meeting with McGowen, Friedman's report agreed with her colleague's: "Tests indicate [Kent McGowen] may be emotionally constricted. He may exhibit little control under stress and may overreact with citizens.

"Based upon this evaluation, I have concluded that he may not be able to meet the requirements for the normal duties of a police officer."

On May 22, an interoffice correspondence reached the desk of then H.P.D. chief Elizabeth Watson: "Re: rejected application of Kent McGowen. Failure to meet the minimum standard psychological requirements after two separate evaluations."

Kent received notification the same day.

He never did file a lawsuit, as he'd so often threatened. Perhaps he knew his chances at H.P.D. had evaporated. And although H.P.D. had a signed release authorizing it to notify T.C.L.E.O.S.E. of his two failed psychological exams, that also never happened.

Again a twist of fate saved Kent McGowen's badge.

Had he failed the exam a year earlier, the agency would have been required to notify the commission. But regulations had changed, and in 1991, Texas law enforcement agencies were no longer obligated to report L-3s, negative declarations of psychological and emotional health, to the commission. Why? "Everyone's afraid of lawsuits," explains a personnel officer. "You cost a guy his job, you can end up in court."

Instead McGowen, his H.P.D. hopes dashed, settled reluctantly back into his work at the jail, complaining bitterly about the political powers that be at H.P.D. that had kept him out. The following month, Sergeant Tom Pruess gave McGowen an above-average rating for his work and noted, "McGowen's initiative and prior law enforcement and training experience have helped with a much improved training program."

Perhaps Sergeant Pruess didn't hear about an encounter McGowen had with another officer that very month, when Deputy Scott Hall of Precinct Four returned home to his apartment at two in the morning, the same complex where McGowen and Acreman then lived. At the automatic gates, Hall noticed a man on foot. When a car opened the electric security gate to leave, the stranger sprinted into the complex parking lot.

"I wasn't the courtesy officer, Acreman was," recounts Hall. "But I wasn't going to ignore it."

Hall, in full uniform, confronted the man, who appeared drunk.

"What're you doing?" he demanded.

The stranger, slurring his words, insisted he was a deputy on his way to visit Acreman. Since the man had no identification, Hall followed him. At Acreman's second-floor apartment door, the disheveled drunk knocked and a woman answered. When he asked for Acreman, she said he wasn't in.

"I thought you said Acreman was here," Hall said. "Don't fool with me."

"Tell him I'm a cop," the guy shouted at the girl, who disappeared inside.

Just then, McGowen burst through the open apartment door, filling the doorway and blocking the light. "Hey, motherfucker, what's your problem?" he shouted down the stairs.

Hall looked up. McGowen held a pistol pointed directly at him.

"Who are you?" Hall demanded.

"I'm a deputy," said McGowen.

"You can tell I'm one," Hall shouted. "I'm in uniform. Put the damn gun up."

McGowen slipped his gun into his waistband.

"What's your problem?" he demanded again.

Hall explained the situation, but instead of being mollified, McGowen growled, "You don't have no fucking business talking to my friend that way."

"Your friend is drunk," said Hall.

McGowen charged down the stairs, demanding Hall's name.

Hall pulled out his card from Precinct Four and handed it to McGowen. "Here's my sergeant's number," he said. "Give him a call."

From his apartment, Hall called Precinct Four to report the encounter. Nothing official came of it.

In the fall of 1991, McGowen appeared frustrated and angry. He complained bitterly to those at the jail about H.P.D.'s refusal to rehire him. He hated working in the jail. "McGowen talked about how he couldn't wait to get on the street," remembers Denholm. "Nobody likes working the jail, but McGowen, if he wasn't hitting on a female deputy, he was just agitating."

Yet Sergeant Tom Pruess gave him another good review that winter, and McGowen took the patrol test, a written and oral exam required before transfer out of the jail to a sheriff's department substation.

Ironically, it was about that time that Detective Curtis Mills, the officer McGowen had worked with in the organized crime unit, first learned his old partner was working at the jail.

"Soon as I heard he was with the sheriff's department, I thought, *Oh, Lord*," recalled Mills. "*Oh, Lord, hopefully they'll never let that idiot out of the jail and onto the streets.*"

But in April 1992, after nineteen months of working at the county jail, McGowen saw his coveted transfer to patrol come through. His co-workers offered congratulations and Kent beamed with enthusiasm. His new assignment: patrolling Olde Oaks, the forested, upscale subdivision Susan White had moved to the previous summer. Her world crumbling about her, she couldn't hear it, but the kaleidoscope had just taken its final twist, and her fate clicked into place.

PART THREE

Summer 1992

10

The sheriff's deputies who worked there called it "Hollywood," the span of well-heeled bedroom communities ringing FM 1960. Here, as in suburbs across the nation, over their morning orange juice and toast, residents read the headlines, tsking at mounting crime rates. Statistics meant little. In the early nineties, experts estimated that a suburban woman had just slightly less chance of being struck by lightning than assaulted by a stranger, yet such assurances paled in the shadow of abductions, rapes, and murders on the nightly news. Pollwise politicians ran on anticrime platforms. Community newspapers warned residents to lock their doors and their windows.

"These neighborhoods are as safe as anyplace in America gets," explains one detective. "In Hollywood, the biggest crime on a Saturday night is usually some kid popping mailboxes with a baseball bat, holding a keg party while Mommy and Daddy are gone, or egging a house—your basic rich kids acting like assholes."

Kent McGowen entered this scene in April 1992 as a

contract deputy, a position considered slightly above that of reserve deputy and security guard in law enforcement circles. Although a contract deputy was employed by the county sheriff's department, seventy percent of his salary was paid by his assigned subdivisions. In McGowen's case, this meant an area spanning the affluent communities of Northgate Forest, Westcreek, and Olde Oaks. The slot probably wasn't what McGowen envisioned. Unlike the department's district deputies, who had the run of the streets—including the main arteries with their clubs and restaurants—contract deputies were expected to spend more than two-thirds of their shift guarding their assignments, far from the action.

"The contracts can bore you to death. There's twenty miles of road to cover. With your foot on the brake, coasting, watching out for spoiled kids making trouble, it takes an hour to make one pass-through," says one deputy. "Eight hours at a time, it's about as exciting as working the jail, except the air is fresher."

Still, for Kent McGowen, the sheriff's department was nearly the only show left, and though Olde Oaks wasn't downtown, it was all he had. He'd reached the end of the line in law enforcement in Houston; had exhausted nearly all venues open to a brash young man who lusted after a uniform and a badge.

It might have been wise, in such a position, to modify the behavior that had cost him so dearly. Yet within months at the Cypresswood substation, McGowen had woven a new jacket for himself, made up of all the distrust and disdain of the ones he'd worn at H.P.D., Tomball, and Precinct Four. When Curtis Mills, his old partner from the organized-crime task force, heard McGowen had a contract job patrolling in far north Harris County, he told another detective, "Mark my words, there's gonna be some shit out there, because this guy is not gonna let anyone alone."

* * *

In District One, McGowen worked the graveyard shift, 10 P.M. to 6 A.M., with Tuesdays and Wednesdays off. His sergeant was Samuel D. Ruggiero, who'd moved up through the ranks at the sheriff's department after coming to Houston from Ohio. In fact, Ruggiero, a wiry, mustached man, had made sergeant just months before McGowen's arrival on the scene. For the most part, his men liked Ruggiero. "He was okay," says one deputy with a shrug. "Green, but okay."

Over Ruggiero was Lieutenant Jay O. Coons, a well-spoken, quiet man with thick dark hair. "I can only say one thing about Coons," says a deputy asked to assess his lieutenant. "He's got more book smarts than street smarts. He stands by his men, sometimes to a fault."

Kent McGowen made an early impression at the substation. He told war stories from his short tenure at H.P.D. and bragged about his undercover experiences, as usual liberally sprinkling references to his father's wealth and his multimillion-dollar trust fund. When more veteran deputies in the district offered to acquaint him with his new beat, McGowen declined. "He was one of *those* guys. He didn't need any help, because he knew it all," says one deputy. "I was going to make the effort, let him know where the kids hang out and smoke dope at the big tree, let him know who the troublemakers were, but he wasn't interested in anything I had to offer."

Quickly McGowen alienated himself from many at the station. The defining incident in his tenure came over an arrest one deputy describes as "borderline." When the sergeant on duty refused to take his charges, McGowen threatened to report him to I.A.D. "Kent got mad," recalls a deputy. "Instead of writing a report saying my sergeant told me to let him go and it was a borderline deal, Kent went to I.A.D. about it. You just don't do that."

In response, Ruggiero developed an intense dislike for his new deputy. "I couldn't trust McGowen," he says. "I didn't want anything to do with him."

Others apparently came to the same conclusion. When Scott Hall, the constable's deputy McGowen had held the gun on from the apartment doorway many months earlier, saw him, McGowen appeared an outcast. "He'd be eating lunch at this coffee shop the deputies all go to," remembers Hall. "Other sheriff's deputies would be there, but McGowen would be sitting off by himself. It seemed strange."

In his contract, two distinct and contrasting impressions of the young officer took hold. The Olde Oaks security coordinator, a homeowner chosen by the local civic association to act as its liaison with the sheriff's department, saw McGowen as a dedicated employee. Yet others, mainly those with teenagers, had a different impression. "I'd heard about McGowen, that he was hard on the kids," says one such mom. "It was not out of the ordinary for him to stop a teenager for no real reason, other than to harass him, demand to know where he's going. McGowen had a Gestapo attitude."

Still, it's likely that Kent McGowen never considered his behavior harassment, rather his badge-given right. Later, one of McGowen's few friends, a deputy from an adjacent county, would tell of afternoon shooting practices on Bill McGowen's land. "Whenever we got together it was war stories," he says, smirking at the memory. "Kent and I agreed things were screwed up—there's this big concern with violating people's civil rights. An officer can't do his job anymore. If officers were allowed to be police—let an officer go out there and do his job—things would be different."

It must have been frustrating for an ambitious cop like McGowen to patrol the streets of a quiet bedroom community like Olde Oaks, where the lights in the big houses turned black, their inhabitants migrating toward bed shortly after the nightly newscast. A long night lay ahead, a deadly quiet one for a cop alone. "A baby-sitter for rich people," some officers called contract jobs, stuck in the silent suburbs while newspapers touted cops who solved the big cases, caught the serial rapists and the murderers. Yet when he surveyed the darkened houses, did Kent imagine husbands and wives and children drifting off to sleep, or drug lords and gun traffickers hiding behind a suburban facade? What thoughts occupied his mind, as his foot pumped the brake of his county-issue squad car, quietly inching his way through the darkness?

Just weeks after beginning his new assignment, Kent McGowen was in his squad car in the early-morning hours and pulled over Gary Roberts, the area's twenty-eight-year-old deliveryman of *The Wall Street Journal* and *The New York Times*. As he threw newspapers in plastic bags from his battered Isuzu pickup truck, Roberts saw blue-and-red lights flash. The deputy motioned him to the side of the road, glaring a spotlight on his face. McGowen wrote him a warning for a burned-out headlight. Days later, he stopped Roberts again, this time to ticket him for drifting through a stop sign on a deserted street.

"It was like McGowen was bored," said Roberts' mother, recalling the incident. "He'd pull Gary over and—without a warrant—search his truck."

On one such night, McGowen found a kitchen knife in the man's truck and booked Roberts for carrying an illegal weapon.

As McGowen cinched handcuffs on Roberts' wrists, the young man, who worked at a Pizza Hut during the day, turned to him.

"Is this fun?" Roberts asked. "You know, it's cops like you who give all cops a bad name."

"I don't like civilians either," sneered McGowen.

In the end, a judge dropped the charges, ruling a kitchen knife was not an illegal weapon. At the trial, McGowen appeared furious.

"He stopped Gary because he was bored and Gary was the only one out at three-thirty in the morning," says Roberts' mother, who operated a small flower shop on FM 1960. "I told deputies I knew in the area, and I called some people at the sheriff's department to tell them they had a demigod with a piece of tin on his chest working the streets. This guy thought he could do whatever he wanted.

"I don't think anyone took it serious."

The month after Roberts' mother complained of the "demigod with a piece of tin on his chest," May 1992, Susan White mentioned the new cop in her neighborhood, her protector, Mac, to Alan Jefferies, the piano player at Resa's. McGowen would later claim she couldn't have been talking of him, that he wouldn't actually meet her for at least another two months.

But according to police files, that May, Kent McGowen indisputably entered her world.

It happened on a Saturday night, while Susan lay in a hospital bed, suffering a relapse of the Legionnaires' disease that had plagued her earlier in the year. Ron had just recently moved out, this time for good, telling her sister Sandra that he was washing his hands of Susan, Jason, the entire marriage.

As he often had done in the past, Jason took advantage of his mother's absence to put out the word that on this weekend the party would be at his house. "Kids invited other kids," he remembers. "I guess there must have been about fifty or sixty of us. It got wild. A bunch out front, on the lawn, smoked weed. I told them to get the hell inside. Someone yelled about the cops."

And, as on so many other nights, the house then disgorged itself of teenagers, who sprinted to their cars and sped into the night. Frustrated neighbors watched as deputies arrived to find only a handful of the revelers, those still fleeing. A cocky Jason met the lieutenant in charge at the door. Confident the drugs had gone the way of the crowd, Jason agreed when the police asked to come inside. McGowen and the other officers fanned throughout the house. They found an empty wine bottle and ashes in an ashtray upstairs. Could the ashes have been from pot? They took the ashtray as evidence, but never tested it. Instead the deputies inspected IDs and settled for arresting a small assortment of drunk and belligerent teenagers.

"There were so many cops, it was like a convention," recalls Jason with an annoyed shrug. "After they left, we just started partying again."

Days later, in the early-morning hours, Jason's best friend, Michael Shaffer, pulled out of the Whites' driveway and onto the street. As he rode off in his battered Ford, his girlfriend, Amy, beside him, another friend in the backseat, the lights of a squad car flashed.

"Shit," he said, pulling over to the curb.

Kent McGowen walked up to the car, shining his flashlight on the three young faces.

"Get out of the car," he ordered.

Shaffer, who hadn't been at the party bust and had never seen McGowen before, had been drinking and stumbled as he pulled himself to his feet.

McGowen ordered the teenager to recite the alphabet, but he couldn't get past "M." Scowling, the deputy turned his attention to the car.

As the three teenagers watched from the curb, Mc-

Gowen searched the car, throwing empty fast-food cartons and crushed soda cans onto the street. Suddenly he spun around, a small pot pipe in his hand.

"What's this?" McGowen demanded with a smile.

Shaffer and the others looked at each other without speaking.

"Then McGowen told me to come with him," reports Amy. "He told me to get in the squad car. He said, 'How old are you?' I was fifteen at the time, but I lied and said eighteen. I couldn't believe it—he started hitting on me, asking why I was hanging around with a couple of losers. He called Michael nothing but a drug addict, a crackhead. He said he was going to take him to jail and I should go back to his house with him. I told him Mike was my boyfriend. I was thinking, *Oh, my God, I'm going to jail, my mom's gonna kill me.*"

Finally, McGowen left the squad car and confronted Shaffer, thrusting out his face until it was but inches away, all the while frantically waving the pipe. Visibly shaken, the teenager appeared to shrink in the deputy's hawklike gaze.

"I've got you dead right here," McGowen snarled.

He paused, letting Shaffer consider his words.

Naive and frightened, Shaffer felt suddenly sober. What would the deputy do to him? He didn't even have enough money to make bail.

Shaffer didn't know that possession of an empty pipe wasn't a crime. McGowen was bluffing.

Then, inexplicably, McGowen slung his arm across Shaffer's shoulders, as if they were suddenly best friends.

"I'm going to let you go," the deputy said, smiling benevolently at the cowering teenager.

Stunned, Shaffer stammered to thank him, but before he could get the words out, McGowen spoke again.

"From now on, you owe me. You're my snitch," he said. "I want to know about what goes on in this neighborhood. Anybody selling drugs, selling guns, especially automatic weapons, you need to tell me. You understand?"

Recounting the conversation much later, Shaffer pauses anxiously, kneading his hands and scowling at the memory.

"I told him I understood," says Shaffer. "But I told him I didn't know anything about anyone selling guns—especially automatics. But . . . I could tell . . . he didn't believe me."

Something else McGowen said that night would ring in Michael Shaffer's memory for years to come.

"Before he left, I asked what I did wrong, why he stopped me," says Shaffer. "McGowen pointed at Susan and Jason's house. He said, 'I'm watching that house. I'm stopping anyone who leaves there.' "

What really happened between Susan White and Kent McGowen that summer?

McGowen would later insist he and White were little more than strangers, that even in the moments before her death, he wouldn't have recognized her if they'd passed on the street.

Did he tell the truth?

Two aspects of what happened that summer, at least on the surface, seem to bolster his claims:

First: Only once would anyone recall seeing them together. It happened in June and was noted on McGowen's duty log at the sheriff's department.

That evening, White called the substation, and Deputy Matt Smith was dispatched to her house. As he pulled up in front, Susan White was waiting for him, clutching a gun, a chrome-plated .25.

"Show me how to load this," she demanded, thrusting it toward him. "I just bought it."

White looked harried, exhausted.

Smith took the gun from her, checked to verify the chamber was empty, and then followed her inside, where a group of teenagers lounged in the den.

"The kids heard we're going to be robbed," she told Smith urgently as she fluttered through the room, puffing on a half-spent cigarette. "I'm all alone here, you know. My husband's left."

Frowning, Smith took a bullet White gave him and demonstrated how to click it into place, simultaneously cautioning her about gun safety and suggesting that, rather than taking any action herself, she should call the substation for a patrol deputy if her information proved true.

Smith unloaded the gun and placed it on the bar just as McGowen strode in through the open front door.

"I saw your car outside," he explained.

Smith gave McGowen a look that said, *Everything's all right*.

Nodding, then turning to go, McGowen noticed Mike Shaffer's girlfriend, Amy. He recognized her from the night he'd stopped Shaffer, the night she says he attempted to pick her up.

"How old are you?" he asked, glaring at her.

"Fifteen."

"You lied to me," he said.

Standing a few steps from White, who sat inhaling a cigarette and staring off into space, McGowen barely looked at her, hardly even acknowledging her presence.

Did Amy notice anything between McGowen and Susan? Any indication they knew each other?

"No, nothing," she'd say later. "He didn't even talk to her. Except, he told her to check the house to find out where Jason kept his stash. He said she should check the bathrooms, behind the toilets. Susan got mad; she told him to shut up about Jason, that Jason didn't use drugs."

Why, if he was the Mac she'd mentioned to Alan Jefferies, didn't she acknowledge him? Was she already afraid of him?

Second: If McGowen harassed her, why didn't anyone notice his squad car in her driveway or lingering in front of her house? Not one of her neighbors would later admit watching him march up the pencil-straight walkway to the imposing threshold of her Amber Forest home, then knock on the massive double doors or ring the doorbell with its crisp chimes.

"That's because it never happened," McGowen contended.

Possibly.

Or could it have been that during the year she'd lived there, White's neighbors had grown accustomed to seeing squad cars parked in front of her home? So accustomed, in fact, that they'd write off a deputy on her front stoop as no more noteworthy than the postman delivering mail?

Did White know McGowen?

White had a well-documented history of stopping deputies' cars as they circulated through Olde Oaks and readily calling officers for help, sometimes just to talk. Why would she not have done the same with McGowen? Or did she? Ron White later told friends he'd seen his wife in her car, talking to an unknown deputy in a squad car at night, during McGowen's regular patrol hours.

What reason would she have had to lie about McGowen? To protect her son and his friends from a gungho young deputy? It hardly seemed that way at the time. When Mike Shaffer first muttered about McGowen to White one night in May, around the same time she told Alan Jefferies of Mac, she defended the deputy. "He's just a young cop, a rookie," she said. "He'll calm down. Give him some time."

Perhaps the most convincing evidence that McGowen had become a presence in White's life was found in her entreaties to friends that summer. As temperatures rose and Houston's unyielding heat closed in around her, she would whisper of him often, claiming he stalked her and threatened her and her son. Was Susan White lying? Or was Kent McGowen the one who had reason to lie?

11

"Susan told me about the first time she met McGowen. She said it was April or May, late spring or early summer of that year, 1992," recalls Helen Bazata, an old friend of White's.

In a bustling restaurant splashed with artificial ivy and latticework wall hangings, giving it the appearance of an outdoor courtyard, Helen sits surrounded by ladies who lunch, housewives in blue jeans and khakis, businesswomen in crisp suits. With her cap of curly red hair anchored by a gold lamé scarf, silver leggings encasing short, curvy legs, a too-big white cotton sweater clumped with gold and silver plastic crystals, she appears a precious-metal peacock in a room of the drably feathered.

"Susan and I hooked up when we were both in real estate, but I hadn't heard much from her in a few years," Helen continues. "Ron didn't like me because when Susan and I went out, we had fun. She kept her distance until that summer, after he left her. We ran into each other, I don't remember where. After that, I took her under my wing.

"The first time Susan brought McGowen up, she didn't seem worried," she says, sipping a mug of iced tea and toying with the clear straw edged in shocking pink lipstick. "Susan just said this young cop named Kent McGowen pulled her over in her car, a few blocks from her house, one night. She said she was speeding— Susan almost always was—but he didn't write her a ticket. Instead he asked her out. He said he'd noticed her before, kind of coming and going. I don't know if they ever actually went out. Susan, well, she told me she told him no. She said she'd married for love when she'd married Ron. Next time she planned to marry for money— big money. And dating some young cop without two nickels to rub together wasn't in the plan.

"But then, things were pretty wild with Susan that summer," Helen recounts, a weak smile edging across her lips. "Between Ron and Jason and trying to figure out what to do with her life . . . sometimes it was like you just didn't know what Susan was likely to do."

Susan would have been difficult to miss in Olde Oaks that summer. No longer working, she sped through the quiet suburban streets in her BMW, its coat as translucent and white as a string of good pearls, its seats upholstered with a yielding tan leather, the very picture of affluence. With the top down, her blond hair waved like ripened wheat slapping against the hot Texas breeze.

Kent McGowen later maintained not only that she never caught *his* eye, but that even if she had, it wouldn't have mattered. "Susan White wasn't my type," he declared smugly. "She was too old for me."

Yet McGowen had already shown interest in a woman not unlike Susan: Sara Williams, the fellow officer he'd had the brief and turbulent fling with at H.P.D. Like Williams, White was older than McGowen, a long-legged blonde. Like Williams' when she encountered McGowen, Susan's sense of security and self-esteem had ebbed to an all-time low.

Her life crashing around her, Susan reached out for help that summer, searching for salvation and escape. She returned to the safety valve of her youth and attended services at Champions Forest Baptist, a mammoth congregation near her home. After one Sunday service, she stopped the minister in the vestibule and confided in him about the disastrous turn her life had taken. A kind man, he brought her into the church library. There he gave her a pamphlet on the saving grace of God's love.

"That little book meant so much to her," says her mother. "She kept it with her, told her sisters and me how she read it over and over."

She also renewed an old friendship, one that had offered her an escape during the darkest days of her life— the breakup with L.J. and the times she'd pined for Jason: amphetamines. Jason and Michael Shaffer both noticed her popping the small white pills early that summer, sometimes washing them down with a glass of wine.

"They're for my lung problems," she told them. "Antibiotics."

But Jason knew what they were. He'd seen his mother on the pills before.

"Mom, well, she just got crazy," he says.

"You wouldn't believe what I found," Susan screeched into the telephone to Helen in early June. "Wait until you see it."

Just on her way out the door to an appointment, Helen pulled off a thick gold earring and pressed the head-set to her ear.

"Well, tell me," she said.

"Ron's charge bills," Susan hissed. "He bought that whore's kid clothes, lots of clothes, and they're on our bill. You know what I'm going to do?"

"What?"

"I'm going to make that bastard pay."

Ron White's American Express bill with a $200 department-store charge became Susan's Alamo, an af-front she'd never forget, and one for which she wanted revenge. With friends, sometimes alone, or with Jason, she hit the stores. Helen brought her to Scruples, a bou-tique with pricey clothes with a penchant for flash, and she indulged in suits and dresses. With Helen to guide her, she chose clothes with "style," gold braid, sequins, tight skirts, and heels so high she tottered.

"She'd see a blouse she liked and buy it in every color," laughs Helen.

Jason, who'd gotten his driver's license months ear-lier, found an '87 Ford Escort in the driveway one after-noon. The car was cheap, five years old, but it had tinted windows, and Susan installed a top-of-the-line stereo.

A news report convinced her there might be added benefits to her shopping spree. A woman in California, so the story went, won back her husband after she ran up their joint credit cards so high he couldn't afford a divorce.

"It worked for her, why not for me?" she asked San-dra one night on the telephone. "Maybe this will make Ron come to his senses. Ron's a rat, but he's my rat. I want him back."

Besides, what did she have to lose?

"Mom said we were going to stock up," remembers Jason. "She said she didn't know how long it would be before we could afford new stuff again."

She filled Jason's closet with Ralph Lauren shirts and

jeans, $200 tennis shoes, and bought him gold chain necklaces.

"What are you doing?" Ron demanded when the bills came in.

He dropped his membership at the country club, where she'd amassed a bill for clothes and sports equipment in the pro shop. He canceled their credit cards. But, days later, she called and reopened them. When he canceled the cards a second time, she searched for an old receipt with the number to his company credit card and called to have her name added to the account. When a customer service clerk hesitated, she assured him that he'd better approve it or her husband, a big customer, would be furious. Although it was just the beginning of summer, Ron, she insisted, had asked her to purchase his corporate Christmas gifts.

With the new card, she bought a lifetime pass to her favorite tanning salon, a membership at a gym, and a $400 Monopoly game. One afternoon, shopping with Helen, she paused at a jeweler's window and lingered over a five-carat diamond tennis bracelet. Maybe the pills made it seem all right, fueling her mood swings, keeping her on edge.

"Why not?" she concluded. "I deserve it."

"This is my time," she told Helen over lunch another afternoon, dressed in a new black suit, her hair in a slick pageboy swinging at her shoulders. "I'm going to enjoy it. If Ron divorces me, I'll get what I can before it's over."

Helen introduced her to her own circle of friends, mostly divorcées who shared her sense of style. At night they met for dinner and drinks at Resa's, where they listened to Alan sing ballads as they searched the crowd for single men. Well after midnight, Susan pulled out Ron's credit card. "My treat," she chirped, slapping it down on the brown leather folder holding the bill.

One afternoon, Sherri Brandt's phone rang in her office.

"I wish we could be friends," Susan mused.

"I don't think so," Ron's new flame answered.

"Well, if you're after Ron for his money, there's something you should know. I wouldn't bother." Susan giggled. "He's not going to have any left."

It was on June 2 that Susan purchased, from a pawn shop, the gun she asked Deputy Smith to help her load—a .25 chrome-plated semiautomatic pistol. She also bought a Texas lawbook, a heavy volume with a thick leather cover.

"I'm going to write a new will," she told Sandra on the phone.

"You don't need one," her sister scoffed.

"Yes, I do," Susan insisted. "To protect Jason."

Night after night, she pored over the text, searching through the table of contents and the index, reading all she could on setting up guardianships and bequeathing estates.

On June 15, Susan met with Kay, Sandra, and her parents at a family reunion in Bastrop, Louisiana. Surrounded by friends and family, some of whom she hadn't seen in years, she relaxed for the first time in months. "She had a blast," remembers Sandra. "Telling stories about the old days. She was the old Susie."

In the quieter moments, she confided in her sisters about her troubles at home. Ron had stopped making house payments and she wondered how long the bank would wait before foreclosing on her dream home. She told them of her shopping sprees and opened her trunk to show off ten pairs of new shoes, still in their boxes, that she'd brought for the occasion. She gave out presents, including a blue topaz ring for O.L. and a gold chain for Kay.

"Now if you need money, you can pawn it next

Christmas," Susan said as she slipped it around Kay's neck.

Kay, who'd had a tough year financially, just laughed.

"But that winter, I did have to pawn it to pay for groceries," she says. "It was after Susie died. I wondered if she knew."

On June 19, just after her return to Houston, Susan was finally ready. She had a pad full of notes as she wrote her last will and testament. "This replaces any previous wills," she scrawled on a long sheet of yellow legal paper. In the will, she left all her worldly possessions to her beloved son, Jason. She named Gloria, the big sister who'd urged her to discipline him, his guardian. Perhaps she hoped Gloria might be able to accomplish what she hadn't been able to. Sandra, the only one of the three Harrison sisters with a college degree, would be the executor, to manage his affairs. At the bottom, she signed her name: Susan Harrison White.

Why the insistence on a will?

"We assumed she was afraid of Ron," Gloria says, rolling her eyes. "We didn't know. We kept asking her, 'Are you safe in Houston? Don't you want to move home?' She said, 'Now, don't you bother yourself worrying. Like I told you, I've got friends in the sheriff's department. I know all the deputies who patrol here, and they're all looking out for me and Jason.'"

Did Susan believe her own words, or were they uttered merely to reassure her family? Four days after she signed her name on the bottom of her will, less than a month after purchasing the gun, Susan White clearly worried about one of the deputies patrolling her neighborhood—Joseph Kent McGowen.

"It was June twenty-third. I'd helped Susie and another friend get jobs as models selling shots of C.J. Wray rum at a couple of clubs. It didn't pay much, but it was fun," says Helen Bazata. "It was late when we finished up, and I asked Susie to take the saleswoman from the rum company to her hotel near the airport. It was after the bars closed, maybe two-thirty."

Helen leans forward in her chair, and the smile she's worn all afternoon suddenly appears fixed by will alone as she recounts the conversation she had with Susan White on the telephone the following morning:

"Did you get her to the hotel and get home all right?" Helen asked.

"Sure. I dropped her at the airport and then went straight home," a sleepy Susan answered. "I got stopped again, though."

"Stopped? By who?"

"That cop in the subdivision. The one I told you about, McGowen," said Susan. "He just wanted to talk, and he asked me out again."

"What'd you say?"

"I don't want to go out with him," Susan said, her raspy voice tinged with concern. "But I don't want to make him mad either. He comes to the house at night, but never when anyone's here. He seems to know when I'm alone. I've stopped wearing little nighties to bed, just in case he knocks on the door after I've gone to sleep. I've been sleeping in old flannel gowns and big shirts."

"What are you going to do?" Helen asked.

"I wish he'd just leave me alone," Susan said. "But I really don't want to make him mad."

After recounting the conversation, Helen's determined smile fades.

"I didn't ask the question," she whispers. "How many times since then have I wished I'd asked the question! Why was she worried about making him mad? What was she afraid of?"

12

At least on paper, all seemed to be going reasonably well for Kent McGowen at Cypresswood substation that summer. His June evaluation by his immediate supervisor, Sergeant Ruggiero, ranked him as average in seven categories and above average in three, and offered this glowing endorsement: "Deputy McGowen works well within the district and with the experience he has gained working for other law enforcement agencies will prove to be an asset to the sheriff's department."

This despite the fact that it was well known within the district that Ruggiero despised McGowen. "He spent most of his time in his contract, and that meant I didn't have to interact with him often," says Ruggiero with a rueful smile. "That was fine with me. I didn't trust him."

Yet the impression among Cypresswood's rank and file was that how Ruggiero felt about McGowen didn't matter. For McGowen had leapfrogged over his sergeant, forging a relationship directly with Ruggiero's superior, the "book-smart if not street-smart" Lieutenant Coons.

"Kent sucked ass," says one detective. "He was Coons' boy and everyone knew it."

Coons liked the young, enthusiastic deputy. Mc-Gowen's bravado might have helped, his continual bragging about working on big cases, busting up drug and gun rings, even though none of the other deputies in the district talked as if such things existed in their slice of Houston. To a young lieutenant on the fast track, such an underling could look like a potential feather for his cap.

McGowen, too, had big plans. He apparently decided that if H.P.D. wouldn't take him back, he'd make the best of working for the sheriff's department, which, after all, was the second-best law enforcement show in town. That summer, he studied for the exam for sergeants. If he passed, with Coons as his mentor he had a chance of getting what he'd bragged to the H.P.D. psychiatrist he deserved—a walk up the ladder to a lieutenant's badge.

Despite Coons' sponsorship, McGowen's status as a loner at Cypresswood didn't change. Scott Hall, the constable's deputy, continued to notice McGowen eating alone, shunned by his fellow sheriff's deputies. Sometimes McGowen would call Hall over to his restaurant table, where he puffed on cigarettes through his break. They'd long since laughed about their acrimonious first meeting. Coffee-klatching at a table near the front, their police radios standing like sentries on the table, their guns in their holsters, Hall and McGowen talked war stories. Kent bragged to the young cop about gunfights and even claimed to have killed a man in the line of duty while at H.P.D.

Hall didn't know McGowen well enough to question him, and initially enjoyed his tall tales. "We started hanging together," says Hall, his blond hair framing a face that could pass for a teenager's. "But McGowen was just looking for trouble. He provoked things. That's the way he was."

One night Hall and McGowen leaned on the bar at Diamondback, a massive country-and-western singles place, drinking and listening to music. McGowen made a pass at a stewardess. When she wasn't interested and her male friends interceded, he feigned a lisp and a limp wrist.

"You're fags, flyboys," he snapped.

Another early morning after a night of barhopping, he sauntered into a Denny's restaurant with Hall and taunted a customer seated alone, eating quietly at the counter.

"Hey, nigger," McGowen shouted. "What the hell you doing here?"

Before long, Hall grew weary of the friendship, and, like so many others, avoided him.

"McGowen was loud. The center of attention," says Hall. "He didn't care what anyone heard. It was like, 'I am the police. You can't screw with me.' "

13

Once Ron White moved to an apartment, Jason's friends overran the house on Amber Forest. Mornings they slept, strewn about, fortifying themselves after a long night of partying. Late afternoons they stumbled into the kitchen in search of breakfast. Often they found little more than stale bread and sour milk. That summer, Susan thought little of food. She lived on her pills: the amphetamines that gave her energy to face each day, the Valium that helped her sleep, and the lithium the doctor had prescribed in March to fight her depression. Left to fend for themselves, her constant houseguests would make a food run to McDonald's or Burger King, and soon empty, abandoned fast-food containers overflowed garbage cans and littered kitchen counters and tabletops.

Jason's best friend continued to be Mike Shaffer. Having Jason as a friend came in handy for Shaffer. Not only did Susan supply him with a place to live, but he and Jason were about the same size, both slight, so much so that they looked years younger than their ages of seventeen and nineteen. This made it convenient for Shaffer, who helped himself to the shopping bags of new clothes charged on Ron's credit cards. And if Mike needed anything, Jason did his best to supply it.

"Jason was bold for as little as he was. He was trying to show off," recalls Bobby Shaffer, Mike's brother. "The other kids, they probably liked him because he'd make them laugh. They'd send him out to do things—just tell him they needed something and Jason would do it. But with his mom, well, Jason was walking all over her. She gave him money. Anything he wanted."

Everyone around Susan that summer understood how desperately she clung to Jason. "I'd see Jason in front of the house and I'd ask, 'Jason, you doing okay?'" says one deputy assigned to Olde Oaks. "He'd say, 'Yeah,' and then, 'I'm doing this and that. Mom's going to do this for me.' I knew Susan was trying with the boy."

"I'm fighting the whole world for Jason," she told one friend that summer. "He's all I've got."

Susan didn't know what would happen to Jason when school began in the fall. The reckless-conduct charge from the gun incident on the school bus still clouded his future. She hired an attorney and the court scheduled the case for mid-July, but in truth, Susan had begun to wonder if she should look for other outlets for Jason. She desperately needed some place where her "beautiful baby" could show off his true abilities. In her eyes, he was an undiscovered star, as handsome and talented as Brad Pitt, Tom Cruise, or any of the actors making millions in movies and on television. And she'd always had dreams of her own of becoming an actress, maybe working on a sitcom.

"Wouldn't that be fun?" she asked friends. "Don't you think I have a knack for it?"

Helen introduced her to APM, the modeling/acting school her photographer-brother operated. She'd left real estate to work there as an agent and talent scout.

Without a second thought, Susan pulled out Ron's credit card and charged acting and modeling lessons for herself and Jason, as well as photo sessions to put together portfolios. The diamond tennis bracelet glittered on her wrist as she signed the receipt.

"Susan had a flare," says Joe Aranki, the school's tall, athletically built instructor. After thirty-five years of working for Bristol-Myers, Aranki had retired to a life of teaching tennis at a local club and acting at APM. Aranki got the APM job based on his B.A. in Fine Arts from Southwestern University and four years as a drama teacher. "Susan had a grace about her, and a natural bent for comedy. We thought she could play mother types," he remembers. "But Jason? Well, Susan tried her best with him."

Aranki's beginning acting class proved a diverse student body that summer. Most, like Jason, were teenagers, some in their early twenties, who hoped to be models. Of the dozen students in the weekly class, Susan and Joe Schultz, a retired chemist, were the oldest.

One of those in class made it big even before the summer ended, fueling the dreams of her fellow students: Anna Nicole Smith, the buxom, blond *Playboy* model who turned Guess Jean model and *Naked Gun* actress before making headlines for marrying an octogenarian Houston oil billionaire. Smith attended only a handful of APM classes before being discovered by a Houston photographer, posing for a centerfold, and moving on to Hollywood.

For Susan, Aranki held lesser hopes. He grew to believe the acting served as therapy for her, a way to relieve her frustration with the chaos in her life. On the surface she appeared carefree. But Aranki sensed Susan struggled to put on a happy facade. "She was the type of person people just gravitated to," he says. "She never had a bad word to say about anybody."

As she'd always hoped, in the classroom she displayed a natural ability for comedy. She prepared, knew her lines, worked on her timing, just as she had studied to be the A student and class president in nursing school years earlier.

In one session, portraying the swivel-hipped, bushy-haired, sex-starved Peggy in a sketch lifted from *Married With Children*, Susan gyrated across the stage, chest thrust forward, eyes glistening playfully, as she coaxed her perpetually reluctant shoe-salesman husband, played by Schultz, to make love.

"Oh, Al," she moaned.

In another sketch she portrayed Sally, Charlie Brown's sister in the "Peanuts" comic strip. Posing as a little girl with ribbons in her hair, she whined, "A C? I got a C on my coat-hanger sculpture? How could anyone get a C in coat-hanger sculpture?"

While Susan shined in class, Jason was a dour presence. He sat, head down, sulking, as he often did in school. He arrived late and unprepared, fumbling for lines, uncomfortable on the stage in front of his classmates. Each time, Susan would jump to his defense, making excuses for his lack of preparation and his uneasiness.

"You can do it, Jason, just relax," she'd call out from the audience. "Take your time, baby."

After he stumbled to a finish, Susan rose to her feet and led the applause.

Aranki pulled Jason to the side more than once after class. "Why not do your work? Come in prepared?" he asked. "Look at your mother. She's always ready."

"I don't have to worry. I can get my mom to do anything for me," Jason replied, smirking. "If I ask her, she'll do it."

Susan felt a heady excitement that summer. She dreamed of glamorous modeling jobs and bit parts in the few

movies that shot each year in Houston. She talked of it
often, telling friends about the classes and the opportunities posted on the bulletin board, mainly TV movies
and shows looking for extras. "Wouldn't I be perfect for
this?" Or, "Jason would be great for that," she'd wist-
fully tell Aranki, fingering notices of a modeling job for
a local department store's ads. "He's so handsome."

For weeks before their photo session, she primped,
priming herself for the event. She'd lost weight on the
diet pills, enough that she bragged she could slip into
size-eight jeans without lying on the bed to inch up the
zipper.

Susan's eccentric reputation on Amber Forest grew
when she showed up at a neighbor's house to ask the
woman to measure her. She needed to document her
proportions for the back of her portfolio photos. By the
time the woman returned to her living room holding a
tape measure, Susan had stripped down to her panties
and bra.

"Start here," she said, holding her head perfectly erect
and her chest jutting out. "Let's get my bust size first."

In early July, they posed for an APM photographer:
Jason and Susan in tennis outfits; Jason in jeans with a
little girl, another aspiring young model; Susan holding
a briefcase, wearing a business suit; Susan, one leg
cocked on a stool, looking like the mom next door in a
sweater and blue jeans.

In a scene radically opposed to real life, the photographer instructed Susan to pretend to scold Jason, cock-
ing her head, sternly shaking her finger with a firm,
parental expression. Susan couldn't pull it off for long.
After two frames, her frown gave way to a smile and
the camera caught her laughing.

While Susan confided to many at APM about her pend-
ing divorce, the only one who would later remember her

mentioning McGowen was the school's director of acting, David LaBelle. A former chemist who quit work in
1982 to spend two and a half years traveling the country
on a motorcycle, LaBelle had fallen into the job at APM
when he worked for the owner as a carpenter. "I found
some talent for Vernon that worked out well, just people
I met with interesting faces," says LaBelle. "I had a
knack for it. I could sit down with someone for five, ten,
fifteen minutes and know if they had a shot."

David liked Susan and they sometimes talked over
coffee in the break room. One night she told him about
a young deputy sheriff. "She said he was harassing her,
that she was unhappy with his attention," recalls David.
"She spurned him and he didn't like it. What really worried her, he was threatening to hurt Jason."

At home, Susan's world continued to erode. Perhaps Michael Shaffer wouldn't have become embroiled in Kent
McGowen's revenge if it hadn't been for an incident that
took place earlier that summer.

In hindsight, it almost seemed inevitable. Michael and
Susan had become so close. Many nights he'd find her
alone, seated on the couch in the den, surrounded by
discarded shopping bags jammed full of expensive
clothes, price tags still affixed; she'd be drinking wine,
lighting one cigarette from another, staring at the television.

On those nights, Michael listened as she recounted the
travails of her life, the poverty she'd escaped, her disappointment in love. Isolated and lonely, she poured out
her heart to him. In Susan's narrowing world, only he
seemed endlessly patient with her, understanding her
fears.

"I was faithful to Ron," she insisted, her voice bitter.
Jason slept upstairs in his bedroom, and the big house,

except for the muted dialogue of an old, forgotten movie, felt empty.

Michael understood her disappointment. In his short life he'd had more than his share of pain. He hoped she'd be all right. At times she seemed almost happy, laughing and clowning with him and Jason, her two boys. But then the phone would ring, a friend calling to say she ran into Ron and Sherri at a restaurant or with her young daughter at the park.

"Are they planning to marry?" the friend asked.

For days after, Susan had to fight to lift her head off the pillow.

"You've been so sweet to me," she said on one such lonely night, her eyes glazed with tears. "May I give you something?"

Michael nodded.

Susan poured him a glass of white wine; the chill coated the clear glass with a frosty sheen.

She walked slowly toward him.

"Here," she said, holding out the glass.

When he took it, she bent toward him until their faces touched, and she kissed him softly on the lips.

"You've never taken advantage of me," she whispered as she lowered herself onto the arm of his chair. "I want to do something for you."

Reaching out for him, Susan laid her lips against his, long and hard. Michael felt his heart pounding solidly in his chest; he sensed her desperation as she pulled him toward her. Susan was an attractive woman, desirable. Yet as they tousled on the floor, he worried, listening for any sound of movement upstairs. *What if Jason comes downstairs?* he wondered. *How could we explain this, his mother and his best friend? What will happen to all of us now?*

"It changed everything," Michael says years later, seated on a park bench near a fountain. "Before that night, things were really good for all of us. It happened one more time. She would have kept it going, but I couldn't. Jason was my best friend. She started acting crazy, saying crazy things, like her and me were gonna be together. That was nuts. After that, I made sure we weren't alone anymore. I just showed no interest. I told her, 'This isn't right.' "

In the days that followed, Michael avoided Susan, often staying away from the house overnight. He knew she'd be waiting for him, asleep on the couch, wanting to talk, maybe more. It aroused him to think of her, yet he couldn't quash the wave of guilt he felt whenever he saw Jason. In his heart he knew he'd betrayed his best friend.

His girlfriend, Amy, had a sense that something had changed at the White house. Before her liaison with Michael, Susan had catered to the girl; now she snapped at her, sometimes ordering her from the house.

"I thought she liked me," Amy complained to Michael. "What happened?"

"She's just tripping out," he said.

Amy wrote it off as another example of the peculiarities of adults.

A few weeks later, Mike Shaffer moved out of Susan White's house.

"I didn't want to be there anymore. I moved back in with my brothers and a couple of their friends in this beat-out house they rented," he explains. "I saw Jason after that sometimes, but not as often. . . . Nothing was ever the same."

Meanwhile, almost as an afterthought in a phone call that summer, Susan mentioned something to Sandra that she'd later look back on and wonder about.

"This cop is harassing me and Jason," Susan said.

"You should let someone know," Sandra urged.

"Oh, it'll be all right," Susan insisted, brushing it off as if it were no more important than if she needed a yardman to weed the flower beds. "I've got friends in the sheriff's department; they're looking out for me. And I bought a gun."

"A gun?"

"Yeah, it's in my bedside table," she said.

Susan talked to at least one deputy she considered a friend at the sheriff's department about McGowen early that summer. She stopped Warren "Al" Kelly, an avuncular deputy who'd been kind to her in the past, someone who'd occasionally inquired about Jason.

"Who does this Kent McGowen think he is?" she demanded angrily one afternoon.

"Why?" Kelly asked.

"He worries me," she said. "I'm afraid he'll hurt Jason."

The deputy, who knew how overprotective Susan could be when it came to her only child, dismissed her fears as those of a troubled parent with teenager problems. Still, Kelly didn't particularly care for McGowen. Like many of his fellow deputies, he doubted Kent's reliability—for instance, the way McGowen kept cornering him at the station.

"Have you seen that kid in the red Beretta?" he'd asked Kelly. "That guy's running guns."

"Can't say I have," replied Kelly, who'd heard nothing of any big operator running stolen guns in the contract.

One night in early July, soon after he'd moved out of the White house, Shaffer, knowing Susan wasn't home, stopped by with friends in a 1981 Chevy truck to see

Jason. He cringed when he noticed McGowen parked on the street.

"That cop's out there again," Jason said, peering out between the curtains. "The one who busted up the party."

"Yeah, we saw him," Shaffer said. "Why's he doing this? We're probably going to get stopped when we leave here."

As he'd predicted, McGowen followed, slowly, as Shaffer and his friends drove away. The deputy tailed them to a deserted street, and Shaffer saw the squad car's red-and-blue lights flash behind him.

"Shit," he said.

The driver pulled over and McGowen ordered them from the truck. He commanded them to put their hands on the truck, then patted each one down.

"What'd we do?" one of the others asked.

"Keep quiet," McGowen ordered.

As they watched, he searched the truck, even pulling out the seats to look underneath. Then, without saying a word, McGowen drove away in his squad car.

"Why'd he do that?" one of the boys asked as they gathered up their belongings, strewn across the grass.

"Beats me," said Shaffer.

A few nights later, McGowen stopped Shaffer again. This time Mike was alone, driving home in his latest car, a dilapidated Toyota, after dropping Amy at her house, a few blocks from Jason and Susan's home.

On this particular stop, McGowen didn't search Shaffer or his car. Instead he acted as if they were old friends.

"You know that guy in the red Beretta?" McGowen asked.

"Yeah, that's Keith," Mike answered. "I've met him at Jason's."

"I hear he's running stolen guns and has automatic weapons."

Mike knew Keith, an older kid who sometimes hung

out at the White house. He also knew Keith collected and traded guns, and that he had a federal dealer's license that allowed him to do so. Mike had never heard of him selling stolen guns or having anything illegal.

"Whatever," Shaffer answered, not wanting to argue with McGowen.

"Can you find someone to sell you a stolen gun?" McGowen asked.

Shaffer shrugged. "I guess so."

McGowen pulled out a card, wrote down his pager number, and handed the card to Shaffer.

"Call me when you get it set up," he said, smiling warmly. "Remember, you owe me."

14

As time passed, the animosity between Susan and Ron White built. He filed divorce papers, urging Gloria and Sandra to convince Susan to sign them.

"It's in her best interest," he argued. "The marriage is over. Why drag it out?"

Much of that summer Ron spent working on a new project, one in Mexico. Sherri Brandt saw him only infrequently. Susan occasionally heard from Sherri's husband, who said she and Ron seemed to be having trouble. "All's not well in paradise," he laughed. Rumors floated through the office linking Ron romantically with a young Mexican woman.

Susan didn't know whether to be happy or sad, she told friends. Now she had two rivals to fight.

Notices from the company that held the mortgage on the Amber Forest house arrived in Susan's mailbox every few days. It'd been a long time since they'd received a payment and the letters threatened foreclosure if the arrears weren't paid. And Ron had finally managed to cancel all their joint credit cards, cutting off for good her access to his money.

"Where will I go?" she asked Sandra one night on the phone.

"You've got to go on with your life," her sister advised. "And remember, you can always come home, stay with family until you get back on your feet."

"I know," Susan said. "But I like it here. And I'm not going to let Ron, Sherri, or that Mexican girl take away all my beautiful things."

Susan had little money left, except for her disability checks from the mortgage company and the $100-a-month money orders she received as child support from L.J. Without Ron's help, how could she make the $1,400 monthly mortgage payments? Yet she was determined to protect what she could.

Telling friends she feared Ron would back a moving van into the driveway and empty the house of their furniture and belongings, she rented a garage-sized storage facility a mile from the house. With Jason's help, she moved her furniture there, as well as her crystal, china, and oil paintings. In their stead she used old, worn furniture from friends, including a black lacquer waterbed in place of the four-poster cherry bed she and Ron had shared. Emptied of its furnishings, the house looked scattered and barren, with hardly a hint of its former opulence.

To Jason, it mattered little. He barely even slept at home that summer, busy as he was with his friends. When Susan wanted him, she called his beeper. But more often than not, he glanced at his home phone number and ignored the page. Susan took to driving to pay phones to call, certain he'd answer an unfamiliar number, afraid of missing a call from a friend.

If she'd known what occupied her son's time that summer, Susan would have been terrified. He continued to seek out teenagers like himself, those from troubled homes. But their play had become increasingly violent. Their parties, laced with drugs, lasted well into the night. Sometimes the drugs mixed with guns and violence. It was at such a party in July, at a run-down house in a neighborhood of run-down houses, that Jason met Maggie.

The noise level rose that night, laughing teenage boys jostling and pushing one another, their girlfriends hanging on possessively close by. Suddenly, gunfire erupted from a nearby house. As they huddled together in the darkness, hoping to elude the shooter, a blond-haired, blue-eyed sprite of a girl caught Jason's eye. Like Jason, she appeared younger than her seventeen years. Also like Jason's, her eyes had the weary look of someone much older.

From that night on, Maggie and Jason were inseparable.

"She's such a responsible young girl," Susan told Jean. "It's a comfort to have her around."

Maggie, who had a younger sister who'd been in and out of trouble, nearly lived at her new boyfriend's house.

"Susan and I talked like friends," says Maggie. "She wasn't like a mother. She worried about Jason and wanted me to help take care of him. She said he'd do whatever his friends told him. She was right. Jason was just that way. He'd do things without thinking just 'cause someone told him to. Especially Shaffer. He was always doing things for Mike."

One person Maggie heard Susan mention often that summer was Kent McGowen. "She talked about him, told Jason to watch out for him. She said he was going to do something to him. When we went out, she'd tell us all the way out the door, 'Now, don't give McGowen any reason to go after you.' Jason and I didn't pay much attention. I thought she was just carrying on."

*   *   *

Happy to defrock herself of the heavy mantle of Jason's troubles, Susan placed her son in Maggie's care as she had once relinquished it to Mike Shaffer. With a new sense of freedom, she met one friend or another for drinks in the late afternoons. On one Monday in July, she met Helen at a bar called Patti's Party Place.

The tavern had been around for decades. A barnlike wooden structure named after a former bar owner who'd moved to Houston from Detroit, then backtracked after a summer's oppressive heat, Patti's catered to many of the same crowd that frequented Resa's. The local shuffleboard club took over the back of the bar on Wednesday nights. Happy hour found realtors, store owners, attorneys, insurance agents, clerks, and company presidents populating the tomato-red tile-topped tables. A glass-door popcorn machine spit out puffed white kernels oozing a movie-theater aroma. Neon beer signs emitted an eerie, fluorescent glow, and the ding-ding of the pinball machines fought the jukebox to be heard.

But in the afternoons, scattered patrons, mainly men with hair in various stages of gray, lined the bar. Overhead, inverted wineglasses hung from racks and clinked each time Mike, the bartender, grabbed a clean one. Rarely did he encounter an unfamiliar face, and most customers were greeted by name. Some retired, others deal-makers unencumbered by offices, Patti's day-timers had little to do but drink and watch stock-market quotes on one television behind the bar and ESPN on the big screen near the dance floor. Most sat alone, empty stools insulating them on either side, their cellular phones propped in front of them on the heavy oak bar.

"Hi, Mike, meet my friend Susan," Helen called out as she claimed a stool at the bar.

Mike, chewing on a toothpick and washing glasses,

glanced up. "Hi," he uttered, a week's growth of beard parting for an unenthusiastic smile.

Helen ordered white wine and Susan requested her usual, a split of champagne.

"Know anyone here?" Susan whispered.

Helen glanced around the room casually, yet absorbing every detail. "Nope," she said. "Except that guy over there, but you wouldn't be interested. By now he's so drunk he probably can't talk."

Just then the door opened.

"Now there's someone I know," said Helen, eyebrows arched, gesturing toward a figure framed by an aura of sunlight.

As the dimness of the bar resettled around him, Susan sized up a darkly handsome, slickly dressed man walking toward them.

"Paul," Helen called out. When he reached her, she lunged forward, embracing him in a hearty hug. "This is my friend Susan. Sit down and join us."

Helen had known Paul, Susan soon learned, for many years. A hairstylist who owned and operated a posh salon on FM 1960, his patrons were local ladies with flash.

That afternoon, they sat together, drinking, talking, and laughing, Susan flirting as Paul returned her attention. When darkness fell and Helen left to meet another friend, Susan and Paul removed themselves to a corner table at Resa's, where they listened to music and danced, pressed together without an inch of room between them, his hand clasping the small of her back.

In Paul's condo later that night, they tumbled together urgently in the heat of a new conquest, hungry for the touch of the other's body. Afterward, locked together and wrapped in a sheet on the couch, Susan gazed through the window into the darkness outside.

"My son's not home tonight. He's with friends," she said, rubbing her blond hair against his bare shoulder. "Could I stay the night?"

"Sure," Paul said, nuzzling her shoulder.

"I don't like going home alone," she said, nestling herself into the crook of his arm. "I had a one-night stand with a young cop in the neighborhood. Ever since, he's been after me, knocking on the door late at night when no one else is home. Sometimes he follows me."

"Could he be out there now?" Paul asked. Suddenly chilly, he pulled the sheet over his shoulder.

"He could be," she whispered.

15

That same month, July 1992, Jason stood before a judge and pleaded no contest to a charge of reckless conduct in connection with the gun incident on the bus. He was sentenced to one hundred and eighty days of differed adjudication, meaning that if he stayed out of trouble for approximately six months, he'd never have to serve a day in jail.

"Maybe things are straightening out for us," Susan told Helen. "I really feel good about the future."

But then, Susan never looked below the surface with her son, his ready smile; at five-foot-seven, he weighed just 120 pounds. How could she have imagined the risks he would take in the name of friendship?

"Jason never wanted her to know what he was doing," says Maggie. "He'd smoke pot out of the green tin container in his bedroom, blowing the smoke out the window. He hung with a tough crowd. They robbed houses and stuff. Did drugs. My parents and me, we'd lived in some pretty crummy neighborhoods, but the kids were actually better there. Most of those kids who were robbing and stealing, they had it made. Their parents would have given them anything they wanted. They lived in big houses, drove nice cars. But they were bored. So they played at being bad, having gangs and stuff. And Jason was right there in it. He thought he was cool. He wasn't a bad person. He just wanted to fit in."

"I just cared about having fun," Jason would later explain. "I'd go to these parties with my friends and stuff and another crowd would show up and my friends didn't like them and they would always fight. The next party, the same thing.

"Some of my pards, my friends, they'd steal purses at clubs and they'd take the credit cards to the mall to buy expensive stuff. We'd buy tennis shoes, a hundred forty or a hundred fifty dollars a pair, the kind those kids in Chicago kill each other over. It was gang stuff, but not really gang stuff. I did it 'cause it made me feel big. Everybody did it 'cause it made them feel big."

As July drew to a close, Susan spent most nights seated at the piano bar in Resa's. Sometimes Jean Morris joined her. As the champagne relaxed her, she blurted out the details of one or another of the liaisons she'd indulged in, men she'd met and accompanied home.

"Oh, you didn't know about that," she'd say with a giggle, the tickling of the wine against her lips.

Jean didn't know what to think, especially when on one night, Susan confided, "Ron thinks Mike Shaffer and I had a little fling."

"Did you?" Jean asked.

Susan simply shrugged.

"Susie, my God," Jean gasped. "He's like your kid."

On another night, Susan opened her purse and showed Jean the small, chrome-plated pistol secreted inside. "It's a twenty-five," she whispered. "I've never shot it, actually I've only got a couple bullets, but I have it with me all the time."

"Why?" Jean asked.

"Protection," she said.

When neither Helen nor Jean joined her, Susan sat at the piano bar alone, listening to the music, requesting her James Taylor song, and attempting to strike up a conversation with anyone who looked her way.

A week or so after their tryst, she noticed Paul at a table with another woman. He'd never phoned after the night in his condo.

"Did I lose an earring at your place?" she asked, leaning over his table and flashing a mischievous smile.

Paul squirmed under the cool gaze of his date, a wealthy divorcée he'd been seeing for months, including during his encounter with Susan.

"You must have the wrong guy," he said.

"Oh, it doesn't matter," Susan said, obviously content that she'd hit her mark. "It wasn't an expensive one. You can keep it as a memento."

On most nights, the restaurant's owners, Jim and Resa Kelly, circulated through the crowd, introducing themselves to newcomers and greeting regulars. They made an odd couple. Resa, thirtysomething, thin, blond, and intense, but with a broad, engaging smile, had once been the head waitress, then found investors and bought the place. With a flair for marketing, she decorated the walls inside with photos and outside with a mural of her most loyal patrons. In a strip center on a quiet side street, the restaurant had little reason for success, other than her business sense and the vision to realize that while low-fat ruled grocery-store shelves, a generation deprived of excess could still be lured with the promise of a stout drink and a thick, tender steak.

In his white, bloodstained cook's apron, Jim, a bulky ex-cop from Cleveland, maneuvered among the patrons, often hobbling from the pain of an arthritic hip.

In addition to their three children, one of the few things the Kellys appeared to have in common was the love of a good story.

"So have you heard the one about . . ." usually accompanied Jim Kelly's arrival at a table.

Susan was a ready audience, laughing merrily at even the weariest jokes. Yet Jim rarely tarried for long. "She was on the lookout," he says. "Running a restaurant, you see it all the time, the newly single woman looking for a man and a bankroll."

On one such night in the restaurant, Jim Kelly stood at the piano bar telling Susan and a cluster of others a joke about three men—a Mexican, an Italian, and a Texas Aggie. The punch line fell flat, leaving some customers rolling their eyes at Kelly, others smiling and walking away. But Susan, as always, threw her head back and laughed enthusiastically.

Kelly turned to leave, but changed his mind.

"Hey," he said, as if something had just occurred to him. "I've got someone I want you to meet." Taking Susan by the hand, he walked her over to the opposite side of the piano, stopping in front of a corpulent, bald-headed man.

"Hey, Ray," Jim said. "Meet Susan White."

Ray Valentine spun around on the barstool and sized up a fortyish blonde with a big smile.

"My pleasure," he said, holding out his hand to shake hers. "Nice to meet you."

Ray Valentine and Susan White talked only briefly during their first encounter. They made no plans to meet again. A few nights later, however, Ray walked into Resa's to find Susan at the piano bar, leaning her head on her hand, listening to Alan sing a soft ballad. Susan perked up the moment she caught sight of him. "Come on, Ray," she cooed. "Sit over here with me."

Valentine lumbered over and pulled up a stool.

"Play something romantic," Susan whispered to Jefferies, who paused for a moment to take a sip of wine before launching into the melody of "Unforgettable," then high on the charts after Natalie Cole's computer-melded duet with her late father.

"What's that?" Valentine asked, pointing a thick finger at a manila envelope on the bar.

"Oh, those are mine," Susan said, flashing a wide grin. "They're photos for my portfolio."

Susan fanned the black-and-whites on the grand piano, like a hand of cards, shoving aside the crystal brandy snifter Alan used for tips. "I'm a model," she said. "I've just started. And I'm doing some acting, too. Not much yet, but my instructor says I have talent."

"Who's this?" Valentine nudged a photo of Jason.

"Oh, that's my seventeen-year-old son," said Susan. "We're taking classes together. Isn't he handsome?"

They mingled at the piano, Susan spilling over with enthusiasm about her career, lowering her voice to whisper of Ron's betrayal. A new audience always seemed to inspire her.

"What do you do?" she finally asked.

"I'm in the circus business," Valentine said, explaining that five generations of his family had worked as aerialists, the "Flying Valentines." The image must have conjured up a contrast for Susan, envisioning this 250-plus-pound, six-foot-two man swinging far above a circus ring. "I've toured just about every country," he said, swigging down a scotch on the rocks. "Except China; never been to China."

Susan ordered herself another champagne and Valentine went on to say that for the last decade or so he'd run a kind of circus-for-hire, which put on fund-raising exhibitions for sponsoring organizations in fifty-four cities in twenty states. In Houston, the Harris County Deputy Sheriff's Association sponsored the circus each summer and received a percentage of revenues. Wearing two heavy gold rings, one domed with diamonds, the other a nugget ring with the initial V, and a thick gold-nugget watch, Valentine wiped his hairless brow and looked at her with eyes that drooped on the outside corners, giving him the appearance of perpetual sadness.

"We've got fourteen semis hauling the circus around the country," he continued. "From May to Thanksgiving, I'm traveling from city to city in a travel trailer." Valentine liked to talk numbers—money, really—and Susan listened eagerly as he rattled off figures, tens of thousands of dollars for insurance, advertising, the cost of running all three rings.

"All the travel makes it hard on my boys," he said, explaining that his latest marriage had broken up eighteen months earlier and he'd been left alone to raise two young sons, aged three and five. At fifty-six, Valentine was thirteen years older than Susan, and he appeared more like a grandfather than the father of young children.

"How old are you?" Susan asked.

"Old enough to know better," said Valentine, grinning. "And too young to resist."

With Ray Valentine, Susan White regained her belief that her life might improve. She continued her acting classes and worked for Valentine at his office a few days a week, doing voice-overs for his commercials: "Coming June thirteenth to the fifteenth, six performances, the Shrine Circus . . ."

The offices, next door to the Harris County Deputy Sheriff's Association, consisted of his secretary and a phone bank of solicitors working telephone sheets to sell tickets at whatever city was scheduled for the circus' next venue. The office door bore the association's emblem and uniformed deputies circulated through it, some on union business, others stopping in Valentine's office to check on ticket sales.

Glad for the distraction, Susan enjoyed the bustle of the place and took an immediate liking to Valentine's secretary, Rita. The wife of H.C.S.D. Captain C.J. Harper, Rita had been with Valentine for more than thirteen years.

Nearly overnight, Susan and Valentine became an item at Resa's. She snuggled up to him, telling friends she enjoyed his bearlike bulk. It made her feel secure. To others, she mentioned his business and the roll of cash, hundred-dollar bills on top, that he pulled out of his pocket to pay their bill. "I think this could go some-where," she told Helen one night.

Helen understood. She knew how determined Susan was to land a husband with money. But she didn't par-ticularly care for Valentine. "He was one of those guys who talked about his money too much," says Helen. "And he had to run the show. Go anywhere with Ray and he takes over."

None of that bothered Susan, who began referring to him as "my Valentine." Yet their days and nights to-gether didn't always go well. From the beginning, ten-sion permeated the relationship every time she mentioned the name of Kent McGowen.

"She talked about him all the time," recalls Valentine years later, seated at an oak booth in a restaurant, drink-ing a happy-hour scotch. "She said this kid deputy was after her and that he was threatening to do something to her or Jason if she didn't sleep with him. I just flat out didn't believe her. I mean, the guy was a cop. 'Come on,' I said. 'He's not going to do anything to you. Cops don't go after people.'

"Some nights after a few drinks, she'd just harp on it to the point I could hardly stand it. I finally told her to shut up about the kid. I didn't want to hear Kent McGowen's name, not ever again."

*   *   *

On August 2, Gloria, O.L., Sandra, and two of Gloria's grandchildren pulled into Susan's driveway for an overnight stay on their way to Austin. She rushed to greet them, greedily throwing her arms around them.

"I'm so glad you're here," she said, tears spilling from her eyes.

Once inside, they were struck by how different the house appeared. It was devoid of furniture, and boxes lined the walls. "I'm still getting foreclosure notices," Susan explained. "I don't know when Jason and I will have to move."

Despite the uncertainty of her future, Susan seemed determined to make the best of their hours together. She brought out her portfolio to show them, and demonstrated a skit from her acting class. She displayed her new clothes, including the business suit she'd bought for the photo session. Then she gave them each a gift, clothing she'd bought for O.L. and Sandra, and for Gloria, now that she had a new one, her old tennis bracelet. Tiny as the diamonds were, they sparkled as she secured the clasp around her sister's wrist.

She rattled on about acting and modeling opportunities, chattered happily about a commercial she'd auditioned for, even pulling in her sweater to show off her slim figure. Gloria stood up, and just like when they were girls, they compared waistlines.

"Why, you're skinnier than me," Gloria whined playfully. Although she'd known about Susan and the diet pills in the past, it never occurred to her that Susan was again addicted.

"I got my girlish figure back," Susan bragged, sashaying her hips. "See here, Momma, I'm like a young girl again."

That night, Susan and Sandra couldn't sleep. Instead, Susan uncorked a bottle of wine. The two sisters sat to-

"I think Susie was always looking for something to fill her up, to make her feel whole," says her older sister Gloria. "I don't think she ever found it." Susan White in the Navy in 1967 and at her graduation from nursing school.

Photo courtesy of Mrs. O.L. Harrison

Susan in happier times, hula-hooping in Gloria's backyard. "Susie had a lot of spirit," says her sister Sandra.

Photo courtesy of Sandra Harrison

Two of Susan and Jason's modeling photos. As in real life, first she scolded him, then she laughed with him.

Photos courtesy of
Kennon Evett Photography

Susan White's dream house at 3407 Amber Forest: the site of her killing.

Photo courtesy of Kathryn Casey

The irony of this bumper sticker, found in Susan's bedroom after the shooting, didn't escape the notice of investigators.

The inside of the house on Amber Forest reflected the dissolution of Susan's life. The upper photo shows the meticulously cared-for kitchen before the divorce. The lower photo records the chaos in her bedroom the morning of the killing.

Top photo courtesy of Sandra Harrison

Bottom photo courtesy of private investigator Rob Kimmons

"I decided to tape-record McGowen's walk-through, something I'd never done before," remembers Assistant D.A. Don Smyth.

Photo courtesy of Kathryn Casey

Steve Clappart, the Houston D.A.'s investigator. Early on, he came to the conclusion that something about Susan White's shooting "didn't smell right."

Photo courtesy of Kathryn Casey

Sergeant John Denholm. He first met McGowen when they both worked in the Harris County jail. "He was a slackard," says Denholm. Later, he headed the sheriff's department investigation in Susan White's death.

Photo courtesy of Kathryn Casey

Edward Porter in the courtroom. Convicting McGowen would set a precedent: the first time a Texas police officer was found guilty of a murder while serving a warrant.

Photo courtesy of Kathryn Casey

Judge A.D. Azios at the bench. "He never liked having his decisions reversed," says one observer. "When it became obvious there might be an error in the McGowen case, you could see the disappointment on his face."

Photo courtesy of Kathryn Casey

Kent McGowen outside the courtroom and with his attorneys:
Brian Benken (*right*), who represented him at his original trial,
and George McCall Secrest, Jr. (*left*), who handled his appeal.
McGowen had received a light sentence for murder. Were they
taking a chance on a longer sentence if they won a retrial?

Photos courtesy of Kathryn Casey

Years after a jury convicted McGowen, their verdict was in jeopardy in the appeals court and he remained free. At their home in Louisiana, O.L. and W.A. Harrison, Susan's parents, wondered if "the man who killed our Susie will ever go to prison."

Photo courtesy of Kathryn Casey

SUSAN D H WHITE
US NAVY
OCT 6 1949 ✝ AUG 25 1992

Susan White's grave in the cemetery near her parents' home, outside Baton Rouge, Louisiana.

Photo courtesy of Kathryn Casey

gether and spoke of their lives. At three in the morning, they munched chocolate chip cookies and laughed over old stories, events transformed into family fables.

Yet Sandra felt uneasy. Something about the nearly empty house bothered her. And her restlessness only increased when Susan jumped up to get something, then came back carrying an envelope marked "Last Will and Testament of Susan Harrison White."

"What's this?" Sandra asked.

"I told you I'd made up a will. I want you to take it," Susan insisted. "You need to have it."

"Susan, honey, you're only forty-two," Sandra protested. "You don't need to worry about this for years."

"Take it," Susan ordered, pushing the envelope toward her. "And there's a key inside with an address. It's the storage place where I've got the furniture. I took it out in your name. If anything happens to me, you're the executor and I want everything to go to Jason."

The next morning, Gloria came downstairs to make coffee. Susan and Sandra were sitting at the table and they had the will between them.

"Gloria, I've named you Jason's guardian if anything happens to me," Susan said. "It's here in my will."

"Okay," Gloria said, still sleepy. "But I've got to tell you, you better plan on living until February, when he turns eighteen."

All three sisters laughed.

Just then Jason walked into the room smoking a cigarette.

"Jason, take that outside," Susan ordered.

"Okay," he said, turning toward the door.

"You see, Jason's not a bad boy," Susan said, staring intently at her sister. "You tell him what to do and he'll do it."

*   *   *

The family had plans for those final hours together, a trip to a pottery warehouse, but the phone rang early that morning. Sherri Brandt's husband called to tell Susan that Sherri was on a plane, going to Mexico to visit Ron.

Shaken, Susan handed the telephone to Gloria. When he explained what had happened, Gloria pursed her lips. "How do you think Susan's doing?" she whispered, hoping her sister wouldn't hear.

"Okay, I guess," he replied. "I think she's just having a hard time right now."

"You know I hate Ron," Susan said when Gloria had hung up the receiver. "I'm through with him."

A few minutes later, in her BMW, Susan led the way as Gloria followed in her van to the interstate ramp to Austin, then motioned them to get on the highway.

"I guess she'd forgotten about the shopping. It was the last time any of us ever saw Susie alive," whispers Gloria. "She was smiling, waving us onto the freeway, waving good-bye."

16

Ray Valentine soon realized he could complain all he wanted, but it made no difference to Susan. She just wasn't going to stop bringing up Kent McGowen. Some nights, it was *all* she wanted to talk about.

"I'm telling you, a deputy sheriff is not going to do anything to hurt you," he insisted one night in her kitchen.

"You know, Ray, someday you're going to believe me," she said, waving her finger in his face. "But by then it'll be too late. I'll be dead, and Kent McGowen's the one who will have killed me."

"Oh, hell," said an exasperated Valentine, spitting out the words. "I'll tell you what I'll do. I'll get Rita and C.J. to go out for dinner and you can tell him all about this kid cop."

A few nights later, Valentine and Susan sat at a candlelit corner table at Resa's with Rita and H.C.S.D. Captain C.J.

Harper. A short man with a fidgety mien, Harper listened intently as Susan confided in him about her fear of McGowen.

"He's threatened to do something to me or my son," she said, her perpetually hoarse voice cracking with emotion. "He says if I don't have a relationship with him, do what he wants, he'll get even with me. C.J., I'm really afraid of this guy. What do I do?"

"Well, you can file a complaint with his lieutenant or captain at the station. You need to do it in writing," Harper said, chewing a forkful of beef. "I can't say I know this McGowen. He must be new out there."

The conversation dragged on, Harper sympathetic as Susan reiterated her fear of McGowen and how vulnerable Jason could be. She told the captain of his trouble at school and reports from counselors that labeled him as having learning disabilities. "Jason's not a bad kid," she said. "It's just he does pretty much what anybody tells him to. I guess you could say he's kind of slow."

Harper would later say he believed he did call someone at Cypresswood a day or two following the dinner, an officer there he would refuse to name, and that he mentioned White and her concerns about McGowen.

"But I can't be sure," he said, his eyes darting around his office at the sheriff's department headquarters, as if afraid someone was listening. "To be honest, I just kind of forgot about the whole thing."

About the same time, the telephone rang one afternoon in the press room tucked inside H.P.D. headquarters. Earnest Perry, a veteran *Houston Chronicle* reporter covering the police beat, answered and heard a deep, raspy woman's voice with a thick Louisiana accent. "I'm having problems with a deputy," she said. "He's going to hurt me."

Perry prodded her with questions, but the woman

gave only sketchy details, not even her name or the name of the agency the deputy worked for. "You've got to give me more information or I can't help you," he said.

"I'm afraid to talk on the telephone," she replied. "What if he has it bugged?"

"Then let's meet somewhere and we can talk in person."

"What if he follows me?" she said. "This guy's a cop. He's harassing me. He's threatened to hurt me or my son if I don't go out with him."

"I need more information. We need to sit down and talk if I'm going to help you," Perry insisted.

"I'll call another time," she said. "I can't talk now."

With that, the phone went dead.

17

Mike Shaffer was on edge. Everywhere he and Amy went, he looked jumpy. What happened at Celebration Station, a small amusement park, didn't help. That afternoon, Amy stood drinking a Pepsi near one of the rides when two scruffy-looking teenage boys approached her.

"You with anyone?" one demanded.

"That's my boyfriend over there," she said, pointing at Mike.

"Hell, he's a little guy," the other teen said, jostling his cohort. "We can kick his ass."

Amy ran over to Shaffer, pulled him into a nearby building, and whispered what the boys had said. Shaky, Shaffer sized up the two, who smirked at him and laughed; then he dropped a quarter into a coin phone and dialed a number.

"Help is on the way," he told Amy when he hung up.

Before long, Jason and a troop of their friends showed

up and escorted Mike and Amy from the amusement park, then followed him home.

Shaffer assumed the confrontation had ended, but it hadn't.

A few days later, he stood in an aisle at Blockbuster, perusing the new releases, when he glanced out the window and spotted a black Mitsubishi Eclipse hovering nearby in the parking lot. Shaffer recognized the driver and the passenger as the hotheads from Celebration Station. He pointed them out to Amy, then pulled her by the arm to the back of the store.

"We'll wait until they leave," he said nervously.

Ten minutes later, he looked out and the car had disappeared.

Shaffer rushed Amy outside, but as they slid inside his Toyota, the black car careened into a neighboring parking space. Shaffer glanced up to find a pistol pointed directly at Amy's face. He slammed his car into reverse and sped away, nearly sideswiping another car as he screeched onto the street.

Shaking, Shaffer wove between cars, accelerating toward home.

"Why're they doing this?" Amy cried. "Why don't they leave us alone?"

Despite Shaffer's attempts to evade the Mitsubishi, it stuck, as if glued to his bumper. Finally, Shaffer pulled into the driveway of the house where he lived with his two older brothers. Alerted by the squeal of tires, Myron, the oldest of the Shaffer boys, raced outside just in time to see the Mitsubishi barrel down the street.

It was all Shaffer needed on top of his uneasy alliance with McGowen. "Mike was afraid of those guys, but there was one thing he was really afraid of," Amy says. "Mike was afraid of going to jail. And McGowen was a cop. He could put him there."

As Amy saw it, Shaffer was obsessed with what the

deputy might do next. He told her McGowen wanted him to set someone up on a gun charge.

"Should I do it?" he asked. "I don't know what to do."

Amy shrugged. "Maybe you should think about it more."

"Yeah," said Shaffer.

As the days passed, he thought of little else. He knew McGowen wanted Keith, the kid in the red Beretta. As he saw it, that presented a problem; as far as he knew, Keith wasn't doing anything illegal. So if he was going to set someone up, he didn't see how it could be Keith.

Desperate, Shaffer asked around. "You know anybody who's got any stolen guns?" he queried friends, teenagers he ran into at the teen club he frequented, where the lights were dim and neighborhood kids as young as fourteen drank Cokes and danced. The rest room doors belched marijuana smoke with each opening swing.

Finally, in mid-August, Shaffer got a break. Through a friend, he learned of a boy with a stolen gun he was willing to sell. But when Mike tried to set up the buy, the teenager insisted the transaction take place inside his house. Still, it was all Shaffer had.

Shaffer paged McGowen and detailed the setup.

"I don't want to do anything inside a house," McGowen said, unimpressed with Shaffer's scenario.

Shaffer felt trapped. He knew he'd disappointed the cop. What if he found no one to sacrifice to him? McGowen wasn't the type to let go.

"I do know this guy Jason," Mike said tentatively. "If I ask him, he might be able to come up with a gun. You know Jason? He lives with his mom over on Amber Forest."

"Sure, I know who he is," said McGowen. "Set it up."

18

She couldn't have known of Mike Shaffer's plot to entrap her son as a way of appeasing McGowen's appetite for a big bust, but that summer, Susan White was obsessed with the young deputy, his name never far from her lips.

"He's getting worse all the time, pushy," she told David LaBelle, APM's director.

"What are you going to do?" he asked.

"I don't know," she admitted.

Yet with Susan's relationship with Valentine blooming, her fear took a backseat to the excitement of making plans for the future.

"It was always 'Ray this' and 'Ray that,' " says Helen. "Susan looked happier than I'd seen her since Ron."

To Gloria, she cooed about Ray and his money. "He'll be good to me, I can tell," she said. "We can follow the circus with Jason and Ray's two boys. Jason will love seeing the world. He won't have to go to school—they have tutors."

Still, Valentine and Susan's relationship was far from

idyllic. They argued often, usually about his continued frustration with her insistence that some young contract deputy named Kent McGowen planned to hurt her. She claimed McGowen had followed her to a shopping center, that he stopped his squad car in front of her on the street and stared at her as she drove around him.

"He's trying to scare me," she said. "He's crazy and I can't get rid of him."

"You've got to stop saying this cop is going to kill you," he countered, his anger rising. "Enough is enough. If Jason gets arrested, if anything happens to him, it's because he's got himself a problem. He's a teenager and he's getting into trouble."

The 1992 Republican convention opened in Houston on August 17, and Ray hired a limo and took Susan and Helen to a political bash at the Ritz-Carlton. Susan wore a sequined dress and rhinestone earrings. She sparkled as brightly as the red, white, and blue centerpieces on the tables. On the dance floor, she and Ray swayed as the room reverberated with music.

"Everything was great until she brought up McGowen again," remembers Valentine, who stalked out of the event and took a cab home alone. "I was tired of hearing it. It was a party. I told her, 'Enough is enough, for God's sake.' "

Their relationship took a second hit a few days later, when Ray's ex-wife appeared at his doorstep.

Susan interpreted the intrusion of a woman out of Ray's past as a threat. Would he abandon her, like L.J. had, like Ron? One night she sat in her bedroom, toying with a yellow legal pad. As a teenager, she'd written an awkward poem to an unrequited love. Now, a middle-aged woman, mourning the loss of her marriage and fearing the loss of new love, she scrawled:

HOW DO I GET IN THESE MESSES. I HAVE ONE WOMAN
WANTING MY EX-HUSBAND FOR HIS MONEY. I HAVE

ONE EX-WIFE WANTING MY LOVER FOR HIS MONEY.
AND I, LIKE AN IDIOT, I'M ALLOWING BOTH MEN TO
TRAUMATIZE ME IN VERY SIMILAR WAYS. I'M IN CEN-
TER STAGE OF THIS FIASCO. WHAT NEITHER OF THEM
REALIZE IS ALL I WANTED WAS THEIR LOVE. BUT YET
THEY HAVE KEPT/KEEP ME IN LIMBO, FEELING LIKE
NEITHER REALLY CARES.

With Ray distracted, Susan made plans to pass a night
with Helen and four of her friends at Resa's. Despite her
inner turmoil, she appeared carefree with them, giggling
girlishly as she boasted about her acting lessons.

"You look just like Teri Garr," one woman gushed.
"You'll be great."

Susan beamed.

As the night passed, they talked about the men in
their lives. To Helen's surprise, she heard Susan say she
hated her ex-husband.

"I'm glad Ron's out of my life," she insisted. "I
wouldn't take him back if he asked me."

The others agreed she'd made the right decision.

Then, as Susan left the table to ask Alan to play her
James Taylor song, Helen turned to the others.

"You know this young cop's been pursuing Susan,"
she said. "I'm glad she's getting a night out like this to
forget her troubles. He doesn't seem willing to take no
for an answer."

All eyes at the table turned to Susan, her blond hair
illuminated by the spotlight over the piano.

"Will she be all right?" one woman asked.

"I hope so," Helen answered.

Excitement tittered through APM Studios that same
week regarding a notice on the job board: One of their
occasional acting coaches, Gary Chason, had taken over
production of a movie. He needed three hundred extras

for a 1931 Rice University graduation scene in *The Trust*, based on the turn-of-the-century murder of the university's founder, Texas multimillionaire William Marsh Rice. It was the quintessential murder mystery, one in which the butler actually did it, albeit with the help of the old man's attorney.

Much of the excitement centered around Chason, who had Hollywood credentials, including casting talent for *Texasville, Paris, Texas, Liar's Moon, Pretty Baby, The Man Who Loved Women, Brewster McCloud,* and *The Last Picture Show.*

"What if I get discovered?" Susan speculated with a friend. "What if they just pick me out?"

On the day of the shooting, Susan and Jason gathered with a crowd of the curious and the ambitious on the university grounds. The courtyard overflowed with a collage of faces. The film's stars, Sam Bottoms and Karen Black, sought refuge from the unrelenting heat in their air-conditioned trailers, while Chason wove through the crowd. He enjoyed mingling with the extras. Looking part surfer and part cowboy, a rumpled man with graying hair, Chason had grown up in Galveston; he was a descendant of the Allens, the two brothers credited with founding Houston. His mother had hoped he'd be an attorney, but showbiz had always dominated his life. As a teen, he'd studied with the Houston Ballet and the Houston Grand Opera. After a fling in New York and Hollywood, he had returned home. His great love, a small independent picture he'd produced, written, and directed, called *Charlie's Ear,* earned good reviews and a handful of awards but failed to find a distributor.

As she'd hoped, Susan stood out on the set. She meandered in and out of the casting tent, watching the actors and the staff. She caught the eye of one actor who asked her to dinner, but she declined, staring instead at Chason, who returned her gaze.

"She was dressed in a long beige dress and a big hat.

She was attractive, but not the most beautiful woman on the set," Chason recalls years later, seated behind a cluttered desk in the downtown Houston loft that serves as his office, studio, and home. "But she was striking. She had elegant carriage, an erect posture, almost regal, a lean body with long legs. I remember thinking she had a strong charisma about her. There was a strong sexual chemistry between us. She honed right in on me, and I found that very attractive."

The scene they shot that day ended up on the cutting room floor, but the following afternoon Susan took Chason up on an invitation to revisit the set. She found him in the holding area near Wardrobe and they drank soft drinks and talked, Susan confiding in him about her troubles with Jason. "But we were distracted," says Chason. "We were more interested in each other."

Susan appeared on the set again later that night, looking for Chason. This time they talked only briefly; then she put her arm around his waist.

"Let's go," she whispered.

She followed him in her BMW to his loft. As the elevator door closed, she drew toward him, pressing her body against his.

"What do you like to do?" she whispered in his ear.

"She was a very erotic woman," says Chason, blushing at the memory. "I poured her a glass of white wine, and she cupped her hands over my ass. She was in charge, and from my point of view, that was perfectly okay. I told her what I liked. She agreed and took it one step further."

Afterward, in a warm, sexual afterglow, Susan wandered naked through Chason's austere quarters, inspecting his camera equipment, a table cluttered with actors' black-and-whites, finally taking the time to sip the now warm glass of wine. She told him of her desire to build a career, to become an actress. Chason watched her. She had the carriage, but did she have talent?

Then the phone rang. The set. Problems had developed while shooting a nighttime street scene.

"I have to go," Chason said, pulling on his trousers. "Let's get together again, when it's not so crazy."

As if reacting to a slap, Susan's mood abruptly changed. Her eyes penetrated him, angry.

"That was another woman, wasn't it?" she charged, grabbing her own clothing. "You're done with me now, so you're going off to see someone else."

"Susan, I'm sorry, but I have trouble on the set. You'd better go."

"Men are all the same," she shouted. "All they do is use you and throw you away. Is someone else coming here, is that why you want me to leave?"

Chason walked toward her and put his hands on her forearms.

"I have to go to work," he said. "I'll call you when things settle down for me. Okay?"

"Okay," she muttered, searching his face for clues.

Chason walked her to the street. As she pulled away in her car, he thought about what had just happened; he enjoyed the enthusiastic sex, he liked her, he wouldn't mind getting to know her, but he realized she hovered on the emotional edge.

I'll call her when we wrap the movie, he thought, walking toward his car. *There'll be time later to sort this out.*

Chason couldn't know how little time she had left.

The day after Susan's encounter with Chason, she and Valentine reunited, his crisis with his ex-wife past. Perhaps to appease him, she kept relatively quiet about McGowen, much to Valentine's relief. She broke her silence only to caution Jason as he left the house.

"She'd say, 'Watch out for McGowen. You've got to look out for him,'" recounts his girlfriend, Maggie. "Jason never seemed very concerned. It was like Jason was not going out of *his* way to avoid trouble."

Throughout that week, Amy had listened to Mike debate whether or not he should do what McGowen wanted and set up Jason in a sting operation. They weren't as close as they used to be, she knew. And Mike seemed angry at Jason's mom.

"One day he'd say he wasn't going to. The next he was going to do it. Then he started saying he should do it, just to teach Jason a lesson and get him to stay out of trouble. I was like, *Why does he want to do that?* But I wasn't going to say anything," she says. "Because *he was my boyfriend.* He was always accusing me of liking other guys, and I was afraid he'd think I had a thing for Jason."

When Mike told his brother Bobby about the sting, Bobby questioned him.

"Do you really want to do this? Jason's your good friend," he said, confused that Mike would even consider setting up someone he'd been so close to. But Bobby knew the cop worried his little brother; he talked about him constantly.

Mike just shrugged.

Jason saw Mike rarely that August, but the cooling of their relationship didn't cause him to hesitate when Shaffer approached him on August 20. They caught up quickly, Jason filling him in on events at home and taking particular glee in making fun of his mother's new beau, describing Valentine as an oafish man.

"She wants to marry the guy and travel around the country with his circus," Jason jeered, dancing maniacally and singing "off to join the circus" to the tune of "Off to See the Wizard," from *The Wizard of Oz*.

Shaffer laughed, but quickly turned serious.

"Jason, I need a favor," he said anxiously.

"What?"

"Can you get me a gun—a stolen one?"

"I don't know," said Jason. "Why?"

"I need one, is all. Some guy's harassing me. Can you get it?"

"Well . . ."

"I can pay," Shaffer said hopefully. "I've got money."

"I'll ask around," Jason agreed.

19

On Saturday, August 22, a tropical depression swarmed in the Gulf of Mexico, threatening the Texas and Louisiana coastlines, the first of the summer to boast the strength of a potential hurricane. But Susan was busy, too busy to worry about bad weather hundreds of miles away. Her relationship with Valentine had survived and she told Helen and others she believed it could be her own survival. Her only concern: his two young sons. Perhaps she considered Jason's troubles and contemplated the responsibility of raising other children.

"I think I could do it, don't you?" she quizzed Gloria on the telephone that afternoon. Ray stood in the kitchen, eating a sandwich.

"You'll just need to have a steady hand with them," counseled Gloria. "But sure, you can do it."

Susan handed Ray the telephone.

"Hello, Gloria," he said, his voice hearty. "Good to finally meet you, even if it's on the phone."

"I've heard a lot about you, too," Gloria said. "How's our Susie doing?"

"Well, as usual she's worried about Jason, and that gentleman is giving her some trouble," he said, handing back the telephone. Valentine was referring to Mc-Gowen, but Gloria assumed he meant Ron.

"He's no gentleman. I've got to go," Susan said. "Ray and I are going over to visit Bill Antley and his wife in a little while. I called Momma and found out they live right near Ray on the other side of town."

A cousin, Antley had grown up with the Harrison sisters and had just recently moved to Houston.

"Well, you have fun, and say hi to Bill for me," Gloria said. "And, Susan, you take care of yourself, you hear me?"

"Yes, ma'am," Susan said, laughing.

Gloria hung up the receiver feeling good about Susan and her prospects for the first time in many months.

Before she walked out the door, Susan grabbed a torn envelope and wrote a note:

JASON,
I AM AT RAY'S HOUSE. PLEASE ANSWER MY PAGES.
I LOVE YOU—

MOM

THE $20 IS FOR FOOD & GAS, ETC.

On second thought, Susan crossed out the "I," making it read, "We love you," then added, "I love you, Jason," followed by a heart in the margin.

Not long after his mother and Valentine left, Jason returned home, trailed by a friend. He picked up the $20, pocketed it, then threw the note to the side.

"Come on upstairs," he said to Pete Rodriguez, a

sixteen-year-old who mimicked Jason's gang look. "Let's hide it in my room."

In his room, Jason opened a drawer, looked under his bed, then decided on a box on the floor. He pulled up some new, never-worn clothes packed inside and ordered, "Put it here."

With that, Rodriguez removed a black, .357 magnum semiautomatic pistol from under his jacket. He'd stolen it from a nearby home and decorated it with Bugs Bunny stickers, giving the gun a deadly comical look.

With it safely hidden, Jason picked up the telephone and called Shaffer.

"I got the gun," he told him. "Pete wants two hundred dollars. Have you got the money? When will you come over to get it?"

"Yeah, I've got it. But I don't want to do it at your house," Shaffer said. "I'll get back with you."

"Okay," said Jason, not even asking why the transaction couldn't be handled at his house.

After finishing his conversation with Jason, Shaffer dialed McGowen's pager number.

"Jason's got the gun," he said when the deputy called back.

"Great," McGowen said.

"He wants two hundred."

An exuberant McGowen didn't quibble, even though the gun had a street value of $50.

"I'll come in a little early," he said. "Set it up for eleven-thirty tonight in the parking lot in front of Cliff's hamburgers. We'll get together later and talk plans."

"Okay," said Shaffer.

After Jason had spoken to Shaffer, he turned to Pete.

"Eleven-thirty tonight at Cliff's parking lot," he said. "We're on."

*   *   *

Across town, Susan and Ray sat on the couch in the living room with Bill's wife, Mickey Antley, drinking champagne and talking about family. Mickey hadn't met Susan before but took an immediate liking to her. And Ray told stories from the circus, keeping all of them laughing. About six, her husband, Bill, arrived home. Susan gave him a hug and they fell into a what-happened-to-so-and-so conversation, resurrecting names from their shared pasts. As evening fell, Ray invited the Antleys to dinner at Resa's.

"We'll meet you there at nine o'clock," he said.

After the Antleys agreed, Susan and Ray drove to her house. She wanted to check on Jason and change before dinner.

When they arrived home, Jason and Maggie were watching television, as if it were any other night. To Jason's annoyance, Susan kissed him and ruffled his hair before heading for the bedroom. While he waited, Ray talked with the teenager about his car—he'd just paid to have the brakes fixed. Susan emerged minutes later wearing an off-white suit, her thick blond hair wound into a French twist. Ray gave her an appreciative whistle.

"Jason, we need to go. Now, we'll be at Resa's if you need anything, okay?" she said, bending down to give him a peck on the cheek and an enthusiastic hug.

"Yeah, sure," the boy said, squirming uncomfortably.

"And don't get in any trouble," she ordered on her way out the door. But then she stuck her head back in. "And watch out for McGowen. Please."

"Yeah, sure," he said again. "Don't worry about me. I'll be okay."

*   *   *

The Antleys arrived at Resa's shortly after Susan and Ray. Seated at a corner table, they ordered drinks. Susan was buoyant, sipping her champagne, jabbering with the cousin she hadn't seen in many years, Ray holding her hand. Insisting she wasn't hungry, she ordered only a salad, then nibbled at a few hunks of Valentine's steak.

It was a busy night, the restaurant filled with conversation, laughter, and music. Alan called to a willowy woman with short dark hair seated at a table with her husband. She wove her way through the crowd, then stood to his right, behind the piano. As he played, in a husky voice she sang an Oscar Hammerstein and Jerome Kern tune from *Show Boat*, "Can't Help Lovin' Dat Man."

On her way to rejoin her husband, the woman felt someone reach for her arm. When she turned, Susan White smiled at her, tears glistening in her eyes.

"You know, I've always wanted to do that," she said. "Get up and sing like that."

"You should ask Alan," the woman suggested.

It was obvious Susan didn't recognize whom she was speaking to. The singer was the woman who'd once stood at the Whites' front door, accusing Jason of ransacking her house and stealing her husband's gold necklace.

For a moment, she considered telling Susan that their paths had crossed years earlier, that they'd been former neighbors when Susan lived on Valley Bend. Then she looked in Susan's face and thought better of it. *Why bring that up when she looks so happy?* the woman decided.

Although Susan was oblivious to it, even here, among so many happy faces, her troubles with Jason had followed her.

"Maybe I will sing here sometime," she said. "Why not?"

"Why not?" the woman agreed.

*   *   *

After McGowen had hung up from talking to Shaffer that afternoon, he called Lieutenant Coons and told him of the impending bust. McGowen had only $40, not enough for the buy money. Coons agreed to bring the other $160 and meet him at the station.

At ten that evening, McGowen and Coons parlayed their finances to make up the needed $200; then Mc-Gowen took the bills to the copy machine, where he arranged them in rows and pressed the button. He stapled together the copies of the bills. Now they had a record of the serial numbers.

That done, McGowen made his way around the station, rounding up four other deputies to work as backup on the sting operation. It must have been a heady night for him, in his plain clothes—jeans and a shirt—running a bust. It must have brought back the excitement of the organized crime outfit, the old days when he didn't "baby-sit for a bunch of rich kids."

Not long after he had arrived, Shaffer paged him. The teenager was jumpy about the sting. McGowen assured him it was a cinch and made arrangements to meet on a small road not far from the site of the bust. Once there, McGowen filled Shaffer in. He told him not to get in the car with Jason, but to make the buy in plain sight.

"When you're finished, run your hand through your hair," he said, demonstrating by running his own hand through the top of his dark hair. "That's the signal. Okay?"

"Yeah," said Shaffer. "Where's the money?"

McGowen handed him ten twenty-dollar bills.

"When it's over, we'll arrest you and put you in the squad car like all the rest," he said. "Then we'll tow your car. Only, while we book everyone else, we'll release you. Got it?"

"Yeah," said Shaffer. "Jason won't know I set him up, will he?"

"No," said McGowen confidently.

The plan set, Shaffer drove McGowen to a nearby church and dropped him off, then rounded the corner into the parking lot in front of Cliff's to wait for Jason to arrive. Since the call about the bust had already gone out on police scanners, wreckers lined up on the fringe of the parking lot, hoping to make a fast eighty bucks hauling a car to the impound lot. McGowen clicked on the radio and asked one of them to pick him up. It was just after 11 P.M., so a half hour remained before the appointed rendezvous. But to McGowen's surprise, when he rounded the corner into the parking lot, he spotted Jason's car, with Jason and Pete Rodriguez inside, parked next to the building. In another car a few rows away, Maggie waited with her sister and a friend.

McGowen jumped out of the wrecker and stood off to the side, his radio in his hand, trying to act inconspicuous, his eyes focused on Shaffer. He saw Jason walk across the lot. At Shaffer's car, they talked, Jason pulled the .357 out of his pocket and handed it to Mike. Then Shaffer handed over the $200.

Jason turned and walked back to his car and handed the money to Pete.

Then, just as he'd been instructed, Shaffer ran his hand through his hair. Into his radio McGowen barked the order to move, and three squad cars roared into the parking lot.

Before Jason realized what had happened, a uniformed deputy jumped him, pushed him to the ground, and handcuffed his wrists behind his back.

"You have the right to remain silent," the deputy recited.

Another deputy pulled Maggie and her sister out of their car and ordered them to throw their arms up against the hood. "Jason," Maggie cried out as the officer pushed her facedown onto the parking lot. They searched her car but found nothing.

"You girls get out of here," McGowen ordered. "Or we'll arrest you and take you in."

As Maggie pushed herself to her feet, then turned to go, she took one last look at Jason. "Go get my mom, she's at Resa's," he shouted.

Maggie and those she'd arrived with sped out of Cliff's parking lot. They sprinted, hearts hammering, through the parking lot at Resa's, then pulled open the heavy carved door. Once inside, Maggie spotted Susan laughing with Ray and the Antleys over after-dinner drinks.

"The cops got Jason," Maggie shouted as she ran toward her. "They're arresting him."

"It's that goddamn McGowen," Susan snapped at Ray. "I told you he'd do this. He's got my son."

On the way to the scene, Ray called Captain C.J. Harper on his car phone.

"I told you he was going to do something to my son," Susan shouted, grabbing at the telephone. "You have to help me."

"Well, McGowen made good his threats against Susan," Valentine said to Harper when she let go of the phone. If she'd asked, he would have had to admit that, for the first time, he truly believed all she'd said about the deputy.

"Fight it out later. You can't do anything tonight. She can't make bail until he's booked and taken downtown for arraignment," Harper advised before he hung up.

"What'll they do to him?" Susan cried to Valentine. "What'll they do to my beautiful baby?"

Just then they pulled into Cliff's parking lot, where the three teenagers, Jason, Mike, and Pete, were handcuffed and stuffed into the backseats of separate squad cars.

As soon as Valentine slammed his brand-new black-cherry Buick sedan to a stop, Susan burst through the door and ran toward the nearest uniformed deputy. She shouted at him, then noticed another deputy who looked familiar.

"Have you been to my house?" she asked.

"No," he insisted.

When Shaffer caught sight of her, he blanched; her face was a mask of rage.

"Shit," he hissed. He'd never acted as an informant before, but things seemed out of whack to him. *Shouldn't they have searched my car like they did the others?* he wondered. *And the gun. I've still got the gun. Why didn't they take it away?*

Shaffer squirmed, attempting to hide from her behind the car door, and he could feel the cold, hard gun, still tucked in his waistband, cut into his gut.

"Damn, Jason'll have this figured out in no time," he muttered, panicked.

Then he saw McGowen walk up and Susan turn to Valentine.

"Call C.J. back," she pleaded to Ray. "Get him on the telephone."

"Now, go carefully. Don't say a word," he cautioned her. "Let me take care of this."

As they approached McGowen, Valentine waved the cell phone before him like a shield.

"I've got Captain Harper on the line," he said. "Do you know who he is?"

"Yeah," said McGowen.

"We just want to see what we can do to help, what procedure we should take," Ray said.

Recalling that night years later, Valentine would shake his head in disbelief. "McGowen said, 'What you can do is get your goddamn head blown off,' and he pulled his gun out. He held it right in my face. I told him, 'Be calm. I'm here as a friend of the family. I'm just trying to help.' Then I got back on the phone and asked

C.J. if he'd heard that. He said, 'Let me talk to him.' But when I told McGowen that Captain Harper wanted to talk to him, he gave me an evil look. He said, 'I don't need to talk to Captain Harper. He's not my captain.' I asked where they were taking Jason, and McGowen said to the Cypresswood substation. Then he said something really weird. He looked at me and said, 'We're not letting him out. He's a gunrunner.'

"Now, Jason had done some dumb things, he was getting in his share of bad trouble, and I told Susan the kid wasn't playing with a full deck and she needed to sit on him, but he wasn't any high-powered gunrunner. I hardly believed my ears. I said, 'He sure looks like a teenager to me.' Then I got Susan by the arm and I pulled her toward the car. I told her, 'We can't do anything tonight.' "

"But he's got my boy," Susan cried, staring back at Jason's face framed by the squad-car window. "McGowen's got my boy."

As Valentine drove out of the parking lot, McGowen turned to one of his fellow deputies. "Did you hear what that woman said to me?" he said. "She called me a son of a bitch. She said she was going to get me."

In his report on the sting, the deputy noted he thought he might have seen her yell something but couldn't hear what.

Despite Valentine's urging, Susan refused to go home and insisted he drive her to the Cypresswood substation.

"We have to get Jason out," she demanded. "McGowen's crazy. There's no telling what he'll do to my boy."

They waited outside the substation until the squad cars from the bust pulled up, and a sobbing Susan watched, a look of utter grief on her face, as a deputy led a handcuffed Jason inside.

Susan jumped out of Ray's car and ran after them, but the thick steel doors slammed and locked before she reached them.

"Do something," she ordered Valentine.

"C.J. says once he's in, no one can get him out, not until he's arraigned. We ought to go home tonight," Valentine cautioned. But Susan made no move to leave. When Valentine eyed a deputy approaching the door from the parking lot, he stopped him.

"Tell Lieutenant Coons Ray Valentine is outside," he said.

The deputy nodded.

Like Harper and many others at the sheriff's department, Valentine had known Coons for years through his fund-raising work for the deputies' association. They'd had lunch a few times.

Minutes later, Coons appeared, surprised to see Valentine with Susan.

As Coons listened, Valentine ran through the situation, explaining that Susan was Jason's mother and that she feared for his safety. Throughout the conversation, Susan stood in the background, wringing her hands and crying.

"Your son is safe with us," Coons said, looking weary with the interruption. "But he doesn't get out until he sees a judge downtown on Monday."

"Are you sure he'll be all right?" she said. Compared to the woman Valentine had whistled at just hours earlier, Susan appeared haggard and tired. There were tears in her eyes.

"I give you my word," Coons assured her.

While Coons talked to Valentine and Susan, inside the substation McGowen had Jason, Shaffer, and Pete seated in chairs in front of the sergeant's office while he filed paperwork and wrote out reports. They could hear the commotion on the other side of the door, voices rising and falling.

"Is your mother crazy?" McGowen, obviously annoyed, asked Jason. "What's she doing out there?"

Coons returned, smirking and shaking his head at the scene he'd just witnessed.

For Shaffer, who fidgeted nervously, Susan's presence outside the substation was just one more thing that had gone wrong that evening. In fact, he was beginning to wonder whether or not being a snitch would be the cinch McGowen had promised. It seemed to him that Coons and his deputies were inept and bungling the entire cover-up.

First there was the gun, the .357 magnum. The deputies hadn't confiscated it when they patted him down at the scene, remembering instead to take it away from him while he was in the car. When they'd pulled the cold black pistol from his waistband, Shaffer noticed Jason watching, his eyes wide.

Then they hadn't searched his car the way they had Jason's and Maggie's. To make matters even worse, Shaffer had watched, his stomach sinking, as McGowen walked nonchalantly around the station waving Xerox copies of the $200 buy money.

"We're missing a twenty-dollar bill," he shouted. "Who's got it?"

Finally McGowen searched Jason and found the money in his pants pocket.

"Why do they have copies of the money?" a suspicious Jason whispered to Mike.

"I don't know," Shaffer protested, feeling the fist of anxiety rise higher in his chest.

As if Jason had needed more proof, McGowen, in Mike's estimation, pulled another blunder; he'd instructed Mike to claim he had asthma, thereby giving deputies an excuse to separate him from Jason and his friend Rodriguez so he could be released and not booked.

"Take this one downtown to the infirmary," McGowen ordered another deputy after Mike used the ploy.

But Shaffer knew it wouldn't work. Why would it? He'd lived with Jason. Jason knew better.

"You don't have asthma," Jason scoffed as deputies led Shaffer away.

Shaffer thought he could almost see Jason weighing evidence. How long before he'd sniff out the sting? How long before Jason concluded his best friend had turned snitch?

Not long, Shaffer thought. *Not long at all.*

Yet in many ways, Jason appeared unconcerned, as if the night's happenings were merely a joke, a minor annoyance. Maybe it didn't seem real, sitting in jail, wondering if his best friend had set him up. Even after Shaffer left, he grinned and laughed.

"You don't have anything on me," he taunted McGowen. "I didn't have the gun on me, and I'm not the one who stole it."

"We'll see about that," McGowen said. "What about this?"

McGowen held up a MasterCard discovered in Jason's pocket during the search, a credit card embossed with a woman's name.

"That's my girlfriend's," Jason bluffed.

"No, it's not," McGowen said, grinning. "We've already talked to the lady. She said it was stolen."

Around midnight, exasperated with Susan and convinced Jason was in no immediate danger, Ray dropped her off at her house and drove on home. But Susan, wanting to be near Jason, simply drove her own car back to Cypresswood. There she sat, hunched down in the seat, staring at the locked door to the sheriff's department—the door that separated her from her son—until well into the night. Finally, she reluctantly drove home.

Susan had already left when a deputy escorted Mike Shaffer to the substation's back door and pointed out his car in the parking lot. He jumped into his car and headed home. Exhaustion ached his body, but he knew he couldn't sleep.

"Everyone knew," he says, still angry when recalling that night. "Jason, he'd figured it out. I could see it on his face. Pretty soon everyone, all my friends, would know I'd turned in my best friend. McGowen said they'd never know it was me, but then they'd just messed everything up, the gun, the copies of the money, that lame excuse. Jason would have had to be a moron not to know I'd fingered him."

Once they'd locked Jason in a cell early that morning, the phone began ringing at Susan's home on Amber Forest.

"Will you accept a collect call from a Jason Aguillard?" an operator asked.

"Yes," Susan answered.

"Mom?"

"Are you all right?"

"Get me out of here," he shouted. "You've got to get me out, tonight."

Jason maintained he was innocent, that Mike Shaffer had orchestrated the entire bust.

"Why'd he do this to me?" he asked. "Why?"

"I don't know, baby," Susan said. "But I'll get to work on it. I'll get you out."

Throughout the early morning hours, the phone continued to ring with collect calls from a holding cell at the Cypresswood substation. What could Susan do? Both Captain Harper and Ray had told her she could do nothing until Monday. But her baby needed her. Susan, who'd always made excuses for Jason, who'd always fixed his problems, was powerless to help.

With each call, Jason repeated the details of what had happened during his arrest: the gun left in Shaffer's waistband, the asthma ploy, the copies of the money. Before long, Susan, too, believed Mike Shaffer had turned against Jason and, through Jason, against her.

"He set my baby up," she told Valentine, crying into the phone. "McGowen used Mike to set Jason up."

The first thing she had to do, Susan decided, was to find Mike Shaffer. Maybe she could convince him to tell Lieutenant Coons how McGowen had used him. Or maybe she could talk sense to him, convince him he shouldn't have turned on Jason. They were friends, best friends.

Still, Susan didn't know where to look. She called Information and wrote down numbers for every Mike Shaffer in Houston and began dialing. She didn't know Mike's brothers, or that the phone wouldn't be under his name. As daylight broke, she crossed one, then another off her list. When she found no one home she left a message, pleading with someone, anyone, to call her.

She called Maggie, who had tossed and turned throughout the night, unable to free her memory of Jason in handcuffs.

"I'm pissed at Ray," a furious Susan told her. "All his big connections and he couldn't pull enough strings to get Jason out of jail. Jason keeps calling, begging me to get him out. I don't know what to do."

Still determined to find Shaffer, Susan rifled through old telephone bills, searching for those covering January through June, when Mike lived with them. She ran her finger down the lists of calls to Ron's parents and to her family in Louisiana, looking for unfamiliar numbers, any

Mike might have called and charged to her bill. She found one, in Killeen, Texas.

"This is Susan White. Mike Shaffer was with my son when he was arrested last night," she said into the answering machine of the house in Killeen. "I'm looking for the Mike Shaffer who is a friend of Jason Aguillard. I need him to call me right away. Because being an informant in Houston is a dangerous business. He needs to know, informants get killed in Houston."

20

Despite the bust, it was a disappointing night for Mc-
Gowen. To his fellow deputies, he crowed about the
sting, how he'd brought in a "major turd" in the form
of seventeen-year-old Jason Aguillard. Yet it soon became apparent that the district attorney's office wasn't
impressed with his evidence.

McGowen contacted Connie Spence, the assistant district attorney on duty, early that morning. He insinuated
he worked on a special sheriff's department gang task
force and that he'd taken down a major gunrunner in
the FM 1960 area. Spence took notes as McGowen described young hoodlums running wild and the sting operation he'd coordinated. He told how he'd cultivated a
snitch and crushed a ring of major criminals.

"I want as many charges as possible against these
two," McGowen insisted.

But when she went over the evidence, Spence found
it lacking. While she agreed to take gun-theft charges
against Pete Rodriguez, who not only admitted stealing

the gun but had pointed out the house he'd taken it from, she insisted they had no reason to file charges against Jason. They had no evidence he was involved in the theft of the gun or that he'd stolen or used the credit card.

Spence hung up, sensing McGowen was furious.

She wondered momentarily why McGowen hadn't gone through the task force to file the charges, but then the intake phone rang again. It was McGowen with another proposal, suggesting she charge Jason with "major organized crime activity."

An exasperated Spence answered, "Because this case doesn't fit the statute."

Within twenty minutes, McGowen called again.

This time he suggested the charge against Jason could be that of transferring a stolen weapon—an offense that, as far as Spence knew, didn't exist in Texas law. Perplexed by the young deputy's insistence, Spence refused.

Only after the fourth call from McGowen did Spence reluctantly agree to accept a charge from the polite yet unrelenting McGowen against Jason Aguillard: possession of a stolen credit card, a third-degree felony, the lowest, with a maximum of $2,000 bond. But to her chagrin, even that didn't appease the young officer.

"Does the U.S. Attorney's office have a twenty-four-hour intake?" he asked. "Maybe he's broken some federal law."

21

What did Susan White mean by "informants get killed in Houston"? Was it a warning?

When Shaffer's aunt heard those words on her answering machine early that morning, she didn't know what to think. Who was this woman, and what was she talking about?

What has that boy gotten himself into? the aunt wondered.

Still, hours remained before she could reach her sister, Mike's mother, Jeannie Jaques, in Austin to relay the message. Jaques and her husband slept in on weekends and habitually unplugged the telephone.

The message didn't seem important enough for her to get in the car and drive the hour to her sister's, but it stayed on her mind, so much so that as soon as Jaques plugged in her phone just before noon, it rang.

"Jeannie, the weirdest thing happened," her sister said. "Do you know a Susan White?"

*   *   *

Jeannie Jaques had never met Susan White, but they'd talked on the telephone a few times while Michael was living with her. She'd been grateful that Susan had taken her son in. Mike's life had been so nomadic ever since he'd dropped out of high school and left Austin to live with his brothers at age fifteen. "I knew Mike was kind of a street kid, but he'd never been in any serious trouble," she says, puffing on a cigarette, her long, straight, light brown hair parted down the middle and pushed behind her ears. Before leaving Austin, Mike had gotten into trouble with the police after breaking into a house with some friends. "I wish they'd made him do some restitution," she muses sadly. "Maybe it would have made an impression on him."

Immediately after the call from her sister that Sunday morning, Jaques called Mike at his brothers' home in Houston. Her middle son, Bobby, answered the telephone.

"Is Mike there?" she asked.

"Yeah."

"Get him," she ordered.

"Hello," Mike said moments later. "Mom?"

"What happened? Did you get arrested?" she asked.

"No," Mike said. "Why?"

"Susan White called your aunt, said Jason had been arrested and you'd been with him."

"I didn't do anything, they didn't arrest me," Mike whined. "Mom . . ."

"Mike, if there's something going on, you need to tell me," his mother said. "Why did she talk about informants?"

"I don't know."

Jaques knew her son wasn't telling her everything. She heard a familiar reticence in his voice. "We're going to call Susan White and find out," she said. "I'm going to add you on the three-way calling. Keep your mouth shut. I'm doing the talking."

With that, Jaques dialed the number Susan had left on her sister's answering machine.

"Hello," a throaty-voiced woman answered.

"Susan, I'm Mike Shaffer's mother. You were looking for me?"

"Do you know where Michael is?" Susan said. Jaques could hear the weariness in the other woman's voice, the worry.

"Why?" she asked.

Susan then told the story of the previous night's arrest. "Michael was there, too, but I can't find out where they took him. There's no record that they arrested him with the others."

"Well, I've talked to him and he wasn't arrested," his mother said.

"He was right in the middle of it," Susan said. "There's a bunch of stuff going on and I can't get anyone to tell me anything."

"Do you know why Jason is in jail?"

"No, but the detectives tell me there was an informant involved," Susan answered, then blurted out, "Something is going on here. You know, down here in Houston, informants don't live long."

"Now, don't talk like that," Jaques cautioned her. "I can't believe they didn't tell you why he was arrested. You need to get a lawyer."

In the background, Jaques could hear Susan's other phone ringing.

"I have to go—that must be Jason," Susan said, hanging up.

When Susan's line went dead, Jaques returned her attention to her son.

"Why was Jason arrested?" she asked.

"I think he had a gun," Mike replied, sounding as if he'd rather not discuss it any further.

Jaques knew she'd never get any information from Michael. She rarely felt as if he ever told her the entire truth.

"Maybe you should go to your father's for a few days," she suggested.

"No," he said. "I'll be fine."

"You sure?" she asked.

"Yeah," he said.

With that, Jaques hung up. She felt confused but not concerned, and thought little of the call for the rest of the day.

Meanwhile, Jason's phone calls continued, as he pleaded with his mother to find a way to get him out of jail.

"I can't be in here," he cried. "What if someone who's mad at me sees me? They're taking me downtown in a little while. I'll be in the big jail. What if they put me on the fag floor?"

Susan, who despite the chaos in her life had always tried to protect Jason, must have felt his fear like physical pain.

"I'm doing all I can," she said. "Trust me. I'll find a way. I'll get you out."

As soon as she hung up, the telephone rang again. This time it was Mike Shaffer calling. Susan quizzed him, but Shaffer seemed reluctant to talk.

"Don't you watch television, Mike?" she asked. "Being an informant is a risky business. They get killed."

The morning melted into afternoon as Maggie arrived at Susan's and listened as she pleaded on the telephone, looking for someone to help. She even called Sherri to tell her what had happened. This time Sherri listened sympathetically, thinking about her own child.

"Maybe someday we can be friends," Susan said tearfully. "I don't blame you for what happened to my marriage."

Throughout the afternoon, Susan popped small white pills and paced the house. Maggie knew she hadn't slept. Her eyes were bloodshot and she rubbed her forehead to mollify what must have been an unyielding pain.

Suddenly, Susan picked up the telephone book, searched for a number, then dialed the home of Don Henderson, the state senator who represented her district. Henderson wasn't in, but she spoke to his wife, Marjorie, telling her that McGowen had sexually harassed her and that he'd set Jason up.

"She sounded punchy with worry," remembers Marjorie. "I felt sorry for her. But I had to tell her there really wasn't anything Don or I could do. She had to handle it with the sheriff's department. Before I hung up, I told her, 'I hope nothing happens to your boy.'"

Attempting to do just that, Susan called Lieutenant Coons twice that day, complaining about the sting and begging him to help her free her son. When he said he could do nothing, she told him what she'd told so many others—that the sting had been a setup to lash out against her, that McGowen had been sexually harassing her, and that he'd threatened to hurt Jason.

Although serious charges were being leveled against one of his deputies, charges that, if proved, could eventually lead to McGowen's termination, Coons paid no attention to White's allegations. Instead he quickly dismissed them as the ravings of an unstable woman willing to do and claim anything to protect her son.

It was early afternoon that Sunday when deputies filled the van from Cypresswood that would take prisoners from the night before to the main jail, where they'd be booked and arraigned on Monday morning. When the van pulled out, Susan and Maggie sat in the white BMW in the parking lot, watching. They followed it for nearly twenty-five miles, like in a funeral procession, until it veered downward into the guts of the massive downtown jail. Then Susan pulled her car over and got out; she stood on the sidewalk smoking and staring at the imposing brick jail looming above her.

"They have everything in the world dear to me in that jail," she told Maggie. "They have my baby."

22

As that Sunday dragged on, Mike Shaffer's already sour mood deepened. He felt physically ill, disappointment and fear eating into his gut like acid. Despondent over his dismal situation, he drove absentmindedly through the thick traffic on FM 1960, not knowing where to go or what to do. Every minute that clicked off the clock on his battered dashboard weighed heavily on him. He knew that somehow Susan would get her son out of jail, if not today, then tomorrow. And then Jason would be looking for him, asking questions Shaffer didn't want to answer.

But that was the future. Right now, he judged he had one priority, to avoid Susan White. He couldn't forget the grief on her face at the sting, or the sound of her frantic voice rising and falling outside the substation door. Her words on the telephone earlier that day nibbled away at him. Informant—she'd talked of an informant. She knew he'd been the snitch who set up the sting. He was sure of it.

Avoiding Susan presented another problem—could he risk driving to Amy's house, just a few blocks from Amber Forest? He wanted to see his girlfriend, he needed to see her to tell her what had happened, but he hated to risk crossing paths with Susan.

Just then, out of the corner of his eye, Shaffer saw the black Mitsubishi Eclipse with the two teenagers who'd cornered him at the amusement park, the ones who'd pulled a gun on Amy at the video store.

"Hell," he muttered.

The driver spotted Shaffer. A nervous smile edged across his face, his young eyes cold, as he held up his hand to the car window, his fingers mimicking a firing gun.

A fist of fear clutched Mike's chest. He swung hastily into the turn lane and wrenched a U-turn in front of three lanes of screeching cars with horns blaring.

"This is out of control," he mumbled as he pulled away, watching his rearview mirror. "Out of control."

By late that afternoon, anger had consumed Shaffer's fear. McGowen had dragged him into this mess, he reasoned, so McGowen owed him, and that meant the deputy had to find a way to make his troubles disappear.

"I paged McGowen. When he called me back, I told him everyone knew I was the snitch, that Jason and his mom had figured it out. I said he'd botched it, the whole sting, the gun, the copies of the money. McGowen sounded ticked that I'd called, said I was imagining things," says Shaffer years later, still seething at the memory. "I told him some guys were threatening me. I told him about the Mitsubishi and the guy with the gun. He didn't even seem interested. I told him he needed to protect me in case that guy tracked me down.

"I told him again that the cops had botched the sting and that Susan and Jason knew I was the snitch, and that wasn't supposed to have happened."

With that, Shaffer hesitates, his anger building. "Then I told him Jason's mom had called my mom and my aunt, how she said, 'Informants get killed in Houston.' All of a sudden, McGowen seemed *real* interested," he recalls. "McGowen said, 'That woman threatened your life. She can't do that. I'm going to get a warrant and arrest her.' I didn't know what to think. The guy was a cop, *he* was supposed to know what he was doing. But I didn't want him making anymore shit out of my life."

McGowen arrived at the substation that night and heard more bad news. Not only did he have a nervous C.I., but Coons informed him that Susan White had leveled serious charges against him, claiming he'd sexually harassed her and that the sting operation and Jason's arrest were orchestrated to strike back at her. Furious, McGowen denied that he even knew the woman.

To McGowen's relief, Coons said he believed him, and that White was undoubtedly no more than a troubled mother lying to protect her son.

Then, McGowen relayed his own afternoon's conversation—with Shaffer, repeating White's statement that "informants get killed in Houston." Shaffer interpreted her words as a threat on his life, McGowen maintained, backing up the danger his C.I. found himself in with the story of the unrelated black Mitsubishi.

"I want to get a warrant for her arrest," McGowen said. "Retaliation."

Although Susan White had just made serious charges against McGowen, Coons didn't hesitate. "Do it," he said.

Once the Cypresswood substation's van arrived at the downtown jail, Jason was unloaded into a web of tunnels that connected the jail to Houston's aging criminal courts building. Jailers made no concessions for a seventeen-year-old from a privileged background as the demeaning and dehumanizing process of booking began. They confiscated his clothing and beat his shoes against a bench to be sure they didn't hide any weapons. From there he was taken to the showers, his body cavities searched, before they issued him an orange jailhouse jumper. Then it was on to Booking, where he was fingerprinted and photographed. Afterward, he was taken to appear before a magistrate, who again informed him of his rights. Hours later, he reached a holding cell.

"You have to get me out of here," he cried to his mother over the telephone throughout that afternoon. "I'm afraid."

"I'm trying, baby," she said, her always hoarse voice crackling and worn. "Just hang in there. I'm working on it. Jason, McGowen came after you to get to me."

For the first time, Susan told Jason what she'd told so many others, that McGowen had repeatedly harassed her throughout the summer, and that he'd threatened to hurt Jason if she rebuffed him.

"And he used Mike to do it?" Jason said, remembering his mother's phone conversations that summer. He'd heard her complaining to friends that some man kept pushing her to have sex with him. He'd never connected the fear in his mother's voice to McGowen.

"It looks that way," Susan said. "It looks like Mike turned on you. When I get you out of there, you need to stay away from Mike Shaffer. You can't trust him. Not ever again. And you need to clean up your act, Jason."

"Yeah," Jason said. "When I get out . . ."

Mike Shaffer swallowed his fear that afternoon and drove to Amy's house. "Mike was scared," Amy says, recalling that day. "He kept talking about Jason and how he'd figured it out. He figured once everyone knew he'd snitched on a friend, he'd be in trouble with all his pards."

As Shaffer drove home, he saw Susan in his rearview mirror, flashing her lights and motioning for him to pull over. She parked behind him as he reluctantly pulled to the side of the road.

When she walked up beside his car, he barely recognized her. He guessed she hadn't slept since before the sting went down. Exhaustion drooped her shoulders and circled her eyes.

"Mike, this cop, McGowen, has been harassing me all summer. He's using Jason to get to me," she said. "If you know anything that can help, I would do *anything* to get Jason out of jail."

Ray, driving down the street on his way to Susan's house, saw Mike in his car, Susan kneeling on the grass and pleading with the teenager through the window. He parked behind Susan and headed toward her, just in time to hear Susan begging, "You can't do this, turn against Jason. How could you do this to Jason?"

Susan stood up and Shaffer drove hastily away.

"What's going on?" Valentine asked.

"Well, Mike did it," she said. "He's the one McGowen used to get my baby."

That night, Susan White tossed sleeplessly as thoughts of Jason reeled through her mind. Unable to rest, she hung on the telephone, hoping to find someone to help her free her son. She called C.J. Harper, who advised her to get her boy an attorney and let the situation run its course. She called an old friend, Philip Riviera, told him about McGowen, and cried.

"This McGowen's joy is stalking me and my kid," she said. "He's just looking for anything to cause him problems."

"Do you want me to talk to him?" Riviera offered.

"No. I'm just going to keep to myself and keep Jason away from him," she said.

Riviera, who ran an oil-field drilling company and occasionally had to bail out a worker, went over the ins and outs of bondsmen with Susan.

"Have you got enough money to post bond?" he asked.

"Yeah," she said. "I scraped it together. But this McGowen, he really scares me."

"Just keep your door locked," Riviera advised her. "And don't open it. Not for anybody."

McGowen also spent much of that night on the telephone. Relieved of his regular patrol in order to concentrate on securing a warrant for Susan's arrest, he sat at a desk at the substation making phone calls. The first number he dialed connected him with the assistant district attorney on duty for intake that night, Jean Spradling-Hughes, who listened intently as McGowen detailed the sting and Susan White's involvement.

Hughes had never heard of Deputy Kent McGowen before that night. She didn't know his jacket and had no reason to question what he told her. When he called, he had all the credibility she gave any police officer inquiring about a warrant. She'd found, over the nearly seven years she'd worked as an A.D.A., that most officers were truthful, but then again, she *had* been disappointed. "On a few, very rare occasions," says Hughes, a fortyish woman with light brown hair cropped short. "But you have to give them the benefit of the doubt. There has to be a presumption that officers are telling the truth. A lot of times they literally call from the scene, tell you what happened, and say will you accept charges. I'm sitting at a desk downtown. I have to rely on what they tell me."

What she later recalled McGowen telling her that night would bear little resemblance to the truth.

"He implied he was on a special gangs-and-guns task force at the sheriff's department," Hughes says, recounting the conversation. "That he'd been working with the ATF on tracking down gunrunners selling automatic weapons. I asked him if he knew other A.D.A.s who'd worked with the gang task force and he claimed he did. He was still angry, complaining that Connie Spence hadn't taken gun charges against the woman's son. He described Susan and Jason as part of a group dealing in guns, implying that they were automatic weapons. He told me about the sting. He described Jason as the head turd in this gunrunning band and said they'd had to go out to the house on other occasions because of neighbors complaining of gunfire and that there were shootings there. He said this woman threatened his C.I. and he said Susan White was a serious threat, she'd threatened to have his confidential informant killed by sunset.

"The call seemed S.O.P., standard operating procedure," she continues. "Nothing gave me any pause, except one thing: McGowen indicated he'd worked with the gang task force, but when I asked him if he'd called the A.D.A. who worked with the task force to look into charges, he said he knew Casey O'Brien. Then he asked me if he could reach him at the same number he'd used to call me in the intake unit. It seemed to me that he should have known Casey's phone number. But then, that wasn't enough to worry me."

Hughes had taken very few retaliation charges over her years as an A.D.A. It had been her experience that in most cases, threats like the one Susan White had uttered were made in the heat of the moment and quickly forgotten. But as she listened to McGowen's litany of stories about the mother and son and their involvement with drugs and guns, she felt this one deserved serious consideration.

"Have *you* talked to your C.I.'s mother to confirm these allegations?" Hughes asked pointedly.

"No," McGowen admitted.

"Well, you need to hear her say Susan White threatened her son and that she's worried about it," Hughes advised him. "Talk to the C.I.'s mother, and if she verifies what he's told you and that she believes the woman is serious, call me back and we'll get you your warrant."

When McGowen hung up, the idea of a warrant for Susan White's arrest must have dangled before him like the golden ring on a carousel, so magical it could solve all his problems.

If he'd truly harassed her all summer, if he'd threatened her safety and Jason's as she'd claimed, the warrant held the power to make his threats real.

But by Susan's actions, she'd raised the stakes. She'd made charges against him to his lieutenant. True, Coons didn't believe her, but McGowen must have feared what could happen if she filed an official complaint with the department, charging him with sexual harassment. It was possible some higher-ups at the sheriff's department wouldn't share his lieutenant's belief in him. What if they believed *her*?

Susan White could cost him his badge and with it his power.

Did McGowen marvel at the irony of what had just happened? Unknowingly, in her frustration, with her hasty words, Susan had handed him what he needed most, a way to discredit her. If she followed through on her threat to file a formal complaint against him, a retaliation charge on her record could go a long way toward tipping his superiors' judgment in his favor.

Did he consider what other opportunities a warrant for White's arrest offered: a way to show her he was the one in charge, a way to exact revenge?

23

By Sunday night, the building tropical depression in the Gulf gathered intensity. Winds up to 140 miles per hour had earned it a name, Hurricane Andrew. Born off the coast of Africa, it became the first named Atlantic storm of 1992. More than a million people fled and four died when it lashed across the Bahamas, before ricocheting back into the Gulf of Mexico, where it eyed the Texas-Louisiana coastline.

Days earlier, Houstonians, well familiar with the destruction of such a giant storm, flooded stores, hoarding dwindling supplies of bottled water, batteries, and canned goods. Now they waited. Where would Andrew hit? When? Television weathercasters displayed maps ranking probabilities, judging its most likely assault on southern Florida early the following morning. Yet they cautioned against Houstonians abandoning their vigilance. After all, hurricanes had been known to suddenly switch course. They could be as unpredictable as they could be deadly.

*   *   *

At the darkened house on Amber Forest, the threatening storm must have given Susan White a sense of impending doom: her son locked up behind heavy steel jailhouse doors miles away in downtown Houston. Did she walk through the cluttered house, littered with unopened shopping bags and fast-food containers, stripped of its beautiful furnishings, like a soldier circling through war debris?

"I'm going to get Jason a court-appointed attorney," she told Ray when he called that night. "I can't afford anything else. The hearing is in the morning."

"Just get someone to get him out, and we'll get him a new lawyer when I get back," he assured her. Ray planned to leave early the next morning to promote the circus when it arrived in Wichita Falls, Texas. "I'll be back Wednesday."

"I'll get him out," Susan said, crying. "I have to get my baby home."

At the Cypresswood substation, Kent McGowen was also too busy to spend the night worrying about the probability of a hurricane in the Gulf pivoting in its path and tracking to Houston. Getting in touch with Michael Shaffer's mother proved more difficult than he might have expected.

"McGowen kept calling me wanting her phone number, but I wouldn't give it to him," Shaffer recalls. "I felt like it was stupid, the whole thing. I wasn't afraid of Jason's mom, and I didn't want him calling my mom and getting her all upset for nothing. But he kept calling and calling."

Finally, just before midnight, Shaffer relented. But by then it was too late. Jaques and her husband would be asleep, their telephone unplugged until morning. When

McGowen insisted he had to talk to her, a hesitant Shaffer gave him directions to her apartment.

"I'm sending an Austin officer to her house," McGowen told Hughes when he called to update her at the D.A.'s intake office. "I'm going to have her call me."

"My shift is over at midnight and I'm leaving here in a few minutes," Hughes said. "But I'll tell Jim Mount, my replacement, about the case. You talk to the mom; I'll tell him to sign the warrant. Then all you'd need to do is get it signed by a judge."

"Great," McGowen said as he hung up the telephone.

Jeannie Jaques and her husband were sleeping soundly when they awoke to urgent rapping on their apartment door, just after midnight.

"Who is it?" Jaques inquired, tying her robe around her.

"Police. I've got a message from a deputy in Houston," someone answered.

"Is something wrong?" Jaques asked as she swung open the door.

"This deputy needs you to call him," the Austin officer in uniform said, handing her a slip of paper.

Jaques slammed the door shut and rushed to plug in the telephone. As her husband watched, she dialed the number and asked for the deputy whose name appeared above it, Kent McGowen.

"This is Deputy McGowen," a man said.

"What's going on?" Jaques asked. "How's Michael?"

"He's okay."

"Then what's going on?" she repeated. "You've scared me to death."

"Do you know Susan White?" he asked.

"No, but I talked to her today. Why?"

"What'd she say?"

"First tell me what's going on," Jaques demanded.

"Well, this woman is evidently crazy. We're getting an arrest warrant right now and we need you to confirm some things," McGowen said.

"I can't confirm anything," Jaques scoffed. "I only talked to her once."

"Yes, you can," McGowen said. "Did she tell you informants don't live long? Did she say that to you?"

"Well, yeah, she did."

"Didn't it worry you?" McGowen asked.

"Not at the time," Jaques said. "But I guess I should have been concerned?"

"Yes, you should have," McGowen said.

Jaques' face flushed. She felt embarrassed. It was obvious from the deputy's concern that she shouldn't have dismissed Susan White's words so quickly.

"What makes you say she's crazy?" she asked.

"White was at the station, acting like she was drunk, going crazy, yelling and screaming," said McGowen. "We had to ask her to leave."

"So she's after Michael?"

"We're going on that assumption, that she's threatened his life. Will you say she threatened his life?"

"No," Jaques replied, wondering why he wanted her to say that. "She didn't threaten him directly. I didn't take it that way."

"Well, she's convinced your son is an informant," McGowen maintained.

"Is he?"

"No," McGowen lied. "He's innocent of all this. That's why we let him go."

McGowen went on to say he'd been watching a gang of teenagers, including Jason Aguillard, for several days. He claimed he'd seen them break into a house and a car, and that he'd found stolen credit cards, guns, and other items.

"I guess I should have been more concerned," Jaques admitted sheepishly.

"Well, don't worry, we're going to get her tonight," McGowen said. "I've got the warrant in progress. I just needed to talk to you."

McGowen assured Jaques she had no reason to worry about her son and that he'd be protected. Then he promised to call her as soon as they had White in custody.

The line went dead and Jaques turned to her husband.

"There's something strange going on here," she said. "That cop seems really gung-ho, but I'm either not getting all the information or there's something really wrong here."

In the Cypresswood substation, after McGowen had finished his phone call, he turned to a fellow deputy and friend, Kevin Stanley. "Kent wasn't outwardly furious," says Stanley. "He was just biting the bit, waiting for her to mess up. And when she made that call to [Mike Shaffer's mom], that was it. He said, 'I got her. All the trash she talked about me, I am going to get her.'"

At 4 A.M. that morning, jailers roused Jason and the other detainees to herd them to breakfast and walk through the tunnels, under the still sleeping streets of Houston, to the criminal courthouse. As soon as he entered the holding cell in the courthouse, he dialed his home telephone number. Court was still hours away, but Susan answered immediately. She was obviously awake.

"Mom, are you coming for me today?" he asked. "Will I get out?"

"I'll be there, baby," she said, her voice spent, her words slurring. "We'll get you home."

Kent McGowen had arrived at the D.A.'s office intake desk, on the first floor of that same criminal courthouse, little more than an hour earlier. Jim Mount, a tall, pale, affable man, waited for him.

"I'm Deputy McGowen," he said.

"Jean told me you'd be in," Mount said. "Let's see what you've got."

Mount wasn't too worried as he looked over the "to be" warrant form McGowen had filled out, nicknamed "to be" because it was "to be served." He'd never known a deputy to flat out lie to him, although they sometimes colored the truth to get what they wanted. He wasn't thrown off when McGowen vehemently complained about Spence and her decision not to issue a warrant against Jason for any charges related to the gun. Mount simply changed the subject, not wanting to discuss another A.D.A.'s decision.

McGowen ran down the details with Mount. Again, as he had with Hughes, he spoke of Jason as the "head turd" in a major gunrunning operation that included automatic weapons, even implying that his C.I. had been used to buy a fully automatic Uzi from Jason Aguillard.

"You're here about the boy's mom?" Mount asked.

"Yeah, she's threatened my C.I.," McGowen answered.

When Mount questioned if White truly intended to harm Shaffer, McGowen recounted the incident with the black Mitsubishi, suggesting the teenager who'd made the threat was connected to White.

Mount looked at McGowen, not knowing what to think.

"We need to get this done right away," McGowen urged, noting that at seven he'd be off duty. "My C.I.'s in danger and I want to serve this myself."

Mount sighed. "All right. Let's get it done."

The A.D.A. escorted McGowen to the clerk's window. There he presented the warrant, which described Kent McGowen as "a credible and reliable person reputably employed as a peace officer" and maintained that White had threatened Mike Shaffer and that his mother, Jeannie Jaques, "believed that White intended to inflict serious harm or death on her son as a result of the statement made to her."

"Raise your hand," the clerk ordered McGowen. "Do you swear the information here is true and correct to the best of your knowledge?"

"Yes," McGowen answered.

"Now you just need a judge's signature," Mount told him. "Judge Shipley will be in at seven-thirty."

"I can't wait," McGowen told him. "I need to serve this warrant myself."

Mount shook his head. "No way, I'm not waking a judge up for a third-degree felony," he said. "Besides, by the time I wake up a judge to sign it, it'll be seven-thirty and Shipley will be here. You'll just have to wait."

"I need to serve this myself," McGowen argued. "My C.I. is in danger."

But Mount remained firm.

"Shipley's your best bet," he said again. "If you can't wait, leave the warrant at the clerk's office and another deputy can serve it."

McGowen looked angry.

"Well, if that's what needs to be done," he said.

"That's what needs to be done," Mount answered.

The lack of a judge's signature essentially took the warrant out of Kent McGowen's control. With no possibility of serving it before he finished his shift, he called Deputy Tommy Moore at six that morning and told him of the progress he'd made the night before.

"Will you get it signed and served for me?" McGowen asked.

"Yeah," Moore answered. "No problem."

Back at the substation at the end of his shift that morning, McGowen ran into Al Kelly, a day-shift deputy who patrolled Olde Oaks. Kelly had known Susan and Jason since they'd moved into the area, and while he felt the boy was troubled, he'd had but a few problems with him. He'd listened as McGowen had complained about Jason over the months, labeling him a troublemaker who influenced other teenagers in the neighborhood. Kelly hadn't paid much attention that summer when White stopped him on the street to complain about McGowen. But he knew she worried about his new co-worker.

This particular morning, McGowen bragged about his big bust, filling Kelly in on the sting.

"His mommy called my C.I. and threatened him," McGowen boasted. "I just got a warrant for her arrest."

"You need to be careful going over there for whatever reason," Kelly warned as McGowen turned his back to him to look through his box. "That woman's afraid of you."

Kelly could hardly believe what he heard next. With his back to Kelly, McGowen sneered, "If I get the opportunity, I ought to kill that fucking bitch."

Still, it seemed Susan White's fate was at least momentarily out of McGowen's hands. Tommy Moore was the deputy who stopped at the clerk's office at ten that morning to pick up the warrant. He was the one who would see that it was served, handcuff White, and bring her in for booking.

But something strange happened, something Moore had never experienced before. When he arrived at the clerk's office at 10 A.M. to get the warrant to take to a judge, he looked it over. Everything appeared in order until he noticed the line marked "Affiant," the person bringing the charges. Somehow, Kent McGowen's signature had been mysteriously obliterated with Wite-Out.

"I couldn't get it signed or serve it without his

signature," says Moore. "So I called Kent and told him what'd happened."

Just hours earlier, McGowen had sworn to Jim Mount that the warrant had to be served immediately, imploring him to wake up a judge. He told Jean Spradling-Hughes that without it, Mike Shaffer could be dead by sunset.

But when Moore called, McGowen's attitude abruptly changed. He no longer seemed intent on having Susan White arrested as soon as possible.

"He said I shouldn't worry about the warrant," Moore remembers. "McGowen said he'd have it signed when he came back on duty. He said he'd serve it himself."

24

At five that Monday morning, Hurricane Andrew slammed the tip of south Florida, leaving behind nine more dead and a thick swatch of utter devastation. It then bounced back a second time, stalling in the Gulf of Mexico, where it mindlessly swirled, building even more deadly strength. Texas and Louisiana hung precariously in its path. No one could predict which city or town, which once quiet beach, the storm would next assault with its unrelenting rage.

Meanwhile, in Houston, Jason sat in a holding cell inside the criminal courthouse, awaiting his hearing, handcuffed and bound to his fellow prisoners with thick ankle chains. He felt someone's eyes bearing down at him, and when he looked up he found Kent McGowen standing outside the cell.

"How do you like the big house?" McGowen asked, smiling. "Even your mommy can't get you out of this."

* * *

The phone rang next to Maggie's bed at six-thirty that Monday morning, August 24, the first day of her senior year.

"Maggie, Jason is appearing in court this morning. I need to have you go with me," Susan pleaded.

"Susan, I can't," the girl answered. "My mother would kill me."

"Please, Maggie, please," Susan begged. "I can't go through this alone."

"Well, I'll see," Maggie said.

As Susan waited, Maggie cajoled her mother. "Please, Mom," she whimpered. "Nothing much will happen on the first day.

"She says I can go," said Maggie when she returned to the telephone.

"Oh, thank you, Maggie," Susan cried. "I didn't know how I could go through this alone."

When Maggie arrived at Jason's house, she sensed immediately that something was wrong. Susan pawed like a nervous animal through her closet, throwing suits and dresses on the floor.

"I don't want to look too nice, no jewelry," Susan said. "If we're getting a court-appointed lawyer, I can't look like I've got money."

She grabbed pills out of a small bottle and gobbled them down with a gulp of bitter cold coffee, then pulled off her Rolex watch and threw it on the table. She yanked on a blue suit, assessed herself in the mirror, then said, "Let's go."

On the way downtown Susan detoured into the drive-through at a nearby McDonald's for another cup of coffee and Maggie's breakfast, then stepped on the gas and sped down the street.

"We're off," Susan said, laughing, as they turned onto the freeway. Just then she noticed her wedding ring.

Maggie held onto the steering wheel while the car swerved between lanes in the rush-hour traffic, Susan sucking her finger to wet it, then inching the diamond off.

"You have to help me, Maggie," she said. "You have to help me keep tabs on Jason. When he gets out, McGowen will still be after him. We have to protect Jason."

At that moment her cell phone rang.

"Ray," Susan said. "I'm on my way to the courthouse. I'm going to get Jason out."

"Keep me informed," said Valentine, who was in his own car driving to Wichita Falls. "If you need anything, let me know."

By the time the BMW pulled into the parking lot across the street from the courthouse, Maggie worried if Susan would make it through the morning. Her eyes drooped and she rubbed her forehead as if trying to silence some great pain. But as they rushed inside the criminal courthouse, a nondescript beige brick building stained with layers of black car exhaust, Susan popped another pill and swallowed. When they finally reached Judge Bill Harmon's courtroom, Susan had rallied.

Inside the 178th District Court, they waited in church-like pews. Jason, still handcuffed, sat sullenly on a wooden bench, chained to his fellow inmates. When Susan first noticed him, she waved her arms and blew him a kiss. A few minutes later, he pointed her out to Blair Davis, his court-appointed attorney.

"You have to get Jason off," Susan implored Davis after he had introduced himself. "He didn't do this. It was a setup. He's innocent."

Susan rattled on, babbling about Mike Shaffer, the sting, and claiming none of what had happened was Jason's fault. He'd simply fallen under a bad influence. Davis wondered what was wrong with the kid's mom.

He'd grown used to distraught parents, but this woman appeared nearly manic.

"Calm down, Mrs. White," Davis, a long-drawn man with an Abe Lincoln demeanor, cautioned her. "We're going to try to get Jason out on a pretrial release bond."

As Susan walked away to wave at Jason, the attorney turned to Maggie.

"Is she all right?" he asked.

"She hasn't slept and she's been taking lots of pills," the teenager confided. "I'm worried about her."

Davis looked at Susan and shook his head.

When Jason's case was called that morning, Judge Harmon, a fatherly man with graying hair and a sympathetic air, had Jason, Davis, and the A.D.A. in charge of the case, Tracey Tirey, approach his bench. After the charge was read, Tirey asked for permission to speak.

"Your Honor, the arresting officer, Kent McGowen, called me this morning and asked us to come down hard on Mr. Aguillard. He says he's been a continual problem in the neighborhood."

"Not him again!" Susan screamed from the gallery.

"Who's that?" Harmon asked.

"The boy's mother," Davis answered, staring back at Susan, who appeared furious.

"Let's go to my chambers," said the judge, who through the years had presided over a long roster of seventeen- and eighteen-year-olds with distraught parents. In fact, most of the defendants brought before him seemed to be in their late teens or early twenties. After age twenty-five, those brought in handcuffs to his courtroom were there either for drugs or for the most serious of crimes, including rape and murder.

In his chambers, Harmon invited Susan to sit. "What seems to be your concern?" he asked.

"This is a setup. Jason's not a bad boy," she said, looking for support on the blank faces of Davis, Tirey, and the judge's clerk. "This boy who set him up, Mike Shaffer, used to live with us. It's not Jason's fault. He's a slow learner, he goes to a special school . . ."

Harmon listened, but at the same time he scrutinized Jason's record. Once he had noted the previous offense, reckless conduct for the gun-on-the-school-bus incident, his jaw set and his kindly smile melted into a stern scowl.

"This is your son's second offense in a situation involving a gun, and I'm not going to give him a pretrial release bond," Harmon declared grimly. "You can bail him out if you want to, but I suggest you leave him in jail. The time will count toward his sentence, and it's time to make an impression on him."

"Judge, please," Susan interjected.

"Your son has bad judgment," the soft-spoken Harmon concluded politely. "Don't spend your money to get him out of jail, because if he's found guilty, I'm sending him to boot camp on this case. You bail him out of this and you're sending the wrong message to this young man. His bond is set at two thousand dollars."

In the hallway, Davis handed Susan his card. "Call me if I can do anything for you, even if you just need to talk to someone," he said, looking at her distraught face. "What're you going to do?"

"I'm going to post Jason's bail," she told him, her expression incredulous, as if she marveled that he could have considered any other alternative. "I'm going to take my baby home."

Susan immediately left the courthouse and walked with Maggie to ABC Bonds across the street. A pretrial release bond would have allowed Susan to free Jason for a $60 fee. With a $2,000 bond on his head, she had to come up with at least ten percent—$200. In the cramped office with black metal bars on the window, she signed papers and wrote out a $200 check. Then she and Maggie went back across the street to a small corner deli to wait for the check to be verified and cleared.

After A.D.A. Tracey Tirey returned to her office, she picked up the telephone and dialed Connie Spence, the A.D.A. who had taken the credit-card charges against Jason.

"Did you take those charges?" Tirey asked.

"Uh-huh," Spence answered.

"Well, thanks a bunch," Tirey said sarcastically. "That kid's mom came to court and caused one hell of a scene."

Spence knew the case was weak, but judged it wouldn't do any good to explain how insistent the deputy had been to get charges, so she shrugged it off and hung up the receiver.

In the deli, Maggie ordered a sandwich and Susan drank another cup of coffee.

"Tell me everything," Susan ordered. "If I'm going to keep Jason out of trouble, I need to know what he's been doing."

At first, Maggie hesitated, but then she opened up. She told Susan about the night she'd met Jason, the night with the gunshots fired at the party. She talked about pot and LSD and how some of the kids Jason went around with burglarized houses. Susan didn't believe her at first. How was this possible? Jason? Then, slowly, as Maggie talked on, Susan began to believe her.

"This is my last chance to straighten that boy out before he lands in a world of trouble," she said, for the first time understanding the seriousness of her son's transgressions. "He's going to be after him. He can't have any excuses to get him. Will you help me, Maggie? Will you help Jason?"

"Sure, Susan," the teenager answered, knowing she was referring to McGowen.

At five-thirty that evening, Jason was brought to the release area of the jail.

"He's here, he's here," Susan squealed, throwing her arms around her son. "Now I've got you."

On the drive home Susan again detoured through McDonald's, this time to buy her son a quarter-pounder, large fries, and a Coke. As he gulped his dinner, she lectured him. He would have to live differently, make new friends, she said.

"Tell me the truth. How bad is this stuff, how deep are you involved?" she said sternly.

Jason hedged, not wanting to answer.

"You spill your guts," she ordered. "You tell me everything. No more secrets."

"The cops set me up," Jason whined. "That's all there is to it."

"I don't care if you complain," Susan concluded. "You're never leaving the house again. McGowen will be waiting to get his hands on you. One mistake and you'll be back in jail. Next time I may not be able to get you out."

As they walked into the house, Susan threw her arms around her son, tears in her eyes. "You're grounded, Jason," she said. "No more Mike Shaffer. No more friends who get in trouble. They're really going to be after you now. You need to stay clean and stay away from your so-called friends. You understand?"

"Yeah." He shrugged, pulling away.

*   *   *

Maggie and Jason wandered off, and when they returned an hour later, they found Susan in bed, talking on the telephone to Ray Valentine in Wichita Falls. The only light in the bedroom came from the flickering television set.

"I've got him home," she said, relief flooding her voice. "He's here now."

"What about McGowen?" Valentine asked.

"He'll be back, he'll try again, but not tonight," she said. "I took a couple of Valiums and I'm going to sleep. I'm too exhausted to worry about anything tonight. Tomorrow is soon enough to figure out what to do about this mess."

After she hung up, Susan pulled the covers about her and nestled into the waterbed. Jason and Maggie gazed down at her. Maggie came forward and gave her a hug and a peck on the cheek.

"Good night," she whispered.

"I'm really glad Jason met you. Maybe you two will get married someday. Maybe the two of us can keep him out of trouble," Susan said, wearily slurring her words as she closed her eyes. "Thank you for being with me today."

"That's okay," Maggie told her.

"Get some sleep, Mom," Jason said.

As she turned to leave, Maggie noticed Susan's gun, the small .25, on the bed. She picked it up and placed it on top of the black lacquer headboard.

Jason walked Maggie to her car, then kissed her good night. Inside the house, he locked the doors and set the alarm.

"Jason," Susan called as he walked past her open door on his way upstairs to bed.

"Yeah," he answered.

"This will all work out," she said, yawning. "But tonight, don't answer the door, not for anyone."

25

Kent McGowen's shift started at 10 P.M. that Monday night, and he immediately headed downtown to the clerk's office to claim the warrant for Susan White's arrest on retaliation charges. Once there, he re-signed his name where it had been covered over. An H.P.D. officer waited in the intake office with another warrant, and the A.D.A. on duty sent the two of them to Judge Donald Shipley's house to have their warrants signed.

The judge was waiting when they arrived. After some small talk, he signed the warrants and the two officers parted at the curb, each going his separate way.

With his signed warrant for Susan White's arrest in hand, McGowen drove back to Cypresswood. The streets were quiet. Hurricane Andrew still stalled in the Gulf, building strength, and an eerie calm had descended over the city.

From the car on his way back to Cypresswood, McGowen bumped Sergeant Ruggiero on the radio, filled him in, and asked for backup to serve the warrant and arrest Susan White. Ruggiero, who also was driving to the substation, had just returned from special duty at the Republican National Convention and had heard nothing about either the sting or Susan White's supposed threats.

"Does Lieutenant Coons know about this?" he asked. It was Coons' night off, and Ruggiero wanted to make sure the lieutenant was aware of McGowen's intentions.

"Yup," McGowen assured him. "He's been keeping tabs on the whole thing. Oh, by the way, this crazy bitch says she's going to file a complaint against me."

"Coons knows about this, too?" Ruggiero asked.

"Yeah, he knows."

"Come on in, then, and we'll get this done," Ruggiero ordered.

When McGowen reached the substation at approximately midnight, he found Ruggiero in his office with District Deputies Mike Malloy and Todd Morong, the two men the sergeant had designated to back McGowen up when he served the warrant and arrested White. McGowen again maintained that not only was the threat against Shaffer real but he'd already "looked down the barrel of a gun."

"I just washed my hands of it, like Pontius Pilate," says Ruggiero, shaking his head as he recounts that night. "I had been told she was a screwball. I don't let Joe Blow-citizen tell me what to do. I get very defensive about my kids . . . If one of my guys works something, it's like sauce for the goose. You busted your ass, you deserve to get the collar. I don't just take it away from them because someone's making claims. McGowen could tell me it's dark outside, and I'd have to walk outside to see, because I wouldn't believe him. But if he was lying, I figured I'd beat his ass the next day."

*   *   *

On Amber Forest, McGowen parked the squad car half a block away from Susan White's home, on the south side of the street. The three deputies then walked toward the imposing double doors of the stately brick home at number 3407. Inside, Susan White, her senses dulled by Valium, slept for the first time in three days.

As planned, Deputy Mike Malloy took a post at the back door to prevent escape. McGowen and Morong approached the front door.

With everyone in place, McGowen rapped soundly.

No one stirred.

"It looks like there's a television on in there," said Morong, pointing to Susan's bedroom window, to the left of the doors. He walked over and knocked on the glass.

Still no answer.

McGowen then rang the doorbell.

With light from a streetlamp illuminating the officers from behind, Susan, wrapped in her worn brown terry-cloth robe, peered at them through the leaded-glass panels on her front doors.

"Who's there?" she called, her words slurred.

"Deputy McGowen," Kent shouted. "I've got a felony warrant for your arrest. Open the door."

What thoughts raced through Susan's mind as the dullness of sleep left her? McGowen was waiting outside her door with a felony warrant for her arrest.

Susan grabbed the telephone in the front hall and dialed 911.

"Nine-one-one county, what's your emergency?" the operator answered.

"Yes, I need the Cypresswood sheriff's department, please," Susan said.

"Stay on the line."

"Go ahead, ma'am," a new voice answered.

"Yes, there's . . . at my door," she said, her voice angry and frightened. "I've filed several complaints with him for sexual harassment and I need some help, *immediately.*"

"Who is at your door? . . . Is this your husband, ma'am?"

"This is a deputy who thinks he owns the world," Susan answered. "My name is Susan White and he's threatened . . ."

Outside, McGowen pounded again on the heavy wood doors.

"What subdivision are you in?" the operator asked.

"Olde Oaks, and I was sound asleep, and I—somebody—I saw somebody through my bedroom window."

"What is going on, Susan? Tell me," the operator prodded.

"I don't know, there's a man standing at the door and . . ."

This time the knocking at Susan White's door was so loud, even the operator could hear it.

"Someone through my bedroom window . . . There's a man standing at the door. He says he's the police and I will not—"

Susan took the phone away from her mouth and yelled to the deputies outside: "I can't hear you. I am getting someone else over here besides McGowen."

Back on the telephone, she heard the operator ask, "Did they identify themselves as police?"

"Yes, but they—I was in my bedroom sleeping and they were in my window, and they said, 'This is the police, McGowen . . .' "

"He's at your front door or your back door?"

"Front. McGowen has made sexual advances toward me and I will not—"

Susan again yelled, screeching at the officers outside. "Who's there? So you can get McGowen away from my house. Get McGowen away from my house. I want him out of my yard and off my property. . . . You don't go peeking in ladies' bedroom windows."

The 911 operator then said, "We're going to get some-one en route."

At that point, Susan asked to be connected with Lieu-tenant Coons, the same supervisor she'd complained to about McGowen. Perhaps she felt he'd understand, that he knew her situation and the reason she couldn't let McGowen inside her home. She didn't know Coons had personally given McGowen the go-ahead he needed to seek a warrant for her arrest.

The operator rattled off the number of the Cypress-wood substation and disconnected the line.

Meanwhile, outside, the three deputies waited, Mal-loy at the back door, McGowen and Morong at the front.

It would later strike Morong as odd that the woman inside knew McGowen's name. But at the time, he made no attempt to question why McGowen was serving a warrant on a woman who seemed to know him.

With his radio on a front channel, McGowen kept in touch with Dispatch. Now a voice over the radio in-formed him that a Susan White, at 3407 Amber Forest, had called 911 begging for help.

"Open the door or we'll kick it in," McGowen threat-ened, yelling at Susan.

"You're going to kick it in?" Susan cried.

McGowen then switched his radio to a back channel to bump Ruggiero.

"She won't let us in," he said. "Can I force entry?"

"You've got a felony warrant, haven't you?" the ser-geant demanded.

"Yeah," McGowen answered.

"Then go ahead and break the door down," Ruggiero ordered. "Break it down."

With their sergeant's okay, McGowen and Morong kicked the door, but the sturdy locks held tight. Malloy ran to the front just in time to hear someone shout from inside.

"Get McGowen out of here and I'll come out," White screamed.

"Come on," McGowen shouted, running toward the back.

Meanwhile, Susan had run to her bedroom, where she cowered, holding the telephone, her one lifeline, and again dialed 911.

"I'm trying to get the Cypresswood substation," she screamed into the phone.

"Do you need a deputy out to your house?" the operator asked.

Outside, Malloy pulled back his foot and let loose with a solid kick; the back door held tight.

"They are trying to break into my house," White cried into the telephone, her voice plaintive and frightened. "*P-l-e-a-s-e.*"

"Who's trying to break into your house?"

"I don't know," she answered. "They say they're detectives, but I have been threatened by one of them . . . Lieutenant Coons is the one I need to talk with. They are breaking my door down."

"How many are there?"

"I don't know," she said. "*P-l-e-a-s-e.*"

On Malloy's third kick, the frame cracked and the back door sprang open. Instantaneously, the house alarm blared a deafening alert.

"They just broke in," Susan screamed to the 911 operator.

From the back door McGowen sprinted ahead of Malloy into the darkened house, through the kitchen. He never stopped to clear the area, the way he'd been taught. He never looked for Susan in the kitchen, the living room, or the dining room.

As Malloy and Morong tailed him through the blackness, McGowen, his pistol drawn, his flashlight glaring into the darkness, ran directly to the half-open door of Susan's bedroom. The only other light came from the streetlamp outside through the window blinds and from the flickering television. McGowen positioned himself in the doorway of Susan White's bedroom, arms extended and crossed, gun and flashlight pointed straight at her.

Morong stood five feet behind him, staring up at the balcony.

With events tumbling so quickly, Malloy stationed himself at the bottom of the steps, waiting for the woman's son, the gunrunner McGowen had warned of, to come barreling downstairs, guns firing.

Neither Malloy nor Morong could see inside the bedroom. Only McGowen had a clear view, down the barrel of his gun, the flashlight shining.

"Drop the gun," McGowen shouted over the thunderous wail of the alarm. "Drop the gun. I said, drop the gun."

Susan's final word on the 911 call: "Okay."

"Ma'am?" the operator asked, just as the line was disconnected.

Seconds later, Kent McGowen squeezed the trigger on his 10-mm police special, once, twice, three times, sending sporadic flashes and three bullets ripping through the darkness.

PART FOUR

The Aftermath

26

The ear-piercing alarm shrieked through the house and awoke Jason, asleep in the second-floor game room, huddled on a couch in front of a television, clothed in only a pair of thin silk boxers. He ran to his bedroom and dialed 911, screaming at the operator over the incessant wail when he heard three loud, popping noises, gunshots, downstairs.

"Is anyone else in the house with you?" the operator asked.

"Yeah, my mom," Jason said, cowering with his arm over his head, attempting to shut out the noise.

"How old are you?"

"Seventeen," he said, his body trembling so violently he nearly dropped the telephone. Then he heard the thud of heavy footsteps rushing upstairs.

Suddenly the door banged open and Malloy and Morong rushed into his bedroom.

"Do yourself a favor and get your hands in the air," Malloy yelled.

"What's going on?" Jason asked, raising his arms over his head just as the alarm cut off. "Are you taking me back to jail?"

"Come on, let's go," Morong said, pulling Jason by the arm.

Downstairs, as the two deputies walked him through the living room, Jason glanced into the bedroom and saw McGowen standing over his mother's bed, shining a flashlight.

"Are you taking me to jail?" he asked again; the trembling in his knees intensified until he feared he'd be unable to walk.

"No," the deputy barked. "Don't say anything."

Outside, he pushed Jason into the backseat of a squad car and locked it. Just then the street filled with squad cars and unmarked cars. An ambulance, its siren howling, turned onto Amber Forest and slammed to a stop in front of 3407.

What's going on? Jason wondered. *Where's my mom?*

"What happened?" Ruggiero shouted as he arrived on the scene within minutes of the shooting. The house was already crowded with deputies, some there to investigate, others merely curious.

"She pulled a gun on me," McGowen said, pointing at Susan's .25 chrome, pearl-handled pistol lying on the bedroom floor. "We found it on the bed, but threw it there because she was still moving."

"Everybody out," the sergeant screamed. "All nonessential personnel out."

Ruggiero noticed the shells, three casings on the floor, the brass from McGowen's fired bullets. He carefully placed a plastic cup over each, then covered the pistol with a box to keep it from being disturbed.

Then Ruggiero heard a medic call out, "I've got a pulse!"

With that, one medic straddled White. He turned her body, which had been curled on its left side in a fetal position, so that she now lay on her back, and began frantically pumping her chest. Another medic hooked her up to an EKG; a third plunged a shot of adrenaline into her vein.

The darkness grated on him, and Ruggiero sent Malloy and Morong in search of a light switch. Soon the house was flooded with brightness.

Another deputy walked over, and Ruggiero ordered him to string yellow crime-scene tape with black lettering across the front of the house.

"Take McGowen to my car," Ruggiero ordered another deputy. "Tell him not to talk to anyone."

As Ruggiero inspected the scene, others arrived, including Clint Greenwood, an attorney who, with his partner, Brian Benken, worked for C.L.E.A.T., the Combined Law Enforcement Agencies of Texas. On a shooting scene, Greenwood's job was to protect the officers' rights.

Guarding the citizens' rights were Assistant District Attorneys Don Smyth and Edward Porter, chief and first assistant in the Civil Rights Division. They arrived within moments of each other, their mandate to determine if McGowen's shooting was justified.

By the time Smyth entered the front door, the ambulance team had driven off with Susan. The front foyer was strewn with blood and gauze where they'd worked feverishly to save her, injecting heart stimulants while administering oxygen and performing CPR.

Moments later, Lieutenant Coons arrived, as did Chuck Leithner, a homicide detective.

"Is McGowen all right?" Coons asked.

"He's in my squad car," Ruggiero answered, but then he looked outside and saw McGowen jawing with a cache of deputies.

"Get back in the car and shut up," Ruggiero shouted.

Outside, blue-and-red lights bounced off the imposing brick homes and the towering pines. Neighbors collected on the curb, murmuring among one another, craning their necks for a glimpse behind the open front door. One stopped a deputy, asking, "What happened?"

He never answered, instead ordering her to cross the street, away from the squad cars. One neighbor spotted Jason trembling in a squad car and pointed him out to the others.

"Guess he started something big this time," someone speculated.

They all nodded in agreement.

Just then a TV-news photographer pulled up in front and ran from his van, his camera capturing the scene for the morning news.

"Do you know what's going on?" one of the neighbors asked.

"Heard it on the radio. Said a deputy's shot someone, a woman," the photographer answered. "Know anything about it?"

The neighbor shrugged. "I always figured it'd be the boy who ended up getting it someday. Not the mother."

While Ruggiero ran down what he knew about the situation for Coons and Leithner, Smyth and Porter circled the house. The call had woken Smyth, a short, ruddy-complected man, from a sound sleep. Nicknamed "Whispering Don" for his hushed manner of speech, an effective tool for making juries listen more closely, he was used to being called out of his bed and away from his wife and three children in the middle of the night. "It comes with the territory," he'd say. "My wife knew when the pager went off, I was gone."

Porter, a round man with thinning dark hair, a bemused smile, and brown eyes that peered over half glasses, lived alone. He'd been married once and had got divorced while he worked as a public defender in Florida. "I decided I'd rather prosecute criminals than defend them," he says, explaining the career change. He'd returned to his hometown of Houston for a job with the D.A.'s office a few years earlier. With his notebook open as he sized up the scene of the shooting, it would have been difficult to visualize him in the sixties, when his hair brushed his shoulders and he marched in antiwar rallies.

"Who's that?" Smyth asked Ruggiero, pointing at Jason, whose eyes were as round as quarters as he sat shivering in the backseat of a squad car.

Ruggiero shrugged. "The woman's kid."

"What was the charge on the warrant?"

"Retaliation," Ruggiero explained somewhat sheepishly.

Something didn't smell right to Smyth. Why serve a third-class felony warrant in the middle of the night? He glanced up at the house. Impressive. The woman didn't look like a flight risk.

Remembering Jason, he shifted his gaze to the car. Smyth sized up the kid one more time. He looked thirteen or fourteen, at the most. He looked scared.

Inside the squad car, Jason shivered in the heat. He watched the activity, pieced together clues. First he saw a deputy take away Kent McGowen's gun and remove and count the bullets. Then he saw his mother on a stretcher. McGowen had shot his mother. A ball of anger grew in his chest until he fantasized about the feel of McGowen's gun in his hands as he pulled the trigger and watched him fall. In that moment, Jason hated Kent McGowen more than anyone he'd encountered in his short life; enough to kill him.

Watching the look of utter hatred on the boy's face as he stared at McGowen, Smyth shook his head. *What the hell happened here?* he wondered. Everything at the scene felt wrong to him, but he'd been an A.D.A. long enough to know that things often weren't as they first seemed. Maybe his instincts were wrong. Maybe it would turn out that the young deputy had had no choice but to shoot.

"Cover it like a blanket," Smyth whispered to Porter, who nodded knowingly. Smyth guessed his gut wasn't the only one acting up. With that, Porter and Smyth parted, Porter to question witnesses, Smyth to assess the crime scene.

On a yellow legal pad, Smyth sketched the scene, noting the back door splintered off its frame and a black shoe print where someone had kicked it in. Once inside the house, he inspected the kitchen and the den, finding no signs of a struggle. He stepped over the medics' debris and bloodstains in the front foyer.

The place is a mess, he thought.

Shopping bags and packed moving crates littered the floor, and towers of spent fast-food containers cluttered tables and counters.

In Susan's bedroom, Smyth found what he was looking for, the scene of the shooting. A Burger King drink cup sweated on the waterbed's headboard; the telephone sat on the bed, atop a black quilt covered in a jaunty geometric pattern of triangles. He had to look carefully to see the coat of thick, wet blood saturating the sheets.

Smyth surveyed the room. Like the rest of the house, it was disheveled. On the nearby dresser he noticed a stack of black-and-white photos, like those in a model's portfolio; they were of an attractive woman, middle-aged, with the name Susan White printed on each.

That's her, Smyth thought. *That's the woman.*

Porter stood at the doorway. "We're ready for the walk-through," he said.

Smyth nodded, walked toward him, then opened his briefcase and pulled out a tape recorder. He'd been bringing one to shooting scenes for years, but he'd never before done what he intended to do now.

"Is he willing to tell us what happened?" Smyth asked Greenwood.

The question was a formality. Greenwood and Mc-Gowen both knew that if McGowen didn't talk he'd face criminal charges and be suspended without pay for the duration of the investigation. Officers almost always co-operated. Plus, Smyth had seen McGowen circling the front yard, talking to whoever was willing to listen, despite his sergeant's continual admonitions to stay quiet in a squad car. It was obvious the deputy was eager to tell his story.

"He's ready," Greenwood answered.

"Let's go, then," Smyth ordered, clicking on the tape recorder.

That action immediately caught Greenwood's eye. He'd once worked for Smyth in the D.A.'s office. He knew tape-recording statements wasn't his old boss' standard procedure. Yet he'd talked to McGowen. The young deputy wanted to do the walk-through. He said he had no reason not to.

He has a warrant, Greenwood thought. *It looks all right.*

The walk-through began at the front door, McGowen telling how he'd gotten the warrant for White's arrest after she threatened his C.I., a kid named Mike Shaffer.

Smyth watched the jowly young cop carefully as he rambled, recounting the events that had led to the shooting. According to McGowen, the kid in the car was a big-time gunrunner, dealing in guns for gangs. After detailing the sting operation, he turned to Porter, who regarded him above his crescent-shaped glasses and smiled.

"You know, the morning of the sting I talked to some stupid A.D.A. who wouldn't take charges on the kid," said McGowen. "She didn't know the law and wouldn't charge him with engaging in organized crime activity," he scoffed, smirking at the woman's stupidity.

Porter just smiled at McGowen. He wanted him to keep on talking.

Meanwhile, Smyth's instincts were on full alert.

This guy's proud of shooting that woman, he thought. *He's delighted.*

This was something Smyth had never seen before. Even seasoned officers forced to fire their weapons on career criminals were depressed and uncertain after having to shoot.

His bearing arrogant, McGowen surveyed White's house as if he owned it, gesturing to show how they'd broken down the back door, talking repeatedly of automatic weapons and drugs.

"She threatened my C.I. We needed to get this woman off the street," McGowen boasted, nodding at Smyth and Porter as if they were part of his club, the inner circle of law enforcement.

Then McGowen mentioned the telephone and White's call to 911.

She called the cops? Smyth marveled at this information. *This major player in a gun ring called the cops to help her? There's something wrong here.*

Moments later, an officer Smyth didn't recognize approached them.

"The woman's dead," he said. "Just came in over the radio."

Smyth and Porter exchanged wary glances. The stakes had just multiplied. If McGowen's shooting of Susan White wasn't justified, they were looking at murder.

Saying nothing, they continued the walk-through, but there was an electricity between the two A.D.A.s. Each knew what the other was thinking: One of them had to get downtown to the sheriff's department to retrieve a copy of the tape of Susan White's 911 call before something happened to it, before it mysteriously disappeared.

Later, Smyth and Porter walked toward their cars.

"The kid says his mom told him McGowen sexually

harassed her," Porter reported, free for the first time to fill Smyth in on what he'd learned from his interview with the boy. "He didn't ever see it, but said he was hitting on her."

"How old's that kid?"

"Seventeen."

"He's a little guy. I'd have made him for fourteen—tops," Smyth said. "I'm going to call ahead and tell them to freeze that 911 tape. This thing smells and I don't want it to get lost. You go to the hospital and check on the position of her wounds."

"After that, I'm going to track down the warrant and check the probable cause," added Porter.

Smyth agreed. Just then the two prosecutors heard someone call out. They turned to see Kent McGowen running toward them, flashing a warm smile.

"Thank you, Mr. Smyth, Mr. Porter," the deputy gushed. "Thank you for coming out to this totally justifiable shooting."

27

Homicide Detective Bruce Johnson arrived on the scene ninety minutes after the shooting. His partner, Chuck Leithner, who'd arrived an hour earlier, filled him in, describing it as an open-and-shut case: The deputy had a warrant, the woman didn't open the door, she had a gun, and Kent McGowen shot Susan White in self-defense. But after surveying the scene, asking questions, and, more important, watching Kent McGowen, Johnson, who'd worked crime scenes for two decades, soon came to a vastly different conclusion.

McGowen's demeanor pricked at him. *Cocky*, he thought.

When Malloy and Morong relayed what McGowen had told them, Johnson became even more suspicious. Though McGowen had led the deputies to believe they'd be entering a dangerous situation, one fraught with mean desperadoes and the possibility of a heavy-duty arsenal, the crime-scene unit found nothing but the .25 "peashooter" the woman had kept near her bed.

"Hell, there are women all over town with those toy guns under their pillows," growled Johnson. "Doesn't look to me like any big gunrunning scene."

As Johnson questioned other deputies, he asked pointed questions about McGowen. The words his peers used to describe the young officer didn't help settle the knot of suspicion in the detective's gut: They called him a know-it-all; some said they didn't trust him and that he had a way of stretching the truth.

Some said he lied.

Something else troubled Johnson. Morong and Malloy said McGowen hadn't cleared the house the way officers and deputies were taught, carefully inspecting each room to be sure it was safe to enter. Instead the kid made a beeline for the woman's bedroom. "He came in, his weapon drawn, and he was after her," recounts Johnson. "Now, how'd he know where she was? If he seriously thought the house was full of guns, how did he know he was safe to chase her down?

"You get that feeling as an investigator," Johnson concludes. "I figured we had a problem here. I thought it was dirty."

A few hours after the shooting, McGowen was ordered back to the Cypresswood substation to make a statement. A'Laine Harrison, who'd never crossed paths with McGowen before, was called in to record it.

Harrison had been a clerk in Homicide for seven years. She'd taken countless statements from officers after shootings, most of them nervous and worried, wondering how their actions would be viewed by the D.A.'s office.

McGowen displayed none of the usual angst. He reveled in the moment, delighted to be the center of attention.

"He showed less concern than if he'd killed a dog," says Harrison.

She felt sickened by the deputy's attitude and escaped outside for a cigarette. In the dark, facing the street, she became aware of the door opening and Kent McGowen standing beside her, lighting his own cigarette.

"He had this look of self-satisfaction on his face," recalls Harrison. "He didn't talk about the shooting. He told me his daddy was rich, that he had a trust fund he'd inherit when he turned thirty-five. That someday he'd be a big rancher and raise cattle. I kept thinking, *Something's wrong here.*"

Inside the substation, Harrison admitted her suspicions to one of the detectives.

"Well, she had a gun. She was going to kill him," the man insisted, incredulous that Harrison could second-guess a deputy with a warrant.

"I don't care," Harrison replied. "This isn't right. I can feel it."

Jason would remember seeing McGowen that morning as the teenager sat in a hard-backed chair against a wall outside Coons' office. He looked up and found McGowen smiling at him. "It was this big, shit-eating grin," says Jason, his voice mirroring the hate visible on his face. "This look like, *I won. I got you.*"

Every few minutes Jason asked what had happened, where was his mother? No one answered him until about 2 A.M., when his mother's closest friend, Jean Morris, and her daughter, Sharon, arrived at the substation. Jason had given her name as a contact, and the women had been called in, without being told what had happened.

The substation's captain greeted them and stood there whispering. Jason couldn't hear what he said, but Jean let out a small cry and Sharon put her arm around her.

Then the three of them walked toward Jason, shoulders bowed, Jean softly sobbing.

"Where's my mother?" he demanded.

"I'm sorry, son, but your mother's dead," the captain told him. "She pulled a gun on one of our deputies."

"McGowen?" Jason asked.

"Yes, son, Deputy McGowen," the captain confirmed. "As a result of your getting in trouble Saturday night, your mom threatened someone. We went there with a warrant to arrest her. She came at an officer with a gun and he was forced to shoot her."

Jason said nothing, just glared at the older man.

Once outside, Sharon, a tall, twentysomething blonde who sometimes modeled, turned to her mother. She'd known Susan well; they'd once worked together, handing out liquor samples in a bar.

"Susan told me about that Deputy McGowen," Sharon said. "She said he was harassing her. She was afraid of him."

Jean turned to Jason. "Is that right?"

"Yes, ma'am," he said. "My mom told me the same thing."

Later that morning, in the substation, deputies crowded around the television for the six o'clock newscast. The report began with the big story of the day, Hurricane Andrew, still stalled, building strength, miles offshore in the Gulf of Mexico.

Then, in a flash of footage, the front of the house at 3407 Amber Forest filled the screen, ringed with crime-scene tape. Susan White, near death, was shown being removed on a gurney.

"According to police, the woman, who died on the way to the hospital, pulled a gun on a deputy serving a warrant," reported the newscaster.

Sergeant Ruggiero, who stood watching with the others, heard a voice behind him.

"Do you believe that crazy bitch?"

Ruggiero turned and stared into the blazing eyes of Kent McGowen.

Homicide Detective John Denholm, McGowen's former boss at the county jail, also caught the six o'clock news that Tuesday morning. After watching the dead woman being wheeled from the house, he called the office. One of his fellow detectives went over the facts as he knew them. But when Denholm heard the shooter's name, he felt suddenly queasy.

"Kent McGowen?" Denholm repeated.

"Kent McGowen," the officer confirmed.

But then Denholm reviewed the facts: McGowen had a warrant signed by a judge; they found the woman's gun. "I thought maybe it was all right," says Denholm, frowning. "Hell, a warrant, that's as good as gold. Sure, I worried that it was McGowen, but I figured even a blind squirrel finds an acorn sometimes. It sounded like a good shooting."

But Denholm's shaky confidence diminished when A'Laine Harrison took the unusual step of seeking him out as he arrived at the office a few hours later.

"There's something wrong with this case," she said. "I've seen a lot, but this guy just plain didn't care. It was like he took out his trash."

With that, the wave of dread that had flooded Denholm at the mention of McGowen's name returned.

Shit, Denholm thought. *That's not what I wanted to hear.*

Meanwhile, at the D.A.'s office downtown, Porter and Smyth sat transfixed, listening to the tape of Susan White's 911 call.

"Anybody but McGowen," they heard her plead. "He's been sexually harassing me . . . threatening me. . . . *P-l-e-a-s-e.*"

"I felt like it was going downhill quick. It was worse than I thought," Smyth says, remembering his first hearing of the tape. "The dead woman knew McGowen by name. Here was a clear indication things were not as McGowen tried to make them appear."

That morning, as the tape recording of Susan White ended in the nagging blare of her home's burglar alarm, Smyth turned to Porter.

"This woman is talking to us from the grave," he said. "Malloy and Morong saw nothing. The only ones who know what really happened in that room are McGowen, Susan White, and God. We can't question Susan White or God, but we're going to find out everything we can about Kent McGowen."

The name Kent McGowen also filled the conversations of Susan White's friends the morning after her death. Jean Morris' daughter, Sharon, called Ray Valentine in his car as he drove down a Wichita Falls highway.

"Are you sitting down?"

"Yeah."

"Susan's been killed."

"What the hell!" Valentine screamed. "I just talked to her last night."

"The police came and shot her last night."

"The police?"

"That deputy, McGowen, the one she'd been complaining about."

Valentine returned to his hotel room, pacing the floor. Finally he called C.J. Harper.

"She's dead," he said. "McGowen killed her."

"I know," Harper replied.

*   *   *

Television reports of a woman from the FM 1960 area
being wheeled away on a stretcher caught Helen Bazata's attention that morning. The front of the home, lit
by television cameras, reminded her of Susan's. Then she
heard the dead woman's name. She put down her coffee
cup and stared, disbelieving, at the television screen.
When she heard that a deputy had fired the fatal shots,
anger welled within her. She knew it had to be Mc-
Gowen, and while he might have had a warrant, she felt
certain that it was murder, plain and simple.

On her way to work, Helen felt drawn to Susan's
house. Once there, she parked, pondering the still un-
folding scene. Yellow police tape flapped in the breeze,
and a few remaining deputies in uniform walked nonchalantly in and out of the open front doors.

No one stopped her when she proceeded inside,
stepped over the blood and debris in the foyer, and
headed toward the bedroom.

I have to see this for myself, she thought.

She did: the bedclothes covered in blood, a spray of
blood surrounding the headboard. Susan's death suddenly seemed all too real.

At the Cypresswood substation, Deputy Al Kelly arrived
for his regular shift, patrolling Olde Oaks. The office was
abuzz, everyone on edge.

"What's going on?" he asked a fellow deputy.

"McGowen shot a woman last night, some crazy
broad who pulled a gun on him."

Kelly swallowed hard.

"What's her name?"

"Susan White."

"Is she alive?" Kelly asked.

"Nah," the deputy replied. "Died on the way to the hospital."

Stunned, Kelly turned quickly and walked away.

In Baton Rouge, at ten that morning, Gloria hummed and tossed a green salad to bring to a women's missionary meeting, scheduled at her church for that afternoon. Then the telephone rang.

"Gloria?"

"Yes, Momma."

"I just got the strangest call," O.L. said, worry edging her quiet voice. "A police officer said you need to call Susan's house."

"Why?"

"I don't know."

After wiping her hands on an old towel, Gloria dialed her sister's Houston phone number. Philip Riviera, a friend of Susan's, answered.

"Susan's been shot," he blurted out.

"What?"

"By a policeman. She was at home in bed," he explained. "Gloria, she's dead."

Back at the Cypresswood substation, McGowen was still reveling in the previous night's events. To anyone who would listen, he cursed the hurricane, blaming it for keeping his shooting off the front page and relegating it to a small article on page fifteen of the *Houston Post* under the headline, "Woman Accused of Making Threats Slain by Deputies."

Ruggiero, who'd fast been losing patience with McGowen's bravado, heard him bragging to a young recruit early in the afternoon. Chest puffed out, face beaming with excitement, McGowen held out a hand, index finger pointing, mimicking the barrel of a gun.

"I popped her three times," McGowen crowed.

Able to take no more, Ruggiero cornered him.

"Shut the fuck up," the sergeant ordered. "You don't need to be talking like that."

Meanwhile, miles away, at the sheriff's department homicide offices on Lockwood, near downtown Houston, Mike Shaffer sat in a conference room, surrounded by detectives and sweating, his thin hands shaking uncontrollably. Jason had called early that morning to tell him McGowen had killed his mother.

Why'd McGowen have to go and kill her? Shaffer wondered.

Again and again, the cadre of detectives asked the same questions. Did Shaffer believe Susan White might injure him?

"I was scared of her, concerned," Shaffer admitted. "I saw her on Sunday, talked to her. I was upset 'cause she and Jason'd figured out I was the snitch."

Did he tell McGowen he feared she'd have him killed?

"No," he insisted.

Always they worked their way around to the teenager who'd flashed a gun on Shaffer, the one he'd seen the morning after the sting operation. Was it possible the incident had anything to do with Susan White?

"No."

Could McGowen have thought that it did?

"No. I told him it was another guy, a guy who'd been giving me a hard time," Shaffer insisted. "It was McGowen who said Susan had threatened me."

The detectives exchanged worried, knowing glances. Denholm, who'd been listening, sighed. The more he heard about this shooting, the worse it looked.

*   *   *

Meanwhile, in Baton Rouge, Gloria sat in her kitchen, staring at the unfinished salad, her heart pounding, her head aching. She glanced at the clock and tried to think of what to do. She had to get the family together; that she knew. How would her mother and father survive such shattering news? They were so old.

"This could kill them," she whispered.

Unable to face breaking the news alone, she called her church and made arrangements for her pastor to meet her at her parents' careworn trailer. Kay would already be there; she lived right next door, along with a menagerie of hens, roosters, geese, ducks, and rabbits. Gloria called Sandra's school and asked to have someone drive her youngest sister to their parents'.

"I'm fixing to tell her something bad," she explained. "Really bad."

In the car on her way to her parents' trailer, where every wall cried out with family photos from her childhood, Philip's news ran like on a continuous recording through Gloria's mind. *Susie is dead. Killed by a police officer. In her own home, her own bed.*

Philip had put a deputy on the telephone, a deputy who said Susan had pulled a gun on a policeman who'd had a warrant for her arrest. For what? How could that be?

Susie wasn't stupid, Gloria thought. *She wouldn't do that.*

The pastor was waiting outside the trailer when she arrived. They talked, then went inside. The moment they entered her parents' living room, she felt her mother examine her face, searching for a hint as to what she would say. Her father looked tired, his eyes downcast, as if he expected the worst but had already seen too much sadness in his life.

"Gloria?" he said.

Gloria took a deep breath.

"Susie's been killed."

*   *   *

In his cluttered office in the district attorney's building, Smyth scanned the records of calls by deputies to 3407 Amber Forest. If Kent McGowen had told the truth, Smyth expected to find a slew of incident reports involving guns and violence at Susan White's address. Instead he turned up nuisance calls, loud music, unruly teenagers, parties with drinking, typical kid stuff. When he ran a criminal check on Susan White, McGowen's alleged gun-toting moll, he found only one offense—that of writing a fraudulent prescription in Louisiana.

It looks like this Susan White had some problems, thought Smyth. *But it sure doesn't look like she needed to die for them.*

About the same time, Edward Porter stood in the 248th District Court, waiting to talk to Jim Mount, the A.D.A. who had signed McGowen's warrant for Susan's arrest.

As Mount finished talking to the judge, Porter approached him.

"Jim, do you remember a deputy named Kent McGowen? He got a warrant on a retaliation charge, a woman named Susan White."

"Sure," said Mount.

"McGowen killed the woman while he was serving the warrant," said Porter. "Don Smyth and I want to have a little talk. We've got a few questions."

28

Upon hearing the news, O.L. let a small scream escape from her lips. W.A. buried his head in his hands. The room felt silent, then quickly bustled with conversation. How could it have happened? Their Susie? Gloria and Sandra made plans to travel to Houston that night, to learn what they could about their sister's death and to claim her body and make arrangements to bring her home for burial.

Al, who'd just arrived from the plant, took Gloria by the shoulders.

"You can't go now," he told his wife. "Not with Andrew ready to hit."

They'd monitored weather reports all week, waiting for Andrew to strike. The killer storm had already lashed through the Bahamas and Florida, leaving behind death and destruction. It now stood poised to hit Louisiana, probably sometime that very morning. The road Gloria and Sandra would travel to Houston, Interstate 10, tracked the coastline, directly in the storm's projected path.

"It's foolhardy to go now. We can't help Susie," he murmured, his arms tight around her. "We'll go later, when it's safe."

Gloria, who'd grown to depend on her husband's common sense, nodded. Houston would have to wait.

L.J. received his own call that morning from a Houston detective.

"Mr. Aguillard, there's been an incident at your ex-wife's house," the man said.

"Is Jason all right?"

"Yes," the man answered. "But your ex-wife is dead. She pulled a gun on an officer with a warrant for her arrest."

After hanging up the telephone, L.J. rocked back and forth in a chair, thinking. He'd expected just such a call, but he'd always assumed the bad news would be about Jason.

Will this cop be back? he wondered. *Was he after Jason?*

L.J. made the flight arrangements, and Jason arrived at the Baton Rouge airport later that afternoon. To his father, the boy appeared to be in shock. L.J. questioned him, but he couldn't answer more than the simplest questions. Yes, his mother was dead. Yes, a deputy had killed her. No, he didn't know why, except that his mother had said the deputy had been harassing her.

Why? L.J. wondered. *Why had he killed her?*

In Houston, as Don Smyth and Ed Porter continued their investigation into Susan's death, Jean Morris called Ron White in Mexico. Ron flew in the next day, but not alone. To the astonishment of Morris and Susan's other friends, he brought along a young Mexican woman, his new girl-friend.

That same day, Hurricane Andrew lashed ashore for the final time, pummeling Louisiana, bringing with it tornadoes and torrents of rain. Newspaper reports recorded a roaring wall of wind and how millions fled to higher ground to avoid flooding. Then, as quickly as it had attacked, the storm retreated to the Gulf, where it diminished to an innocuous front, leaving behind one more person dead and a hundred-mile swath of destruction.

"Deadly calm after the storm," read the Houston Chronicle headline.

The following Saturday in Houston, in a Southern-mansion-style funeral home with white pillars, a small band of Susan's friends held a quiet memorial service.

Ron sat in the front row with his new girlfriend, the body of his estranged wife in a casket before them. Helen, Jean, Ray, and those who'd come to know Susan so well that summer fanned out behind Ron. Less than thirty mourners attended. Only during the brief service did the whispering cease.

"Who killed her?"

"A deputy."

"Why?"

"Is this the same deputy, the one she kept talking about, the deputy Susan said stalked her?"

A friend of Susan's from acting class whispered to the organist, and the melancholy strains of "Amazing Grace" filled the opulent room as he sang the hymn in a clear yet mournful voice.

*   *   *

In Louisiana, Gloria and her family waited for Susan's body to arrive for burial in a small cemetery just up the road from Kay's house. Her death still seemed unreal to them. When she finally had the opportunity to talk to Jason, Gloria quizzed him about McGowen and everything that had happened. She got little information.

"Mom said this cop was harassing her," he told his aunt, staring down at his hands.

But when questioned, Jason admitted he'd never seen the two of them together.

Why didn't Susie tell me if she was in trouble? Gloria wondered. Then she remembered they hadn't been as close this past year, with Susan hurt by her insistence that she needed to rein in Jason.

Maybe she just didn't want us to know how out of control her life was, she mused.

The Harrisons were simple people. For the most part, they believed in what they could see and touch. But because Susan's death seemed so monstrous to them, so impossible, they felt themselves afloat, with little to hold onto.

The day before the funeral, one of Susan's nieces saw what appeared to be her aunt Susan standing at her bathroom door.

"I'm all right," the apparition said. "Tell everyone I'm all right."

That night, it happened again. In bed, Susan's father felt a hand as light as a breeze on his shoulder. He heard his lost daughter's voice.

"Daddy, I'm all right."

"Susie?" W.A. said. He turned, but found no one there.

Much of the Harrison family—the cousins, aunts, and uncles—attended Susan's funeral that steamy morning in early September. The talk, as it had been in Houston, gravitated toward the circumstances of her death. How could it have happened? By then, O.L. had a theory: that Susan had feared the three deputies were home-invasion robbers, the type O.L. heard about on television newscasts while staying with Jason the previous spring, the kind who dressed up as police and then robbed homeowners when they opened their doors.

"That's why she didn't open the door," her mother concluded.

"Maybe, Momma," Gloria allowed. But to her, that didn't quite make sense. Susan had known this deputy; she'd been afraid of him.

The day after the funeral, the telephone rang in Gloria's house. When she answered, the funeral director she'd hired for Susan's services said he had something to tell her.

"The funeral-parlor people in Houston asked us to pass along a message," he began, nervously clearing his throat. "Someone at the coroner's office wanted them to tell you something."

"What?" she asked.

"They want you to know that whoever shot your sister wanted her dead. They shot to kill."

The week after Susan's funeral, Sandra, Al, Gloria, and her parents drove to Houston. Sandra brought along Susan's will, the one she'd handwritten not quite three months earlier. They pondered Susan's insistence on the will, her decision to buy a gun. Had she had a premonition that danger lurked not far away?

Dwarfed by the skyscrapers of downtown Houston, they walked from one official county building to the next. They attempted to get a copy of Susan's death certificate, only to learn it hadn't yet been filed. At a window in the district clerk's office, they tracked down a copy of the arrest warrant and read and reread it, hoping for clues.

Why would Susie threaten this Michael Shaffer? they wondered.

From there they walked to the sheriff's department main office, on the first floor of the jail, where a spokesperson detailed the situation as he knew it, insisting Susan had threatened a confidential informant and refused to open the door when the deputies came to her house. She'd held a gun on one of their deputies, and he'd shot her. The spokesperson said he was sorry for their loss, but it was a simple case of self-defense. The deputy had had no choice.

When Gloria requested that the man put his account of the events surrounding her sister's death in writing, he refused and excused himself.

At the D.A.'s office, Don Smyth was out of town and Ed Porter was at a trial, so Gloria made arrangements to call them later from Louisiana. Tired but still determined, the family headed to the courthouse to find Judge Harmon, whom Susan had talked to the morning before her death.

As they stood waiting outside his courtroom, where a frantic and exhausted Susan had stood only two weeks earlier, helplessness and grief weighed on them. Gloria wondered what they had come in search of, what they hoped to find in the tangled web of bureaucracy that constituted government in Houston. The city had once seemed welcoming to her, but now it felt harsh and foreign, frightening, as she warily watched deputies in uniform circulate throughout the courthouse. She wondered if one of them was Kent McGowen, Susie's killer.

Sandra, as weary as her sister, bent down to drink from a hallway water fountain. Suddenly a familiar scent enveloped her, a heavy perfume, sweet and rich—her dead sister's perfume.

She searched about her for the source, but found no one but her mother near.

"Momma, did you smell that?" Sandra asked O.L.

"I did," her mother said, smiling. "Our Susie's with us."

On the six-hour drive home, Gloria, Sandra, and the others recounted everything Susan had ever told them about Jason's troubles and Mike Shaffer, the boy whom police said she'd threatened. For a brief moment, they speculated that Susan's death could have somehow been the work of Ron White. But that didn't make sense. What connection could he have with this deputy, this Kent McGowen? But if Ron wasn't behind Susan's death, what had happened?

"Why would anyone kill our Susie?" a weary O.L. wondered, her eyes wide and spilling over with tears. "The whole thing just flat doesn't make sense."

"Somebody at the coroner's office in Houston told our funeral director the person who shot Susie shot to kill," Gloria informed Don Smyth when she called him from home later that week.

"Mrs. Hamilton, don't worry. As I've told you before, our office is investigating your sister's death," Smyth said matter-of-factly. "We'll get to the bottom of it."

After he hung up, Smyth reviewed the medical examiner's photos of Susan White's body. Three bullets. One grazed her face, entering from the right through the bridge of her nose. The second shattered her right arm. The third sliced into her chest, again from right to left. It was the third wound that had proved fatal, severing a main artery into her heart.

Smyth discounted the relevance of the coroner's message, even doubting it had come from the medical examiner's office. It sounded more like the type of thing someone at the mortuary in Houston could have said. M.E.s understood that police were taught to shoot for the body's biggest target, which was consistent with the fatal wound.

Yet something else Gloria had mentioned during their conversation piqued his interest: Susan White was left-handed, so hopelessly left-handed her family teased her about not being able to wave good-bye with her right hand.

The reason that one fact meant so much to Smyth lay in his walk-through with Kent McGowen. When he'd asked the deputy to reenact White's position at the time of the shooting, McGowen had stood at the side of the bed, pointing a gun at the bedroom door. Only McGowen, pretending to be White, had held the gun in his *right* hand—not his left.

"Curious," Smyth whispered. "Very curious."

Something else gnawed at Smyth: Which of McGowen's shots had hit White first? The one to the chest, the arm, or the face? If the latter, Susan White had had her face turned from McGowen, not staring at him, pointing a gun.

Could she have been turned away from McGowen, hanging up from her second call to 911? Smyth thought that scenario seemed possible. The tape ended with little more than six seconds of the blare of the house alarm, more time than McGowen himself estimated had lapsed between breaking down the back door and standing at White's open bedroom door.

On the tape, White had said, "Okay," before the line went dead.

Could she have been responding to McGowen ordering her to put down the gun?

Had she then reached over to hang up the receiver, on the upper left corner of the bed? If so, that could explain why she'd turned to the left, positioning the right side of her body toward McGowen at the door.

If he could only confirm the order of the shots.

"Impossible," Smyth whispered. "Only McGowen knows that."

But other aspects of the case continued to fall into place for Smyth. White's friends were flooding his office with telephone calls. They claimed White knew Mc-Gowen, that she'd feared him. That would explain her knowing McGowen's name, the fear evident in her voice on the 911 tape as she pleaded to have someone save her from a cop "who thinks he owns the world."

To get to the bottom of the case, Smyth knew he'd need cooperation from McGowen's fellow deputies at Cypresswood, and that could be a problem. He sensed the wagons had begun circling at the sheriff's department. No one there wanted to admit it could be a bad shooting. They had a lieutenant who had given Mc-Gowen permission to serve the warrant, a sergeant who'd authorized him to kick in the door. And cops were loyal. Smyth had a feeling that Sergeant Ruggiero had second thoughts about the shooting, but Lieutenant Coons, even now with the woman dead, had expressed no second thoughts about sending McGowen to White's house that night. He didn't even seem to question the wisdom of allowing a deputy whom the woman had made sexual harassment charges against serve a warrant and break down her door.

With the lieutenant solidly behind McGowen, Smyth knew the sergeant and deputies McGowen worked with would think twice about opening up. The legendary tightness of the Blue Brotherhood was something Smyth had grown used to in his years of investigating and prosecuting police officers.

Still, it wasn't as tough as it had once been to charge a bad cop with his crimes.

In the seventies, a spate of highly publicized disclosures of H.P.D. officer misconduct, including illegal wiretapping and questionable shootings, some involving throw-down guns, had made headlines throughout the city and the country. Federal prosecutors had moved in, spearheading investigations and prosecutions.

In response, the D.A.'s office set up a civil rights division in 1979. Smyth was named its chief in December 1983. At first, deputies and officers looked on him as a headhunter out to get cops. Over the years, he'd earned a reputation as a fair prosecutor, one who pursued the truth. "My code of ethics is to see justice is done, period," says Smyth. "If that means the case needs to be dismissed, I dismiss. If that means the guy needs the death penalty, then that's what we go for. We're not bought or sold."

As his reputation for fairness spread, Smyth detected a metamorphosis. Officers emerged who trusted him enough to come forward to testify about crimes committed by others. It was no longer a case of "my fellow officer, my brother, right or wrong."

He only hoped that in this case, too, he'd find enough of McGowen's peers to clear up the mystery surrounding the case. If McGowen was telling the truth, so be it. If he wasn't, Smyth wanted him on the witness stand, where a jury could judge whether or not Susan White had had to be killed.

With the file on her death open on his desk, Smyth assessed he had three major questions he wanted answered.

First: What was White's relationship with McGowen? Jason and Susan's friends agreed she feared him. Why?

Second: What was the hurry in serving the warrant, a third-degree felony? Why 12:30 at night? Mike Shaffer said he didn't fear White, so where was the urgency? Was Jeannie Jaques, Shaffer's mother, upset about White's call? Did she give McGowen reason to move so quickly?

Third: Why, when White refused to answer the door,

didn't McGowen leave the arrest to Malloy and Morong? Was it because McGowen saw White's arrest as settling something personal?

It had quickly been apparent to Smyth that this was not a chance shooting. Something had happened between McGowen and White. It could have been a romance gone bad. On the other hand, could White's obsession with McGowen be the posturing of an overprotective mother against a deputy who'd arrested her son?

Smyth needed to know a lot more about both McGowen and White, and he would before this investigation ended. Even now, Steve Clappart, the D.A.'s investigator, was questioning McGowen's co-workers and White's neighbors and friends, documenting the events that had led their lives to so fatally intersect.

In the meantime, Smyth judged his best tactic was to keep the investigation as quiet and as separate from the sheriff's department as possible. As far as he was concerned, he was relieved that the hurricane news had pushed the shooting off the front page. He wanted McGowen to feel secure.

"Kent McGowen thinking the investigation was over and he was in the clear?" says Smyth. "Edward Porter and I agreed it sounded like heaven. Because that's when guys screw up, when they think it's all a done deal."

29

Meanwhile, at the Sheriff's Department Homicide Division, Sergeant John Denholm, McGowen's former supervisor at the county jail, pored over the same evidence Smyth and Porter had before them. Like Clappart, he and others in his office were asking questions about McGowen and Susan White.

Together with Detective Ronnie Robertson, Denholm compiled a profile of McGowen. From Tomball, he learned of McGowen's claim of threats by Colombian drug lords. Leroy Michna told him that as far as he was concerned, the entire episode had been a ruse. At Precinct Four, Denholm heard an account of the gun butt McGowen had administered to Daniel Newrones' forehead, and how he'd lied about working security at the apartment complex. Finally, at H.P.D., he learned of McGowen's jacket formed of dishonesty and ego, his unsuccessful attempts at rehire, and his scalding exit evaluation.

What Denholm discovered only reinforced the opinion of McGowen he'd formed during their months working together at the county jail: that McGowen was a womanizer and a habitual liar, a man whose opinion of himself far exceeded the opinions of others.

"What I'd felt all along was true," says Denholm, shaking his head in disgust. "McGowen was someone who squeaked into the department, someone who never should have been wearing a badge."

At the same time, Steve Clappart, the D.A. investigator, wove together a similar profile of McGowen. "I'd never investigated an officer shooting before where the victim knew the officer," remembers Clappart. "I got a funny little feeling. Something was wrong."

At first, the deputies at Cypresswood were reticent to open up with Clappart, all except Ruggiero. To Clappart, the sergeant appeared troubled by what had happened, that he gave the order to break down White's door. And it was plain that he didn't like McGowen.

Slowly, Clappart made inroads. At times the telephone in his office would ring, or a deputy would pull him to the side at the courthouse.

"I heard this guy knows something about McGowen," they'd say. "But don't tell anyone I'm the one who told you."

When he followed up on the information, the deputies Clappart confronted would at first deny they knew anything about Kent McGowen that might help Clappart's investigation, but when he pressed just a bit, they opened up, eager to tell all they knew. "McGowen's coworkers weren't volunteering anything," says Clappart. "But no one was willing to lie for him either."

One deputy Clappart didn't hear from was Al Kelly, who worked days in McGowen's old contract. Kelly was sitting tight. "If I get the opportunity, I ought to kill that fucking bitch," McGowen had told him. Kelly disliked

McGowen, that was true, but he knew telling anyone what he'd heard would drag him into the fray, forcing him to testify against a fellow deputy. Kelly decided if anyone asked him, he'd tell the truth, but he wasn't offering any information.

Still, before long, enough deputies had come forward for Clappart to feel he understood the situation at Cypresswood on the days preceding White's killing. He realized how few of McGowen's fellow deputies trusted him and that so many openly questioned his ability to distinguish the truth from a lie.

Equally important, none of the other deputies at Cypresswood had any information involving gunrunning at 3407 Amber Forest. Although many had quelled loud parties there or dealt with a distraught Susan or a rebellious Jason, not one besides McGowen claimed to have even heard rumors about automatic weapons.

After building a profile of McGowen's time at Cypresswood, Clappart polled friends at H.P.D., where he'd worked for twenty-four years before retiring and joining the D.A.'s staff. He again heard the word "liar" repeated by nearly everyone he interviewed about McGowen. "The badge was important to McGowen," Clappart assesses, piecing together the threads he collected of McGowen's character. "That McGowen didn't step back and let other officers handle Susan White's arrest when she offered to open the door if he left—that smacked of a personal deal, like he was teaching her a lesson."

When he interviewed Sara Williams, the H.P.D. officer with whom McGowen had once had a fling, Clappart saw a picture forming. Like Susan White, Williams was older than McGowen, tall, and blond. With McGowen's love of wealth, Clappart thought he could envision how the young cop's path had crossed with the troubled woman in the big house: "I grew to believe that Mc-Gowen had a fixation on Susan White. She was an attractive woman he knew to be single [separated at the time], driving a classy little car. He hit on her like policemen do. Maybe it was flattering to her to have this younger guy hustle her, but he didn't have anything she wanted. I figured she rejected him. Susan White wanted any new husband to have money, and McGowen didn't have shit. I figured McGowen went after the boy to show her he was the one in charge. He thought, 'I'll fix that rich bitch.' "

As far as Clappart was concerned, it seemed all too clear: The reason McGowen had made a beeline to the bedroom, ignoring his training to carefully check each room, tied in with his obsession with White; he knew where she'd be that night because he'd watched her house; he knew the layout.

When Clappart reviewed McGowen's spotted record, another possible motive for killing Susan White became clear: White's threats to file a formal complaint against him. "McGowen couldn't risk that. He'd already moved so far down the rope he was nothing more than a glorified security guard. To a guy with a big ego, who'd battled Colombian cartels and all in his mind, that's quite a comedown," says Clappart. "It was obvious McGowen had watched too many episodes of *Miami Vice*. He saw himself driving a Ferrari and wearing designer clothes. H.P.D. did the most wonderful thing H.P.D. had ever done—they didn't rehire Kent McGowen. His gig with the sheriff's department was Podunk, but it was his last grab at being a policeman, his last little grasp at a decent policing agency."

Another ominous possibility presented itself to Clappart when he heard that McGowen had lied about having killed someone in the line of duty while at H.P.D., and that he'd sometimes carried a briefcase with photos of corpses at crime scenes. To his abhorrence, Clappart judged he was dealing with a cop who fantasized about taking a human life.

*   *   *

When Clappart reported to Smyth and Porter, the two A.D.A.s drew similar conclusions. "The whole thing smelled bad," says Smyth. "None of the evidence pointed to McGowen's version being the truth."

While Smyth didn't know if McGowen intended to kill White when he arrived at her home late that night, he felt certain of one thing: When the opportunity to shoot to kill presented itself, McGowen took it.

But another factor impressed Smyth and Porter even more as they reviewed Clappart's evidence: his interview with Mike Shaffer's mother. During the conversation, Jeannie Jaques repeatedly insisted that she had no fear Susan White would injure her son. "I'm just a normal human being. I don't deal with cops every day of my life. I rely on them to tell me what is needed, what's fixing to happen," she told him. "Susan White was a stranger. McGowen, a deputy, tells me there's this crazy lady talking about killing Michael. I'm not worried until he tells me I should be worried."

Yet when Porter interviewed Jean Spradling-Hughes and Jim Mount, the two A.D.A.s who'd taken McGowen's charges against White, they insisted he'd stressed Jaques' fear, repeatedly saying that she felt Susan White could kill her son. Mount recalled how determined the deputy had been to get the warrant signed immediately, to the extent that he wanted to wake up a judge. In fact, McGowen seemed determined to serve the warrant on White personally.

After the interviews with Jaques, Mount, and Spradling-Hughes, Smyth and Porter believed they might have a case worthy of a trial. If the warrant was bad, if he lied to get it, they reasoned, McGowen had no more right to break down Susan White's door than did a burglar. Then, even if she pulled a gun on him, she was justified in doing so, not unlike any citizen awakened in the middle of the night by an intruder with a gun.

Still, Smyth had no illusions about the strength of his case. First, there was Susan White's own history. She was a troubled woman, a portrait McGowen's defense attorneys would paint in broad strokes during a trial. And she had a history of addiction to prescription drugs, documented in her autopsy blood work, which found traces of not only Valium but amphetamines.

Second, try though they had, they'd uncovered neither evidence nor witnesses to substantiate White's claims that McGowen had sexually harassed her. In fact, they couldn't even prove that White and McGowen had known each other, beyond their brief official encounters.

In his prosecutor's gut, Smyth sensed something *had* happened between White and McGowen, but all he had as evidence were her allegations to friends, three months of whispers that she feared McGowen, that he'd threatened to hurt her or Jason if she refused a relationship with him. And Smyth was painfully aware that with Susan dead and unable to testify and be cross-examined, such statements, as tantalizing as they might be, constituted hearsay, inadmissible in a court of law.

Looking over the evidence, Smyth, Clappart, and Porter all agreed it seemed likely that Kent McGowen had murdered Susan White. Yet they wondered if they'd ever be able to prove it. They knew juries preferred to believe that police officers didn't break the law, that a deputy wouldn't hunt down a woman and kill her in her bed.

In Smyth's mind, McGowen had put in motion all the events leading to the confrontation in Susan White's bedroom, and the warrant he'd lied to get for her arrest was worthless. But that McGowen had a warrant, even a tainted one, presented a particular problem: Never in the history of the state of Texas had a deputy serving a warrant been convicted of murder.

As damaged as that warrant might be, Smyth wondered if it was damaged enough.

Then, a month after the killing, the A.D.A. got a call—a call that would lead to an answer Smyth had hoped for but feared he'd never find.

"I've got some information," said Detective John Denholm. "We need to talk."

In Smyth's office that afternoon, the husky cop with the blunt manner sized up the two A.D.A.s sitting across from him. He knew they didn't trust him. There'd been plenty of indications that the D.A.'s office wanted its investigation separate from his at the sheriff's department. In fact, Smyth had taken the unprecedented step of submitting a written request to the head of the Homicide Division for all records and copies of tapes involving McGowen and the case. Denholm judged that Smyth and Porter were worried that someone in the department, some friend of McGowen's, might destroy evidence. Plus, he knew they didn't want anyone leaking information to McGowen. They wanted him to feel he was in the clear. A relaxed suspect felt freer to talk, not compelled to watch every word.

Denholm had taken similar steps to keep his investigation as quiet as possible. He didn't want an alarmed McGowen any more than Smyth and Porter did. In fact, when Denholm ran into McGowen while working a second job at a country-and-western nightclub two weeks earlier, he'd even reassured him.

"Is everything all right with that shooting?" McGowen asked. "Have they finished looking into it yet?"

"The way I heard it, you had a warrant, Kent," Denholm answered. "Why wouldn't it be okay?"

"Yeah," Kent said, smiling.

Now it appeared that maintaining secrecy might have

given Kent McGowen the rope he needed to tie his own noose.

"I got a call," Denholm began. "Kent's been shooting off his mouth to friends working the jail. He's saying some pretty bizarre things."

"Like what?" Porter said, his eyes burning with sudden interest.

"Seems McGowen came into the jail the other day with a copy of the nine-one-one tape and played it for a bunch of his pals," he said.

"We already heard that," said Smyth. "Steve Clappart heard the same report." What Smyth didn't add was that when Clappart related the event to him, he did so with disgust, commenting that McGowen's fascination with the tape reminded him of a serial killer who collected an ear from a victim.

"Well, Kent did something else," Denholm continued. Ruggiero, he said, had heard through the jail grapevine that McGowen had concocted a bizarre story involving the brass, the shell casings from the bullets that had killed Susan White. In truth, they remained in departmental custody, awaiting the outcome of the investigation. If McGowen was indicted, they'd become evidence. If not, they'd be destroyed.

But McGowen, alleged Ruggiero's source, had told something vastly different to a young deputy named Jeff Copeland. As the story went, while at the jail, Kent McGowen had bragged to Copeland that he was there to pick up a souvenir of White's killing.

"He told Copeland the department mounts the brass to commemorate the event whenever a deputy kills a citizen," said Denholm.

The two A.D.A.s looked at each other with knowing glances. If Ruggiero's source was right, Kent McGowen had bragged about getting a trophy as a memento of killing a human being, much like mounting a deer head with antlers to hang on the wall. What better evidence could there be that he viewed the warrant he'd held in his hand that night as a hunting license?

"Thanks, John," Porter said, holding out his hand. "We appreciate it."

"No problem," Denholm answered, sensing from Porter's extended hand and the new respect he saw in Smyth's eyes that he'd just passed a test. If they hadn't been sure they could trust him when he'd walked in the door, they now understood he was on their side, not McGowen's.

The day after Denholm's visit to Smyth's office, the two assistant D.A.s sat across from Jeff Copeland, a tall, broad, moon-faced deputy who worked at the county jail.

"We understand Kent McGowen made a visit to the jail," Smyth began.

"Kent?" Copeland answered nervously. "Sure, he stops in sometimes."

"We understand he came in to pick up a trophy," Smyth continued. "The brass casings from the shoot."

"Nah," Copeland said, fidgeting in his chair. "I didn't hear him say anything about that."

Smyth glanced with disappointment at Porter.

"He didn't say that to you?" Porter asked pointedly, staring down at Copeland over his half-moon glasses.

"No, sir," Copeland said.

"Well, we understand McGowen talked to you," Porter continued. "What *did* he tell you about the shooting?"

"Just about the way he shot her, that's all," Copeland replied flatly.

"The way he shot?" Smyth said, reining in his excitement. The order of McGowen's shots was a mystery Smyth never thought he'd solve, a mystery that could answer many questions.

"Yes, sir," Copeland said.

"What did he say?" Porter asked.

"He said he shot the reverse of the way the Feds do."

"The Feds?" asked Smyth, who'd never heard of any such special order of shots. "How do they shoot?"

"Well, Kent says he saw a D.E.A. movie and that they shoot to the body first," said Copeland with a shrug. "But he said he did the opposite, to the face first and then two to the body."

"Hmmm," said Porter. "He didn't shoot to the chest first?"

"Nope," said Copeland, oblivious to any importance attached to the information. "He said the first shot was to the head."

Before he left the office that afternoon, Copeland signed a statement recounting his conversation with McGowen. Once they were alone, Smyth turned to Porter, his smile broad. "That boy doesn't have a clue to what he just handed us."

Porter nodded.

McGowen's admission that the first shot fired was the one to White's face was a powerful piece of evidence. That first bullet could only have grazed Susan White's face from the right side, as it did, if she was turned away from him at the time he squeezed the trigger. With this bit of information, Smyth and Porter had evidence to place before a jury proving that Susan White was not, as McGowen had claimed, standing at the side of her bed, facing him, threatening him with the .25 at the time he fired.

For the two prosecutors, the scene in the bedroom that night now fell into place: They felt even more certain White had turned to her left, away from McGowen, probably to put the telephone down, when the first shot rang out. That bullet tore right to left through the bridge of her nose. McGowen's second shot tore through her chest, also with a right-to-left slant. The third shot shattered the bone in her upper right arm.

Their conclusion: Kent McGowen's claim of self-defense was a lie.

30

News filtered through the circle of Susan White's friends and family in late September and early October that prosecutors were getting ready to move, and that the facts surrounding her death would soon be put before a grand jury. In Louisiana, O.L. and W.A. Harrison and their family received a personal call from Don Smyth.

"There are no guarantees," he cautioned. "But we feel we have enough to go with. Then, whether or not to indict will be up to the grand jurors."

"Everyone involved believed there should be an indictment, but no one knew what a grand jury would do with it," says Steve Clappart, recalling that day in mid-October when Don Smyth and Edward Porter brought the McGowen case to the grand jury.

The twelve citizens of Harris County called upon to consider the killing of Susan White had been impaneled in August and considered nearly 1,400 cases, most of them drug-related, during the first two and a half months of their ninety-day tenure. Most of the twelve jurors were middle-class and white, including a dog groomer, an architect, realtors, and a small contingent of retirees. The grand jury had the power to no-bill: in essence, to conclude that the D.A.'s office lacked sufficient evidence to indict McGowen with a crime. But if nine of the twelve agreed, they could formally charge McGowen with a crime that ranged from manslaughter to murder.

As he addressed the grand jury on the McGowen case during that first afternoon, Smyth distributed a notebook to each. Inside were signed and notarized witness statements, a copy of White's autopsy, a diagram of White's home, and a sketch of the bedroom and the angles of McGowen's shots.

From Clappart to Denholm to Porter, all involved in the investigation worried that though they'd collected evidence they believed showed a pattern of behavior on McGowen's part that led to murder, a grand jury would have a difficult time getting past the fact that McGowen had a warrant signed by a judge for White's arrest.

Afternoons passed slowly as the grand jurors reviewed the evidence and issued subpoenas for witnesses. The first to testify was McGowen, whom a juror would later describe as arrogant, as if "we were wasting his time." When Smyth asked him to demonstrate how White had confronted him with the gun, as he had done at the walk-through, McGowen held the gun in his right hand and stood straight, pointing the gun at a make-believe bedroom door. Smyth pulled out a camera and snapped photos.

"Is there anything else you'd like to tell us?" one juror asked McGowen as the session ended.

"Just that I've had lots of other chances to kill people, and I didn't do it," he said, to their astonishment.

Uniforms filled the waiting room as Lieutenant Coons, Sergeant Ruggiero, and others from Cypresswood waited to testify. During one session, Smyth asked Coons if he had any second thoughts about allowing

McGowen, whom White had said she feared, to gain a warrant for her arrest and break down her door.

The lieutenant maintained he'd never second-guessed his decision. Many on the grand jury were stunned as he insisted he couldn't let a citizen's claims dictate his office's actions.

"It was pure macho," says one grand juror.

On other days, Susan's friends, including Helen Bazata and Ray Valentine, recounted the last months of her life. In the grand jury room, unlike in an actual trial, hearsay was allowed, and Valentine dabbed tears from his ample cheeks as he repeated White's warning to him during one of their final conversations.

"I didn't believe McGowen was after her," he said. "I thought she was just being dramatic. She told me one day I'd believe her, but that by then she'd be dead and McGowen would have killed her. And that's exactly what happened."

Despite the testimony, as the days passed, something seemed missing. The jurors grew to believe McGowen had known the woman he'd killed, possibly had threatened her. Copeland's testimony and evidence that White was left-handed made them question the truthfulness of McGowen's claim that she'd held a gun on him and, therefore, that he'd shot in self-defense. Yet the deputy *did* have a warrant signed by a judge, and a gun *had* been found in Susan White's bedroom. How could they know whether it was murder or a sloppy arrest gone wrong?

Then, on a Tuesday, just days before they were set to disband, one juror mentioned the notarized statement of Jeannie Jaques. "I stayed up half the night thinking about it. The darn thing seems vague to me," he said. "Let's get her in here."

The next afternoon, Jaques, who'd driven in from Austin, stood before them. When they asked the petite woman with the long, light brown hair the question she'd been asked so many times—Did she fear Susan White would injure or kill her son?—she replied as she had consistently since the shooting. "No," she declared. "Until Kent McGowen told me I needed to be worried, I wasn't worried."

"If you believe it was a good warrant, Kent McGowen had every legal right to be in that house. If you believe she pulled a gun on him like he says she did, he had every legal right to kill her," Smyth advised the jurors before they began their deliberations. "But if you believe the warrant was a lie, then Kent McGowen is a murderer."

With that, Smyth and Porter withdrew to allow the grand jurors to consider the evidence before them. In hindsight, Smyth would say this was one of only a few cases he'd presented to a grand jury where he had no clear indication of what they might do. He hoped for a murder charge but was concerned that if he got an indictment at all, it might be for a lesser offense.

Meanwhile, as the jurors deliberated behind closed doors, a lively argument ensued miles away at the sheriff's department. The McGowen case had ignited many a bitter exchange since Susan White died two months earlier. A contingent of deputies believed McGowen—right or wrong—shouldn't be charged with murder. They insisted that whether or not he had lied to obtain the warrant, it was signed by a judge and therefore valid. They argued further that it was undisputed that White had resisted arrest and that no one but McGowen could say if she'd threatened him with a gun. Any deputy in such a situation, they declared, had an implicit right to shoot to kill.

But others, like Denholm, saw the very same warrant—which some labeled as McGowen's salvation—as a law officer's gravest sin, a bastardization of the legal system they all served. McGowen had manipulated the system for his own purposes, they argued, to hunt down White and kill her.

Still, in the end, the only opinions that mattered were those of the twelve grand jurors considering the case. Finally, on October 28, 1992, the day before their in-panelment ended, news spread that the grand jury had reached a verdict. Not knowing what to expect, Smyth rushed to their meeting room, where the foreman handed him their decision. As he read the words before him, a smile spread across "Whispering Don" Smyth's face. In his hand he held a formal indictment, charging Kent McGowen with murder.

That afternoon, Internal Affairs ordered McGowen to report to headquarters for a meeting. Denholm and others who knew his fate gathered to watch as the young deputy walked jauntily down the long corridor to I.A. He appeared not to sense what awaited him.

Minutes later, another McGowen emerged from Internal Affairs, handcuffed, head bowed. As he passed his former boss, he shot Denholm a timid glance.

"He looked like someone had hit him with a sledgehammer," remembers Denholm, who returned McGowen's gaze with a satisfied smile.

Within hours, Houston's newspapers and television stations heard the whispers—a deputy indicted for murder. At 5 P.M. that same afternoon, a spokesman for the Harris County Deputy Sheriff's Association called a hasty press conference to contend that McGowen was an innocent pawn in a political battle between Harris County D.A. John B. Holmes Jr. and Sheriff John Klevenhagen.

"It's all a big political game," he charged in a sound bite picked up by the nightly news. "Don Smyth pressured the grand jury into indicting this officer because Smyth is biased against the department."

By that evening, McGowen was free on $20,000 bond. At home that night with his family, Denholm thought back to the afternoon's events, remembering the vanquished look in McGowen's eyes.

"He really believed he'd get away with it," says Denholm. "I don't think it ever occurred to him that he'd finally gotten himself in a mess he couldn't talk himself out of."

31

In the delay-ridden, Dickensian bureaucracy of the court system, it took more than a year before Kent McGowen stepped before a jury. From Louisiana, Susan White's family, usually Gloria, called often, beseeching Don Smyth for a date when they could expect to see the man accused of murdering their Susie stand before a jury.

Smyth reassured her that they needed to be patient, their day in court would come.

Six months before the trial was scheduled to begin, a shake-up hit the rank and file at the district attorney's office. Smyth was transferred to head one of the D.A.'s trial divisions, in charge of a group of felony courts. The new head of civil rights and his replacement on the case was quickly named. Belinda Hill, an A.D.A. promoted from overseeing prosecutors assigned to a district court, was the first woman and the first African-American to head the office.

Smyth would later insist that he wasn't worried about the McGowen case or the others he left behind. Hill had a reputation as a bright and able prosecutor. And Edward Porter knew the McGowen case front to back. "I knew Ed, I knew he could handle it, with or without me," says Smyth.

In fact, Porter had latched onto the McGowen case from the beginning. A one-time public defender in Jacksonville, Florida, who'd moved to Texas to join the D.A.'s office, Porter had won a high-profile case two years earlier, the prosecution of the son of a wealthy Houston car dealer who'd fled with his two young sons, violating their mother's custody order. The case had made headlines as the man traversed through Scotland and Switzerland, to Greece, and finally to Mexico, avoiding prosecution.

In some ways, Porter didn't fit the stereotype of a typical prosecutor. He'd grown up in a military family and liked to call himself a "Navy brat," usually with a good-natured chuckle. An antiwar protester during the sixties and an amateur photographer who loved to backpack through the Texas tundra, Porter was a Bruce Springsteen fan who'd played in a hybrid rock-and-roll-and-blues band right after high school. Yet those who paused at his office door often heard him humming along with Puccini's *Madama Butterfly* on his office stereo.

Porter relished his work in the D.A.'s civil rights division. "Officers are human, they make mistakes," he explains. "But we trust them with so much. We give them a tremendous amount of authority over us. When you have a truly bad officer, it's a service to boot him out."

Of course, with McGowen, Porter hoped to do more than deprive an officer of a badge. With McGowen, it was a question of murder.

On the last Saturday night in February 1994, just three days before McGowen's trial was scheduled to begin, Ray Valentine hovered at a corner table in Resa's. Alan

Jefferies had left the year before, and the new piano player pounded out Roy Orbison's "Pretty Woman," singing over the din of a crush of laughing patrons.

While others might have been celebrating, Valentine was in a foul mood, shooting down drinks and eager to talk to anyone who'd listen about the miscarriage of justice he felt certain would soon take place. "Far as I'm concerned, it's a waste of time," he blustered. "There's no way they're gonna pin shit on McGowen. Whole thing's a charade."

Valentine then contended that it didn't matter if the deputies McGowen worked with hated him—and he knew many of them did; they would never testify against him under oath. And without them, Porter had a tough case.

"I've worked with cops for years, running the circus, raising money. I know how they think. Cops stick together. Bottom line," he said, looping together his right and left index fingers like links in a chain. "Cops don't break the code. No way *any* cop is going to testify against McGowen. Not a rat's-ass chance. That sniveling coward's gunned down a woman in cold blood and, no doubt about it, he's going to go free."

32

The gavel sounded in the austere courtroom of the 232nd District Court of Harris County, Texas, on the morning of Tuesday, March 1, 1994, calling to order case number 647,853, The State of Texas vs. Joseph K. McGowen.

The previous day, a panel of forty-three potential jurors had lined the wooden benches, there to be questioned by Edward Porter and Belinda Hill, for the state. And for the defense: Clint Greenwood, a man of medium height, his face roughed as if he'd had his share of childhood playground altercations, a man who looked as if he relished a good fight; and Brian Benken, his partner and his antithesis, tall and blond, with patrician features.

They'd asked potential jurors a series of questions: Do you believe a deputy on duty can commit crimes? Could you find an officer guilty of murder? Have you had any negative experience with law enforcement officers? Have you or your families or friends ever been in trouble with the law? With the Harris County sheriff's office? The prosecutors needed to weed out jurors who were so pro-police, they'd be unable to come down hard on an offending officer; the defense team had the opposite duty, to identify anyone with an ax to grind against deputies in general or the sheriff's department in particular.

One by one, jurors were excused, until only twelve remained, the eleven men and one woman who raised their hands and were sworn in by Judge A.D. Azios.

Kent McGowen and his attorneys stood at attention as Edward Porter read the charge for the jury: "On or about August 25, 1992 . . . did then and there unlawfully, intentionally, and knowingly cause the death of Susan White, by shooting her with a deadly weapon, namely a firearm. . . . Joseph K. McGowen did then and there unlawfully intend to cause serious bodily injury to Susan White and did cause her death. . . . against the peace and dignity of the state."

"Mr. McGowen, how do you plead?" asked Azios, a short man with dark eyes framed by a somber face, his hair graying at the temples.

"Not guilty," McGowen answered.

"All right," Azios answered. "All the witnesses in The State of Texas versus Joseph K. McGowen please stand, raise your hand, and be sworn."

The trial of Kent McGowen had officially commenced.

Valentine had been right about one thing: Porter had a tough battle ahead of him. Despite months of pretrial preparation, prosecutors still had no one to swear that Susan White and Kent McGowen even knew each other. Without a witness who had personal knowledge of what had transpired between Susan White and Kent McGowen, hearsay regulations on testimony, barring second-hand information, would restrict much of what Porter could put before the jury. In fact, under the laws of evidence, it would be a fight for prosecutors to introduce any evidence of Susan's fears to the jury.

That first day set the scene for the two weeks to follow. Ed Porter and Belinda Hill, surrounded by boxed files, conferred at a table to the right of the judge, near the jury box. Porter sipped throughout the trial on water from a white-and-pink plastic Weight Watchers mug, intent yet seemingly unconcerned, as Hill, with her matter-of-fact gaze, assessed the gain or loss to their case with each witness' testimony.

Susan's family, her sisters tall and blond, her aging parents, their eyes often misting over with tears, positioned themselves in the gallery, just a few rows away. Gloria's husband, Al, came every day. It would take a toll on the family, traveling from Louisiana once a week, staying in a hotel or with family, but they were determined to see it through, clinging to each other and each bit of evidence.

At a table to the left of the prosecutors sat Kent McGowen, scribbling notes on a legal pad, wearing a gray suit and a quiet tie. At times he appeared glassy-eyed, and his father would later say that Kent was on antidepressants, a byproduct, he claimed, of the anxiety caused by the "unfair" charges and subsequent trial.

Beside their client sat Greenwood and Benken, surrounded by their own crates of meticulously organized files. Later, a source close to the two attorneys would say McGowen had left them woefully ill-prepared. "McGowen lied about everything," the man explained. "They had no idea what Porter had against him."

From their first witness—namely, the assistant medical examiner, Dr. Vladimir Parungao, a native of the Philippines who'd worked in the M.E.'s office for some thirteen years—to each succeeding witness, the prosecution attempted to build evidence discrediting McGowen's version of White's shooting.

The defense, conversely, painted a picture of McGowen as a dedicated officer doing his job that night eighteen months earlier, and Susan and her son as unstable criminals. Kent McGowen, they argued, had no motive other than self-defense.

With Porter asking the questions, Parungao dissected autopsy number 92-5567. Aided by prosecution exhibits numbers 1 to 8, photographs of the three gunshot wounds through White's body, the doctor traced the path of each bullet, using Porter as White's stand-in and a pen to illustrate the paths of the bullets: one through the bridge of her nose; one to her right arm, shattering the major bone and artery; the third on a diagonal right-to-left route through the chest.

"You can't tell which bullet is the first bullet, second bullet, third bullet?" Porter asked.

"That's correct," the physician replied. "I can't tell."

Aligning his body with his right side facing Parungao, his right arm tucked at his side, Porter asked if that position matched, according to the bullet paths, the one in which Susan White must have been at the time of the shooting.

"That's correct," Parungao agreed.

"If I'd been facing you, could. . . . the one through the nose have entered the way it did?"

"No," he answered. "If you're facing me, I'm going to hit the nose direct, going [front to] back."

Porter smiled.

When he asked Parungao the cause of death, the A.M.E. targeted the gunshot wound to the chest, which, he explained, cut through the lungs, the pericardial sac, slicing twice through the aorta, the pulmonary artery.

"Would she have died instantly?"

The wound would have caused an immediate drop in blood pressure that most likely threw White into unconsciousness, explained the physician, leaving her body to helplessly convulse.

"What you're talking about is called death tremors, where the body just kind of shakes?" Porter asked. O.L.

and her daughters could be heard quietly sobbing in the gallery.

"We call them convulsions, but you can call them that," concluded the doctor.

After Parungao, Porter called Deputy Daniel Rinehart of the Sheriff's Department Identification Division, the crime-scene investigator at 3407 Amber Forest the night of the shooting. Rinehart testified that White's telephone/answering machine had been found on the left side of her bed, which fit the theory Porter would later lay before the jury—that White had turned to her left to hang up the receiver as McGowen pulled the trigger. The deputy went on to identify the casings found on the scene and the bullets taken from White's body. Then, just before lunch that first day of trial, Rinehart testified to a startling fact: White's .25-caliber semiautomatic pistol, found on the bedroom floor after the shooting, the one McGowen claimed White had pointed at him, bore only one fingerprint—not Susan White's, but Kent McGowen's.

After the jurors were dismissed for lunch, Clint Greenwood addressed Azios. "It's just been brought to my attention by someone in the courtroom that the family of Ms. White, sisters or whatever, female relatives sitting back there, are sniffling, booing, crying. They're all displaying a picture of Susan White so the jury can see it. Would you admonish . . ."

Azios, the first Hispanic judge elected in the county, looked at Greenwood and frowned, then turned to the Harrisons and their daughters. O.L. gingerly concealed the black-and-white modeling photo of her dead daughter on her lap. Her eyes still glistened with the tears that had clouded them throughout the morning's testimony.

Sternly, Azios instructed O.L. and her family to retain their composure throughout the trial. "If you want to cry or express any remorse or sadness, go in the hall," he said. "I don't want that picture shown." He concluded by assuring Greenwood that at the slightest show of emotion, Susan White's relatives would be removed from the room.

With that, the courtroom broke for lunch. Once outside the beige brick building with its heavy glass doors, the Harrisons just stood there, dejected. How could they listen to such testimony without their emotions overtaking them? They'd already learned many lessons about the court system, that it moved slowly and, at times, seemingly without common sense. Now they knew it to be heartless.

Porter's examination of Rinehart continued as the afternoon session began, lasting only long enough to establish that of the weapons on the scene—including Morong's and Malloy's—only McGowen's had been fired. It was therefore the weapon used to fire the fatal shots.

As defense attorneys are trained to do, once Clint Greenwood took on Rinehart for cross-examination, he concentrated on what wasn't done on the scene that night in August. Why hadn't the bedclothes been collected as evidence? Why weren't fiber samples taken from Mrs. White's clothing? Why hadn't Rinehart noted the positioning of the blood on the bed? Greenwood was implying for the jury that the crime-scene unit had done a shoddy job. When it came to the fingerprint on White's gun, the attorney ran through a litany of the people who had handled it after the killing, and implied that there should have been many sets of prints on it, not only McGowen's. Finally, he turned to a theme he would repeat throughout the trial.

"The area of the bedroom was pretty trashy, is that an apt description?" Greenwood asked.

Displaying photo after photo of the rooms in White's

house, Greenwood repeated his question. "How about this room? Is that neatly kept?"

"No," Rinehart replied each time, appearing confused by the question. "It's not."

"Is that a neatly kept bed. . . . a neatly kept floor. . . . a neatly kept bedroom? Did it strike you as odd that that quality of a home located in that neighborhood was sparsely furnished, that there were not the accouterments in the house that you would expect with that type of a home?"

At this point, Porter objected, disputing the relevancy of Greenwood's questions. Azios overruled the objection, allowing the defense attorney, who appeared to just be hitting his stride in complaining of the unkempt nature of Susan White's house, to continue. Was Greenwood implying that White's untidy house branded her a criminal ripe for killing?

Next, Steve Clappart took the stand and, under questioning by Porter, narrated a video he'd made of the scene just days after the shooting. On a courtroom television, Clappart could be seen stringing a line from a bullet nick in a television cable box near the bedroom door to the hole in the wall where a bullet had been recovered. The bullet was the only one not found in White's body, the one that had grazed her nose. The string hung low over the left upper quadrant of the bed—more proof, Porter insisted, that Susan White had been low to the bed and turned toward her left when McGowen fired that particular shot. To illustrate, he lay down diagonally across the defense table.

"Is this the way she must have been to be hit by that bullet after it hit the converter box and before it hit the wall?" Porter asked.

"Yes," Clappart answered.

After Clappart, Porter called C.E. Anderson to the stand, a senior examiner in charge of H.P.D.'s firearms laboratory. With Anderson, Porter confirmed that the bullet that killed White had identical markings to those shot through Kent McGowen's pistol during a test. That done, he returned his attention to the trajectory of the bullets. From a large, clear-plastic evidence bag, Porter took the blood-soaked pink nightgown and thick brown robe Susan had worn the night she died. As he displayed them for the jury, their stunned eyes trailed down the once-red blood now cured a faded brown. Some quickly averted their gaze, while others openly stared, transfixed at the evidence.

With her own blood, Porter had brought Susan White into the courtroom, for the first time making her real for the jury.

33

The following morning, Judge Azios called the court to order as both a U.S. and a Texas flag quivered in the breeze of the air conditioner. Although his courthouse reputation pegged him a kind man, the judge objected to any characterization of him as defendant-friendly. In a mention he seemed most proud of, his appearance in *Daddy's Girl*, a 1988 book by Clifford Irving on another Texas murder case, Azios had raised an aging, balled-up hand and warned, "Don't characterize *me* as compassionate. If a man's violent and I smell no remorse. I give him *la chingada* [an expletive]."

After the gavel fell, C.E. Anderson resumed his position in the witness box, microphone before him. Anderson's testimony would prove long and tedious as Porter and Greenwood, an amateur gunsmith, questioned him at length about holes that McGowen's bullets had torn through White's bathrobe. Greenwood scored points as a confused Anderson admitted he'd once wondered if White's bathrobe was worn inside out. He seemed unsure of the position of White's right arm at the time of the shooting. Could it have been extended out, as if she'd held a gun on Kent McGowen? Anderson, for all his years in ballistics, didn't know.

Next, Porter recalled Rinehart and Clappart with minor points, and then turned his full attention to Rhonda Watson, a custodian of records overseeing 911 tapes. Watson was an important witness for Porter. Susan White could be heard in the courtroom only if he were allowed to play the emergency calls made to 911. But would Judge Azios agree with the defense and rule the tape containing the phone calls constituted hearsay, secondhand information inadmissible in court because Susan White could not be put on the stand for cross-examination? Porter needed the judge to buy his argument, that the tape fell into an exception in the laws of evidence.

With jurors closeted in the jury room, Porter and Hill passionately argued in favor of the admissibility of the tape. During her frantic conversation with the emergency operator, White had made serious allegations against McGowen, charging he'd harassed and threatened her, the types of claims that could go a long way toward swaying the jury.

Conversely, Benken began the argument against admitting it by questioning Watson's function as a witness: "The tape certainly doesn't fall under the business record [exemption to hearsay] and should not be admitted through this witness."

Porter replied that Watson's only purpose in the courtroom was to testify to the integrity of the tape, which he asserted accurately recorded the conversation of August 25. He insisted the tape itself fell under various exceptions to hearsay exclusions, including that it was an excited utterance, that with police pounding on her door, Susan White would have been in such an ag-

itated state that she could not have had the presence of
mind to manufacture an untrue story.

"It is admissible because the integrity is that, at the
moment that this is occurring, she doesn't have time to
reflect and make up things as to why she's engaging in
that conduct," Porter said. "Her state of mind at that
point is that she is afraid of the man."

"Asking the jury to hear an allegation of sexual harassment which has no basis . . . that's not an excited utterance," Benken countered. "It just does not fit, Judge,
and is too highly prejudicial."

Both sides cited cases. Finally Azios spoke: "[It goes
to] state of mind to call nine-one-one to stress as a present situation a knock on the door, but not to any allegation that the defendant had sexually harassed her
before." His ruling—the tape was admissible with the
charges of sexual harassment excised.

Benken and Porter continued their posturing, but
Azios stood firm. In truth, each side had won a victory.
Benken had deleted the most damaging of Susan White's
words, and Porter would play the tape. The jury could
hear the fear in Susan White's voice for themselves, her
claims that Kent McGowen was "a cop who thinks he
owns the world," one who'd threatened her in the past.

After using Watson to introduce the tape to the jurors,
Porter excused her, explaining that they'd hear the tape
itself the following morning. Then, as his final witness
of the day, Jason Aguillard was sworn in and took the
stand.

The Jason who sat before the jury that afternoon looked
markedly different from the mug shot in his police file.
With his light brown hair cut short at the neck and
combed boyishly to the side, dressed in a trim shirt and
pants, the earring abandoned, he projected an appearance that supported what he told jurors he'd become: a

student at a Christian boys' school near his father's home in Louisiana. Timid and easily confused, sometimes mumbling his words until the judge or prosecutor admonished him to slow down and speak up, Jason looked, as he had throughout his life, like a boy years younger than his actual age, which now was nineteen.

"Do you recognize that photograph?" Porter asked, showing him an eight-by-ten, black-and-white modeling shot.

"Yes," Jason answered.

"And who's that a photograph of?"

"Susan White, my mother," the boy said.

Introduced into evidence as prosecution exhibit number 52, Porter handed the jury a photo of a smiling White staring into the camera. She appeared the all-American suburban mom, wearing jeans and a sweater, her blond hair cut in a shoulder-length pageboy.

"Had you been in trouble with the law?" Porter asked Jason.

"Yes," he said.

Porter grazed lightly over Jason's record, that he'd been sentenced to probation for bringing a gun—which Jason described as a BB gun—on the school bus. Jason had a calm, almost deadened demeanor as Porter led him through the events of the weekend preceding his mother's death, a skeleton-thin summary of the sting operation that ended in his arrest.

"Who arrested you?"

"Officer McGowen," Jason said, at Porter's direction pointing at a jaw-clenching McGowen seated at the defense table.

In response to Porter's questions, Jason recounted how he'd been released from jail early in the evening of August 24, and the events that night: returning home; saying good night to his girlfriend, Maggie; checking on his mother, her door partially closed; then going upstairs to bed. The next thing he remembered was the blaring of the house alarm system, followed, seconds later, by three gunshots.

"Bang, bang, bang," Jason intoned, demonstrating how quickly the shots had been fired.

"Were you arrested?" Porter asked.

"No," Jason said.

"Jason, which hand did she use to write?"

"Left."

To play tennis, golf—Jason replied, "Left."

"Did you *ever* see her use her right hand for *anything*?" Porter asked, looking directly at the jury, as if willing them to remember this particular point.

"No," Jason answered.

On cross-examination, Brian Benken returned to Jason's troubled history and the chaos at 3407 Amber Forest that summer. Yes, his mother and stepfather argued, even fought. They were getting a divorce. Yes, he was in and out of trouble.

"This was a bad time in your life?" Benken asked. "Did you mean to tell the jury that you were getting in trouble during this period?"

"Yes," Jason replied.

From the incident on the bus to the crowd he hung out with, friends he admitted stole purses in clubs and burglarized houses, Jason answered Benken's questions. His mother took prescription drugs, didn't she?

"Yes," Jason said. When asked how many, he recalled seeing four or five different pill bottles in her bathroom. He agreed he'd felt angry and upset when he learned Mike Shaffer had betrayed him by setting him up for the sting, yet he showed no hatred. Though the defense attorney prodded, Jason gave the impression, not of a cold-blooded, homicide-ready criminal, but of a young boy deeply hurt by a friend's betrayal. At one point when Benken asked if he felt angry at Shaffer, Jason replied. "Well, it's heartbreaking, you know."

Under redirect, Porter illustrated that Jason had only

suspected his best friend's involvement in the sting because of sloppy police work.

"When you first saw Shaffer after the sting, after your mother's death, did you punch him or anything?" Porter asked.

"No."

"Did you want to hurt Michael Shaffer?"

"No."

For all his confusion, the teenager made a compelling witness. If Jason fell so far short of the defense's description of a suburban gang member, could they persuade the jury Susan had the credentials of a gun-toting moll, a woman so dangerous she required killing?

"Yes, I need the Cypresswood sheriff's department, please." Susan White's voice resonated through the courtroom the following morning as Edward Porter played the 911 tape for the jury, the words "sexual harassment" deleted.

"Thinks he owns the world. . . . McGowen has made sexual advances toward me and I will not. . . . Who's there? Get McGowen away from my house. Get McGowen away from my house. . . . They are trying to break into my house, p-l-e-a-s-e. . . . They're breaking down my door."

In the hushed courtroom, the house alarm screamed unnervingly, until it seemed to shake the very walls. Seconds later, the telephone went dead.

A woman, the middle of the night, police officers breaking down her door. Jurors knew moments after the tape ended that Susan White lay dying, the blood they'd seen earlier seeping from her body, staining her pink nightgown. Some of the men stared at McGowen. The sole woman gazed resolutely at her hands.

Edward Porter rose behind the prosecution table.

"Your Honor," he said. "The state of Texas rests."

His words sent a shock wave through the courtroom. Judge Azios appeared stunned. It was a move the defense hadn't anticipated. Porter had dozens of uncalled witnesses on his list.

With the jury removed from the room, Brian Benken stood before Azios. "We have a motion for an instructed verdict, Your Honor," he said, outlining what he said Porter had failed to prove: there'd been no serial number on the gun; no one had testified McGowen even fired the weapon that killed White.

"Mr Porter?" questioned Azios.

"Judge, we presented a circumstantial case," Porter countered. "It's a circumstantial case, a prima facie case that the defendant shot Susan White and caused her death."

Clint Greenwood approached the bench and took up Benken's argument. "There were other deputies at the scene that night," he insisted. "There is absolutely no evidence that, as alleged in the indictment, he did the shooting."

Porter, Hill, Benken, and Greenwood hovered before the judge, attempting to persuade him. Azios appeared worried.

Like a poker player cuffing his hand, Porter centered his strategy on hiding much of his case. He felt certain, from all he'd heard about the former deputy, that McGowen would lie on the stand. That would open the door for Porter to hammer his testimony in rebuttal, to introduce conflicting evidence and witnesses. But now he held his breath. What if Azios ruled against him and declared McGowen not guilty?

"The state's case just fails," Greenwood said, shrugging as if Azios' only possible ruling was the one *he* had presented, to acquit Kent McGowen.

Azios hesitated. The attorneys waited.

"The motion is denied," he said finally. "Ready for the jury?"

"State's ready, Your Honor," said Porter, relieved. The assistant D.A. had just dodged a bullet, but he didn't realize until later that another waited nearby.

With that, Brian Benken announced the defense wished to make an opening statement. Edward Porter objected.

"Judge. . . . the state made no opening statement, and I don't believe the defense is entitled to make an opening statement unless the state has made an opening statement."

Azios barely paused. "That's sustained."

"Your Honor," said Benken. "For the record, I would object to the denial of being able to make an opening statement to the jury."

"All right," said Azios.

That motion would later haunt Porter. There would be many a day when he'd wish he had the power to expunge those moments from the trial.

Porter had relied on a Texas appellate court decision he'd read only days earlier, one that stated if prosecutors opted against an opening statement, defense attorneys weren't entitled to one. But Porter had made an error. He'd forgotten the justices' caveat. What the decision had actually stipulated was that the defense wasn't entitled to an opening statement *at the beginning of the trial.* The decision in no way prevented the defense from giving an opening statement later in the trial, before it began its case. Porter had had a simple lapse in memory, but it would prove a costly error.

As his first witness, Clint Greenwood called Tommy Welch to the stand, a contract deputy who worked a subdivision within a few miles of Olde Oaks. Using Welch, the attorney set the scene, explaining the difference between contract deputies and officers who worked the entire district. Then he turned his attention to the night of Saturday, August 22, 1992, and the sting operation that ended in Jason's arrest.

McGowen was in charge, Welch testified. He knew little until he showed up for a pre-sting conference. It appeared a regular buy-and-bust. McGowen's C.I., Mike Shaffer, would buy the stolen weapon from his contacts, and Welch and the handful of other deputies on the scene would swarm in for the bust.

Everything went as planned until Susan White arrived on the scene. Welch said she came over to him, but he waved her off to talk to McGowen. Later, he heard White screaming, cussing at the officers.

On cross-examination, Porter spent little time on the events of that particular night. Instead he asked if Welch had ever heard of Susan White before that night in the parking lot.

"No," the deputy replied.

Never anything about her being a "major turd and a gunrunner?" Porter prodded.

"No," Welch said.

Porter then turned his attention to the use of confidential informants like Shaffer, and whether being a C.I. was a dangerous occupation. Welch agreed that it was.

"Informants get killed in Houston, don't they?" Porter asked.

Welch shrugged. "I would guess they would if they got found out."

"That's kind of a fact of life . . . dangerous business?"

"I would say it is," agreed Welch.

After Welch, Deputy Chris Gwosdz took the stand. In response to Greenwood's questions, he described the scene of the sting. Picking up where Welch left off, Gwosdz said that an intoxicated Susan White approached him, confusing him with Kent McGowen.

"She called me Deputy McGowen," Gwosdz testified.

"And did you tell her that you were not Deputy McGowen?"

"Yes."

Gwosdz described Susan White as angry and testified that at the time she and Ray Valentine drove away from the parking lot, he distinctly heard White scream out the car window.

"It was directed at Deputy McGowen," he said, ". . . a loud, threatening statement."

Gwosdz' testimony was important to Greenwood for two reasons: His assertion that White had confused him with McGowen implied that White didn't know McGowen well enough to recognize him at the scene, backing up McGowen's claim that he and White had never met and he therefore, harbored no animosity toward her. And the threat? The defense planned to draw a scenario in which White's claims of harassment were revenge against McGowen for arresting her son.

But when Porter took over the questioning, Greenwood's carefully laid image of the events on the scene that night quickly eroded. "Yes," Gwosdz said when asked if he was McGowen's friend, if he wanted to help him.

"Nothing unusual about mothers getting upset about their sons getting arrested, right?" Porter asked.

"No," Gwosdz admitted.

Porter then handed Gwosdz a copy of a voluntary sworn statement he'd given police six days after the sting operation and three after White's killing, a statement that drastically contradicted much of what he'd testified to on the stand.

In that statement, Gwosdz had written that when White approached him, she didn't call him McGowen but simply asked if he was the deputy who'd come to her house.

"Do you have any idea how many deputies have been to this lady's house?" Porter asked.

"She meant McGowen," Gwosdz insisted.

The prosecutor smirked, a tendency that ultimately

earned him the nickname King Edward from amused jurors, who grew to enjoy his self-assuredness. Looking at the witness over his shoulder, Porter seemed to imply such claims could be expected by a "friend" of the accused.

Returning his attention to questioning, he asked Gwosdz to repeat what he'd heard White shout.

" 'I'll get you, you son of a bitch,' " Gwosdz answered.

"You heard that?" Porter repeated.

"Yes," the deputy said.

But in his statement Gwosdz had written that he couldn't hear what White said. Instead it was McGowen who had turned to him and claimed, "Did you hear that? She threatened me. She called me a son of a bitch."

"That's substantially different, isn't it?" Porter asked.

"Yes, it is," admitted the deputy, looking embarrassed and angry. It didn't alleviate Gwosdz' chagrin that Porter pointed out that he had been the one in charge of arresting Mike Shaffer that night, the one who had failed to relieve him of the .357 magnum tucked in his waistband.

"We pass the witness, Your Honor," said Porter as he finished with the deputy, who looked nearly shrunken in his highly starched uniform.

Jean Spradling-Hughes and Jim Mount, the two assistant district attorneys who had secured the warrant for McGowen, were next on the stand. Brian Benken led them through the events of the night eighteen months earlier, specifically of Sunday, August 23, and the early morning of Monday, the twenty-fourth. To the jury, it must have seemed everything was in order. They were calm and respectful in their answers. Yes, they'd issued the warrants. They cited nothing out of the ordinary.

Edward Porter opted not to cross-examine either witness, but stipulated the right to recall both at a later time. His tactic: to allow McGowen a false sense of security, to conceal damaging testimony from the A.D.A.s until after McGowen testified. He knew that, with no other witnesses, McGowen had no choice but to take the stand in order to claim self-defense. Only he could claim that Susan White had held a gun on him and he'd fired in self-defense.

Next, Benken introduced into evidence the written warrant for Susan White's arrest, signed by a judge, dated the day before her death.

Again Porter made no objection.

The foundation leading to the night of the shooting having been laid, Greenwood then called to the stand Michael Malloy, one of the two deputies who'd accompanied McGowen to White's house that night. The defense attorney needed Malloy to recount the events just prior to the shooting.

From Ruggiero's assigning him to accompany McGowen to serve the warrant to his arriving at the house, Malloy told the story of that night. Yes, they'd looked in the garage; there were two cars there. He'd gone to the back door, but heard McGowen and the third deputy, Todd Morong, shouting at the front door: "Open up, we have a warrant."

Over the back channel on his radio, Malloy heard Sergeant Ruggiero authorize McGowen to kick in the door. Morong and McGowen tried kicking in the double front doors, but they were too solid. They came running to the back, and Malloy kicked the back door three, four times before it gave way to the shrill scream of the alarm. McGowen led the way at a "fast walk," Malloy said, until they reached the bedroom. Then McGowen stepped into the doorway. Malloy couldn't see what happened inside, but he heard McGowen shout: "Drop the gun. Drop the gun. Drop the gun."

Gunfire: one, two, three shots, all in a span of four fast seconds.

McGowen rushed into the room; Malloy followed. Malloy testified, "The first time I saw [Susan White's] weapon was after it was picked up off the bed and thrown on the floor."

"Did you hear him say, 'Drop the gun,' three times because [Deputy McGowen] asked you if you heard him [say that], or did you hear him say, 'Drop the gun'?" Greenwood asked, leery of what had happened to Gwosdz on the stand.

"I heard him say three times, 'Put the gun down,'" answered Malloy.

Greenwood passed the witness.

Porter moved slowly with Malloy, deliberately making his points. No, Malloy admitted, McGowen wasn't on any gang task force, and they didn't usually serve warrants at night. No, he'd never heard of Susan White or Jason Aguillard before that night and had never heard rumors of a major gunrunner living in Olde Oaks. Would he have expected to hear of such an operation, perhaps one converting semiautomatic weapons to automatics? Porter asked.

"It seems like I would have heard if there were major gun dealers in the Olde Oaks subdivision. Yes," said Malloy.

In fact, the only information Malloy said he had on White before he broke down her door was what McGowen had told him that night, that she was "crazy," and that there could be guns in the house.

"You heard someone inside the house say, 'McGowen, go away and I'll come out,' didn't you?" asked Porter. "Strike you as odd?"

"Yes," Malloy conceded.

Malloy also admitted he'd never encountered a situation where a person he'd been sent to arrest called the police for help.

Once inside the house, Malloy admitted feeling uncomfortable with the speed McGowen had moved, not checking each room to see if it was clear.

"Could you see what [Susan White] was doing [inside that bedroom]?"

"No," Malloy said, he couldn't see White; he didn't know whether or not she held a gun on McGowen.

At 3:05, the judge declared a short recess and the jurors left the room. The spectator benches were filled with a smattering of curious attorneys, killing time between their own trials, and the occasional deputy in uniform. As the recess ended, Kent's mother approached O.L.

"I'm sorry for your loss," Carolyn McGowen offered. "But I want you to know, our family has suffered, too."

O.L. Harrison looked at the stocky, gray-haired woman and frowned.

"You still have your son," she said, her eyes blazing. "My child's dead."

When court reconvened, Brian Benken called the third deputy on the scene that night, Todd Morong. The defense attorney used Morong to flesh out the circumstances of the shooting. At first, he recounted, White seemed confused about who they were. Her speech slurred, she asked them to slip their IDs under her front door. When McGowen said that wasn't possible, she shouted that she wanted McGowen to leave. As if agreeing to her demands, Morong said he told her that McGowen was gone.

"Did she open the door then?" Benken asked.

"No," said Morong.

Morong also testified that after the shooting he saw White's gun on the bed.

"McGowen yells, 'Secure the weapon,' " Morong recounted. "McGowen says, 'There it is.' McGowen grabs the handgun and throws it to the back of the room."

When Benken passed the witness, Porter hammered again at what were fast becoming his themes. Morong had never heard of Susan White or Jason Aguillard as troublemakers or gunrunners, he conceded. Like that of Malloy, the only information he had on them came from McGowen, who referred to them both as "stoned lunatics."

"When you hear a voice inside [the house], do you recognize the voice?" Porter asked.

"No."

"Deputy McGowen do anything that indicated to you that he recognized the voice?"

"Yeah," said Morong. "At that point he said, 'Mrs. White, this is Deputy McGowen. I have a warrant for your arrest.' "

Analyzing those moments when Susan White said she'd open the door if McGowen left, Porter postulated that streetlights lit the officers from behind. If so, wasn't it probable that Susan White could see them on her front stoop? That she knew McGowen hadn't really left?

Looking uncomfortable on the stand, Morong admitted that with the light behind them, they would have been silhouetted and easily seen through the front doors' glass panels.

Morong also agreed with Malloy that he'd felt uncomfortable with the speed of McGowen's entry into the house that night.

"[McGowen rushed like] he had his eye on something?" asked Porter.

"Yes," said Morong.

"A target," said the prosecutor, looking sternly at the jury. "He's got his eye on some kind of a target."

Greenwood and Benken appeared surprised by the testimony Porter consistently elicited from their own witnesses. Even the deputies who'd accompanied McGowen

on August 25, 1992, admitted uneasiness with his behavior.

Outside, the late-afternoon sun hovered low in the
sky as Benken recalled Jason Aguillard, still under oath,
for another round of testimony. Porter objected, saying
the matter was irrelevant, when Benken asked the boy
how he got along with his neighbors. But Azios ruled
that he'd allow the line of testimony.

Yes, Jason said, he had attended an alternative school,
one for teenagers who were discipline problems. He had
loud parties, and the police were called. When Mike
Shaffer said he wanted to buy a stolen gun, Jason had
no trouble finding one to sell.

"Did you sometimes carry a gun?" Benken asked.

"Once," Jason said.

"When?"

"The day we sold it."

During a brief cross-exam, Porter put into the record
one small piece of evidence, evidence he believed the
jurors, especially those with teenagers, would understand—that unsupervised children sometimes did things
their parents wouldn't allow.

"In May 1992, when you were having these parties,
where was your mother?" he asked.

"In the hospital," replied Jason.

Jason Aguillard left the stand for the last time, and moments later, a hush settled over the courtroom as Clint
Greenwood announced his next witness. Kent McGowen
strolled confidently toward the box and stood before the
judge's bench. He raised his right hand.

"Do you swear or affirm to tell the truth, the whole
truth, and nothing but the truth?" the court clerk asked.

"I do," McGowen answered.

Edward Porter smiled.

34

"Could you introduce yourself to the jury?" Greenwood asked.

"Yes," McGowen said, looking directly at the faces in the jury box. "My name is Joseph Kenton McGowen."

"How old are you?"

"Twenty-eight years old."

So began the testimony of Kent McGowen that Thursday afternoon. He appeared anxious, rushing his words, tendencies understandable for a man on trial for murder.

Clint Greenwood smiled fondly at the nervous young man before him in the dark gray suit, leading him through a chronology of his pre-badge years, a brief stint in the Air Force, his years in the Air National Guard and Air Force Reserves. McGowen had been a military policeman specializing in nuclear security. Greenwood looked toward the jury, his face earnest. Surely Kent McGowen was a man to be trusted.

As his testimony continued, McGowen sketched out

his years in law enforcement. He left H.P.D. to go to college, he said. Yes, he'd tried to return.

"And were you accepted?" Greenwood asked.

"No, sir," said Kent. "I wasn't."

Greenwood didn't ask if he knew why not.

From H.P.D. to Tomball to the sheriff's department. In this oral résumé, McGowen left out one position, that of his short tenure in Precinct Four, the one that ended with his pistol butt to Daniel Newrones' forehead.

Using police jargon like "beat integrity," McGowen told of his contract position with the sheriff's department. He'd developed sources, he said.

"I had spoken to several other teenagers in the neighborhood and they informed me [that] some teenagers [who] lived in the neighborhood were dealing guns."

He described stopping Mike Shaffer and enlisting him as a C.I. The teenager set up two buys; neither worked, McGowen said, but then Shaffer mentioned Jason Aguillard.

Before proceeding into the sting, Greenwood backtracked, allowing McGowen to maintain that he'd been at Susan White's house twice in his time as an Olde Oaks contract deputy, the first time to break up Jason's May party, where he said he'd found dime bags of marijuana with traces left in them. Other deputies at the same party would remember confiscating only an ash tray that might or might not have held a residue of marijuana ash.

McGowen maintained he'd met Susan only once, on his second stop at her house, the night he dropped in on a deputy instructing her on how to load her pistol. In Kent McGowen's version of that summer, he had no further contact with Susan White. It seemed he had no idea why she would complain about him, other than that, after the sting operation, she might have been lying to protect her son.

McGowen's excitement built even on the stand as he

spoke of the sting. "I asked if I could come in plain-clothes and bring my uniform to put on later," he said, gushing like a teenager describing a rock concert. "[Lieutenant Coons] approved it."

"Even though you're a contract deputy, your lieutenant okayed it," said Greenwood, nodding importantly at the jury.

"Yes," said McGowen. "I looked at it as my responsibility. It was in my contract."

McGowen's enthusiasm escalated. After the sting, he claimed Jason, the confused teenager who'd just been on the stand, said he knew how to get his hands on a fully automatic, laser-sighted Uzi. McGowen said he'd called an ATF agent. "They were interested."

He told of the Xeroxed bills, finding $20 of the buy money in Jason's pants pocket, and then honed in on Susan White's calls to Mike Shaffer's aunt and mother.

"Informants in Houston don't live long," McGowen said, repeating White's words, looking meaningfully at the jurors.

When he recounted conversations with Shaffer, he insisted his C.I. said he feared White would carry out a vendetta against him. When McGowen had taken White's threat to the district attorney's office, he said, Jean Spradling-Hughes told him, "Sounds like a case."

Body language is a difficult thing to read with jurors. Attorneys pay thousands for consultants who do just that, often guessing wrong. In the jury box, this group of McGowen's peers sat back in their chairs; a few had arms folded across their chests. Were they absorbing the testimony, piecing together McGowen's version of the events that led to White's death? Or were their pensive expressions filled with skepticism?

Court ended that afternoon, but early the next morning McGowen again took the stand, this time recounting his quest to obtain the warrant, the trip to White's house that night, the breaking down of the back door, and the

dash to her bedroom. He said he looked inside and saw
Susan White holding a gun on him.

"Were you in fear of your life?" Greenwood asked.

"Yes, I was," said McGowen.

"Did you think she was going to shoot?"

"Yes, I did."

"What did you do?"

"I fired."

"What is the picture you have of her in your mind
before you fired?"

"Pointing a gun at me."

"At that instant, right before you fired, what did your
whole world consist of?" asked Greenwood.

"Her right hand with the weapon in it."

"And you were afraid?"

"Yes, I was," McGowen said, staring directly at the
jurors.

Edward Porter rose solemnly from his chair behind the
prosecutors' table and paused momentarily, eyeing the
man in the witness stand.

"Mr. McGowen," said Porter, "when you were introducing yourself to the ladies and gentlemen of the jury,
you gave a list of the various law enforcement agencies
that you have been associated with, did you not?"

"Yes," McGowen said.

"Left one out, didn't you?"

"I'm not sure," said McGowen, looking down at his
hands.

"Precinct Four?"

"Yes, I was employed there as a reserve deputy,"
McGowen admitted.

Porter then turned his attention to H.P.D., noting that
McGowen had worked there for just under three years.
It was important to Porter that the jury realize the man

on the stand was a gypsy cop, one who'd jumped from agency to agency.

"And you resigned to take this great opportunity that was available to you, is that correct?"

"Yes."

"That was your *only* motive for leaving the Houston Police Department?" Porter prodded.

"Yes," said McGowen.

"You weren't having problems out there?" suggested Porter. "Were you?"

"Objection, Your Honor," Clint Greenwood called out. "It's irrelevant."

Azios ordered the jury removed from the courtroom.

With that, the argument ensued. Like the dispute over admitting the 911 tape, the trial's outcome could hinge on who prevailed. Both sides knew that. Greenwood needed to keep the jury from hearing even an innuendo that McGowen was anything but a solid member of the law enforcement community. On the other hand, Porter wanted a whiff of his jacket in the courtroom, enough so that jurors understood whom they had before them.

As the sides squared off, Porter argued that Greenwood had opened the door for limited testimony on McGowen's employment history by giving the "false impression with this jury that [his client] has peacefully and wonderfully traveled from police agency to police agency without really letting them know what the deal was. He was, at the time he left [the] Houston Police Department, under investigation for various allegations of misconduct."

The defense team insisted they hadn't opened the door, and that McGowen's testimony merely outlined his background. "He didn't say he went peacefully," countered Greenwood. "He just simply said, 'I went from this agency to this agency.' Okay? That's it."

Azios struck a thoughtful pose, pondering the ceiling as the attorneys argued, finally telling Porter to ask the question he'd intended for McGowen—if he'd been in trouble with Internal Affairs at the time he resigned from H.P.D. Without blinking, McGowen maintained he knew of no such trouble. Porter rolled his eyes and shot him a look of exasperation.

With no further hesitation, Azios ruled: Porter would not be allowed to ask questions probing McGowen's past. If Porter and Hill were going to be able to get the stench of McGowen's jacket before the jury, they'd have to do it another way.

With jurors again in the courtroom, Porter restarted his cross-examination, concentrating again on the brief careers McGowen had had at the various agencies. Houston police wouldn't rehire him. He left Tomball after five months, Precinct Four after two months. Porter then asked if his contract at the sheriff's department wasn't "pretty boring," patrolling such a quiet part of the city.

"I made some traffic stops," McGowen said.

"Don't officers want to make felony arrests?" quizzed Porter.

McGowen denied he was concerned with such things, but Porter's insinuation that he was a bored cop looking for action hung resolutely in the air.

Porter then led McGowen through an analysis of the three statements he'd given about the shooting of Susan White: one during the walk-through, a written statement early the next morning, and his grand jury testimony. McGowen, said Porter, had contradicted himself, changed testimony as he learned more facts about the evidence against him. During the first two statements, McGowen knew of only one call White had made to 911, but before his grand jury appearance, he'd obtained a copy of the 911 tape and discovered White had actually made two calls.

"Susan White sound scared on that tape?" Porter asked.

Greenwood hastily objected.

Porter then asked McGowen to recount his first meeting with Mike Shaffer, the teenager who'd become instrumental in Jason's arrest and White's death. McGowen described a "friendly traffic stop," but under questioning admitted he'd ordered Shaffer and his friends from the car and searched it, finding a pipe with what might have been traces of marijuana inside.

"You [search the car] in all your traffic stops?" asked Porter.

"It depends," answered McGowen.

"Do you think they're sticking Uzis and machine guns under their seats?" Porter mocked.

"I didn't think they were sticking weapons there," replied a defensive McGowen. "They were making furtive actions."

"Furtive actions," repeated Porter. "That's a term used by courts to justify searches, isn't it?"

McGowen blanched. "I'm not sure if it is."

"And this was a friendly stop?"

"Yes."

Porter then asked if the marijuana found in the car was of an illegal amount, defined in Texas as a "usable quantity." McGowen said it wasn't.

"Did you threaten to take Mike Shaffer's girlfriend in because she was sitting closest to it?" Porter asked.

"No," McGowen replied.

"Did you tell him he owes you a favor because you didn't take his girlfriend in?"

"Not that I recall," said McGowen.

By McGowen's second traffic stop of Shaffer, he said, he'd heard rumors of fully automatic weapons being sold in the neighborhood to teenage gangs by two white teenagers in a red Beretta.

"Tell me what gang was out there," instructed Porter.

"I have no idea," admitted McGowen.

Over the following weeks, Mike Shaffer, his new and, McGowen said, eager C.I., came to him twice with information on guns—first, about two men with a box of AR-15s that McGowen labeled as fully automatic; next, about the very same teenagers in the red Beretta he'd heard about earlier with AK-47s. Yet McGowen admitted he did little to investigate. He wrote no offense reports. He didn't warn other deputies, not even fellow officers who might need to beware when making traffic stops of such a car. He didn't call the ATF, the federal agency in charge of investigating such cases.

In fact, Porter pointed out, Mike Shaffer had never given him either names or addresses to go with his claims. "Not a good C.I., is he?" asked Porter with a smirk.

"I wouldn't be able to judge that," replied McGowen.

In addition, Porter continued, the guns Shaffer described, unless converted to automatic, were legal to own.

"Is it illegal for a citizen to sell a gun to another person?" Porter asked.

"I don't know," said McGowen, biting off his words with tightly controlled anger. "I'm not clear on the law."

"When you heard the 911 tape, you heard Susan White on there complaining about you in particular," said Porter as the afternoon session began. "Is that correct?"

"Yes," answered McGowen.

"But you're telling us you didn't have any contact with her except on two occasions prior to the night of the shooting?"

"That is correct," said McGowen. "Two times on a professional basis."

"You heard her on the tape say to 911 that she wanted you off the property?"

"I did," answered McGowen.

Porter picked up the black-and-white modeling photo of Susan White he'd earlier entered into evidence and, after asking Azios for permission to approach the witness, handed it to McGowen. The former deputy barely glanced at the image.

"She an attractive woman?" Porter asked.

"Average," said McGowen.

"Average?"

"Yes."

McGowen said he wouldn't have recognized Susan White if he'd passed her on the street. Even with her photo before him, he insisted he didn't recognize her as the woman he'd shot and killed. He didn't even know what car she drove.

"You never stopped her on the street for a broken headlight or an expired sticker?" asked Porter.

"No," insisted McGowen.

Porter then reviewed the record of calls made to the substation regarding disturbances at 3407 Amber Forest: fireworks on the Fourth of July; teenagers causing a disturbance, once banging the trees out front with a baseball bat.

"I guess you'd call these criminal mischief?" asked Porter.

"Yes," said McGowen.

No, he admitted, there'd been no reports of gunfire at the house or teenagers playing with guns on the front lawn. In fact, the only gun he'd known of on the premises was the small .25 he'd seen on the bar the night he stopped over to find another deputy teaching Susan White how to load it.

"Do you remember telling Don Smyth [during the walk-through] of people playing with guns and all?" asked Porter.

"Not that I recall," McGowen answered.

Over the course of the following hours, McGowen denied many things: that he'd told the two assistant D.A.s who issued the warrant that he was a member of a gang task force; that he'd claimed there'd been gunplay at White's house; that Jason was the "head turd" in a gun ring involving automatic weapons; that he'd implied the driver of the black Mitsubishi, who'd threatened Mike Shaffer early in the morning after the sting, was connected to White; that he'd told Jeff Copeland the order of the shots he'd fired at White.

"Did you tell Mike Shaffer that Susan White had threatened him and he needed to be concerned?" asked Porter.

"I didn't tell him that," said McGowen.

"He told you that?"

"Yes."

Later, Porter planned to put witnesses on the stand to refute each of these points.

Equally puzzling were McGowen's omissions, Porter suggested. Fearful for his C.I.'s life, he didn't suggest Shaffer leave town or find a safe place for the teenager to stay. When it took longer than expected to get the warrant issued and served, why didn't he tell Coons he needed overtime to get it done? If he feared Shaffer's life was in danger, why did McGowen let the warrant sit for an entire day in the clerk's office? Twenty-six hours had lapsed from the time he first heard of Susan White's alleged threat until he had the signed warrant in his hand, yet he'd shown no urgency in protecting his C.I. On the stand, McGowen had no answers for Porter's barrage of questions.

"So your main concern was arresting Susan White?" Porter asked.

"No," insisted McGowen.

"Well, you're working on getting an arrest warrant for Susan White, aren't you?"

"For Michael's safety," said McGowen. "Yes."

"Susan White's complaints to Lieutenant Coons about you make you angry?"

"No," said McGowen.

As the afternoon wore on, Porter asked McGowen to physically position him just the way White had been that night. The deputy rose and walked around Porter, taking the district attorney by the arm and sitting him gingerly on the edge of a table. He then put the gun in Porter's right hand and thrust his arm awkwardly forward, keeping his right upper arm tight to his side and turning his head and body to the left.

"This is exactly what you saw that night?" said Porter.

"Yes," said McGowen.

With that established, Porter introduced into evidence state's exhibits 62 through 67, photos taken during the grand jury testimony. In each, McGowen, in uniform, stood or sat on the edge of a chair, positioning his body the way he then said White had stood on the night of the shooting, facing straight forward, his extended right arm pointing a gun. Of course, McGowen had learned much about the evidence against him since his grand jury testimony, including the autopsy findings that the bullets had traveled at an angle through White's body—an impossibility if she'd confronted him as he'd initially claimed, facing him squarely.

"Your testimony at the grand jury was different than what you showed us here today, isn't it?" Porter asked.

"It's the same."

"It is?"

"Yes," he insisted.

As another day's testimony drew to a close, Porter concentrated on one final point: McGowen's claim that as he entered the house through the back door, he saw Susan White running into her bedroom. To set the scene so the jury could see it unfold, he again asked McGowen to review his written statement and grand jury notes. In the first, McGowen estimated it had taken as few as two to three seconds for him to reach the bedroom door. In the second, that estimate jumped to five to seven seconds. Now, on the stand, he said he'd been wrong, and that it had taken him eight to twelve seconds to run to her bedroom door.

"Now, if it took only a matter of seconds to . . . get to the door where you're confronting Susan White, then she couldn't have been running from anywhere in the living room . . . into her bedroom. Could she?" asked Porter.

"I don't know," McGowen answered.

Porter then produced photos showing the two telephones on the first floor, one in the foyer, the other in the bedroom; neither was portable.

Porter pulled out his tape recorder once more.

"Do you have a watch, Mr. McGowen?" Porter asked.

"Yes, I do," he answered.

Porter then pressed the Play lever on the tape recorder and the house alarm blared through the courtroom yet again, loudly reverberating off the walls.

"How long did that take?" Porter asked.

"Six and a half seconds," said McGowen.

"So if Morong and Malloy are right [that it took only a few seconds to get to her bedroom door], she's on the phone when you're going through the den, getting to her bedroom door?"

"No," insisted McGowen. "Morong and Malloy are incorrect in their statements."

"They lied?"

"I'm not saying they lied; they might have been mistaken," he concluded.

"You've got to get eight to twelve seconds now in order to see Susan White running in there, right?"

"When I look back on it?" McGowen said. "Yes."

"She's got the gun in her *right* hand?"

"Yes," McGowen said. "She did."

"You didn't have any hard feelings toward Susan White, did you?" Porter continued.

"No," said McGowen.

Again Porter went through a laundry list of statements McGowen denied: that he'd told Jean Spradling-Hughes that White warned Shaffer's mother her son would be dead by the end of the day; that he'd said there had been gunplay at White's house; that he'd told the second A.D.A., Jim Mount, that Shaffer had been used to buy fully automatic Uzis.

"Did you tell Jim Mount that you wanted to personally serve the warrant on Susan White?" Porter asked.

"Not that I recall," said McGowen, looking defiantly at Porter.

35

"The defense rests," Clint Greenwood announced the following morning, and Edward Porter called his first rebuttal witness. Michael Shaffer shuffled into the courtroom. His hand raised to be sworn in, Shaffer appeared as frightened as if he stared down the barrel of a gun.

With Jason's former best friend, the prosecutor repeated much of the testimony already heard, but then centered on the most germane issue of the trial: Had he been frightened by Susan White's words, frightened enough to feel his life was truly in danger?

The jury that day would receive no clear answers. On the stand, Shaffer vacillated. When asked by Edward Porter, he denied worrying about White, recounting how he'd talked with her that Sunday, that she'd made no threats and attempted in no way to harm him, even though for much of the weekend he had his car parked on the street in front of his girlfriend's house, just a block from White's home. But under cross-examination by Brian Benken, the by-now twenty-one-year-old testified that at the time, he was concerned and frightened by Susan White's words.

"I just felt like everybody knew," said Shaffer, lamenting the lack of protection the deputies, especially McGowen, had given his confidential status. "I wasn't scared of her; I was scared of everybody knowing."

In two ways Shaffer's testimony remained relatively consistent: that it had been McGowen who told him Susan White had threatened him and needed to go to jail, and that he was in a panic, worried that his friends would discover he'd "snitched" on Jason.

His only other consistent testimony revolved around the black Mitsubishi that had stalked him the day after the sting. Shaffer insisted he'd told McGowen about his ongoing fear of the car's driver much earlier, and that the deputy had shown no interest, simply suggesting he try to get a license number. He also denied ever insinuating the car could somehow be connected to Susan or Jason.

"Do you remember what you asked McGowen when he told you he was going to pick Susan White up?" Porter asked on redirect.

Stunned, Shaffer had asked, "What for?"

Jeannie Jaques followed her son into the witness box. As she had been with the grand jury, Jaques would prove a powerful witness. McGowen had cited her fears when he signed the warrant. Yet on the stand, Jaques testified that while she felt concerned about Susan White's remarks, she had never taken them as a threat to her son. It was McGowen, she said, who alarmed her.

"I began wondering to myself, *Why wasn't I more concerned?*" she said.

After Jaques came Jay Coons, McGowen's lieutenant. No, he said, the department had no provisions allowing officers to misrepresent facts to assistant district attorneys when filing for warrants.

"Is that permitted in any circumstance?" asked Porter.

"No, none whatsoever," Coons snapped back angrily, obviously still fiercely loyal to McGowen.

Before Coons left the witness box, Porter used him to establish one more point, that Susan White's complaints could have been a serious threat to Kent McGowen's job. If proved true, the department had penalties that included possible termination.

"Was she complaining about Deputy McGowen?"

"Yes," said Coons.

But Coons, who described White as sounding intoxicated, admitted he paid no attention to her assertions and gave her no information on how to file a formal complaint. He did, however, recount his conversation with McGowen concerning his meeting with and telephone calls from White.

"Was McGowen angry?" Porter asked.

"There was some anger," Coons said.

"Was he cussing mad?"

"The exact words out of McGowen's mouth I do not recall," said Coons.

Yes, Coons testified, McGowen told him about a black Mitsubishi and tied it to White's threat. In fact, Coons remembered McGowen saying the teenage driver who held the gun on Shaffer had said, "Snitches get killed."

"Pretty direct reference to an informant, isn't it?" asked Porter.

"Yes," said Coons.

Since witnesses are banned from the courtroom during the trial, Coons had no way of knowing that Michael Shaffer had just denied that the two incidents were connected, or that McGowen himself had sworn while on the stand that he'd ever made such a statement.

As testimony continued, the prosecutors' attack on the warrant—which bore the judge's signature that gave Kent McGowen authority to break down Susan White's door in the middle of the night—kicked into full assault. Not for a moment had Hill or Porter forgotten that to convict McGowen of murder, the jury had to brand the warrant a lie, as worthless as a blank sheet of paper.

Belinda Hill, who'd spent the trial thus far perched behind the prosecution's table monitoring testimony for Porter and scribbling suggested questions on a pad of legal paper, now took center stage, recalling to the witness stand her colleague Jean Spradling-Hughes. Under Hill's cut-and-dried cross-examination, the assistant D.A. testified that McGowen had used much stronger words than "informants die in Houston" when recounting White's words to her. In fact, she said, over the phone that night, McGowen had told her something vastly different. That in her conversation with Jeannie Jaques, Susan White had said: "I'm going to kill the C.I. for having my son arrested. He'll be dead before the day is over."

McGowen also misrepresented himself, Spradling-Hughes said, identifying himself as a member of a special unit. He'd claimed Susan White had a history of violence, that he or his supervisor had once had to disarm her, and that he'd been called to the house at 3407 Amber Forest in the past for complaints involving gunfire. McGowen had described his collar, Jason, as nothing less than the head of a gang of teenagers who converted guns to automatic weapons.

District attorneys rely on officers for their information, Spradling-Hughes admitted, and based on those statements from McGowen, she'd authorized the warrant for Susan White's arrest.

"If I walked into your office, Ms. Spradling-Hughes, and I simply said Mr. Benken called someone up and said, 'Informants in Houston die,' are you going to give me a warrant on that alone?" asked Hill, gesturing at the tall, blond defense attorney as she spoke.

"No," said the woman.

Brian Benken did nothing to waver Spradling-Hughes' powerful testimony. His concern must have amplified when he heard Jim Mount being recalled to the stand. The second A.D.A. to testify that day backed up much of what his colleague had said. Yes, McGowen claimed the buy/bust had been of a fully automatic Uzi, not a .357 magnum. The first was an illegal assault weapon, the second a gun not uncommon for protection in homes across the nation. In intake that night, McGowen had expressed anger toward Susan White and repeatedly indicated he wanted to be the one to arrest her.

"He wanted to personally run this warrant on Susan White, didn't he?" asked Hill.

"Yes, ma'am," Mount agreed.

"If you learn that a police officer had lied to you at intake, would you ever accept another charge from him?"

"No."

"Would you ever accept another charge from Deputy McGowen?"

"No, ma'am," said Mount.

Deputy Al Kelly, in uniform, appeared uncomfortable on the stand later that afternoon. What McGowen had said to him the morning before Susan White's death nagged him. Still, Kelly had told no one for more than a year. Finally, just two weeks before the trial, he sought out Sergeant Ruggiero, who called Porter.

"I think you need to talk to Al Kelly," Ruggiero advised the assistant D.A.

When Porter met with the deputy, Kelly's reluctance hung heavily on him. As much as he disliked McGowen, he understood that officers didn't testify against brother officers; to do so jeopardized the solidarity of the Blue Brotherhood. But Kelly took a deep breath, steadied himself, and blurted it out. "The morning before she died, McGowen told me, 'If I get the opportunity, I ought to kill that fucking bitch.' "

It was all Porter had hoped for. He now had that elusive carrot all prosecutors chase—a smoking gun showing intent, a window into Kent McGowen's soul the night he killed Susan White.

In the courtroom, Porter began slowly. Kelly described his encounter with McGowen at the substation. They'd talked about Jason's arrest, the warrant McGowen was seeking against White. Had Kelly advised McGowen of anything involving White's arrest?

"Told him to be careful," Kelly answered. "Because she was scared of him."

"How did you learn that Susan White was scared of Deputy McGowen?"

Kelly paused. "Because she told me, several times. Real strong the last time I talked to her."

But when Porter asked what McGowen had replied to Kelly that morning at the substation, Brian Benken objected. Azios instructed the bailiff to remove the jury from the courtroom, and the attorneys squared off on yet another issue. Benken argued he had an agreement signed by the D.A.'s office promising they would turn over all incriminating statements made to police before trial. Porter countered that since this particular testimony had come in only weeks earlier, it wasn't covered by the agreement. In addition, he argued that McGowen's words weren't elicited by an investigator but in a friendly conversation with a co-worker. Azios, as always, listened patiently, then asked Porter what Kelly was about to say. When he heard the quote, Azios grimaced and shook his head.

The attorneys' debate raged on. Azios asked questions. Finally he ruled: The discovery agreement was all-inclusive and binding. Deputy Al Kelly's testimony regarding McGowen's statement would not be allowed.

A disappointed Edward Porter returned to the prosecution table and dropped his yellow legal pad with a slap. Benken and Greenwood strode to their seats, grinning as if they'd just dodged a bullet. In a sense they had. The jury returned and Kelly again took the stand. Despite the setback, Porter continued, determined to get all he could from McGowen's co-worker.

"Were you left with an impression as to Mr. McGowen's feelings toward Susan White?" Porter asked.

"Yes."

"Were those feelings good or negative?"

"Negative," said Kelly, who left the courtroom after a brief cross-examination.

As the trial wore on, Porter called one witness after another to refute McGowen's testimony. Next came Don Smyth, the former head of the Civil Rights Division, who testified about McGowen's walk-through on the scene the night of the shooting. According to Smyth, McGowen had said he knew White's car and that, after breaking through the door, he saw Susan crossing the den into her bedroom, holding something in her right hand. Then came Jeff Copeland, who testified, as Porter knew he would, that McGowen had told him the order of his shots that night—the reverse of what he'd said the Feds shoot—the first to the head, the second to the chest, the third to the arm.

While Jeff Copeland was on the stand, Porter placed one more image before the jury, that of McGowen in the jail, retrieving a copy of the 911 tape and playing it for friends.

"The prosecution calls C.J. Harper," Porter announced next, and the career officer entered the courtroom and walked resolutely to the witness stand. In full uniform, Captain Harper told of his dinner with Susan and Ray Valentine in the piano bar at Resa's, just weeks before her death. Yes, he said, Susan White did talk to him about Kent McGowen.

"Was it a pleasant conversation about Officer Mc-Gowen?"

"No," said Harper. "It was not."

"Was it the type of information that could subject a person to disciplinary action?" Porter asked.

"Yes."

Before the trial's first day, Ray Valentine had made a prediction: that none of Kent McGowen's fellow officers would break the code and testify against him. He was wrong. As Harper left the courtroom, Porter called his next witness. Officer Theresa Barr, in full H.P.D. uniform, walked confidently to the stand. Barr had worked with McGowen at Westside.

"Do you consider him to be a truthful person?" Porter asked.

"No," she said, her voice firm, unyielding.

"In your opinion, is he a person who should be believed under oath?"

"No," she answered.

"Based on your discussions with those other persons [you work with at Westside], did you form an opinion and have you an opinion today as to his reputation for being a truthful person?"

"Yes."

"Is that opinion good or bad?" asked Porter.

"Bad," said Barr.

Barr's attack on McGowen's character thundered through the courtroom. For days Porter had put witness after witness on the stand to contradict McGowen's sworn testimony, but now this officer blatantly labeled him a liar. Porter wasn't finished. Following Barr he called C.J. Grysen, McGowen's supervisor at H.P.D.; Curtis Mills, his partner in the organized crime task force; Leroy Michna, his chief in Tomball; J.R. Jones, his chief at Precinct Four; even Sergeant Ruggiero, his supervisor at the sheriff's department. All agreed with Barr. Kent McGowen, they testified, was not to be trusted; he could not be counted on to be truthful, even under oath.

The following morning, Wednesday, March 9, the seventh day of the trial, Porter called two more witnesses to the stand. The first, Scott Genovese, a deputy who'd worked with McGowen, testified as his peers had the day before. McGowen, he said, could not be counted on to tell the truth.

After Genovese, Belinda Hill recalled A.D.A. Jim Mount to make one final point: The bond set on the warrant he'd written for Susan White was $2,000 on a third-class felony, the amount given for people who had no felony convictions on their records. That piece of information made clear to the jury that Susan White had never before been in any serious trouble with the law.

When Porter again rested, Clint Greenwood took over for the defense, calling a deputy who worked the area. Steve Lasky would give no new evidence, just reiterate that the White house had been a magnet for teenagers in the neighborhood, loud music, parties, disturbance calls. Based on his dealings with her, he labeled Susan White as overprotective of her son, unwilling to accept that Jason was troubled. He called her "unstable."

On cross, Porter asked if White had ever refused to open the door for Lasky when he was called to her home. Did she ever appear afraid of him, as she was of McGowen?

"I don't believe she was afraid of me, no," he answered.

Greenwood called his final witness, Susan White's former next-door neighbor on Amber Forest. Yes, she said, Jason was a problem in the neighborhood; they worried about the parties and wondered if there could be drugs involved. She and her husband constructed a fence to keep him out of their backyard and put an iron gate across their driveway. She recounted his odd behavior, like the day he vacuumed bees from a jasmine bush in her front yard with a Dustbuster, an image that sent a surge of stifled laughter through the courtroom.

The boy's mother, too, was odd, she said, citing the afternoon that Susan, in her kitchen, dropped her pants and wiggled out of her shirt, asking her neighbor to record her measurements for a modeling assignment. She recounted another afternoon when Susan, furious with Ron, threw all his clothes and possessions out the front door onto the lawn. With that image, testimony ended.

Belinda Hill began closing arguments that same afternoon. After thanking the jury, she reviewed the court's charge, the twenty-page document explaining the law the jurors were entrusted to consider. She highlighted three main areas, those in which they had to rule in favor of the defendant if they were to judge him not guilty on the basis of self-defense. When it came to police officers, the law had special rules. One: that the arrest was lawful and was made under a warrant McGowen reasonably believed to be valid. Two: that he identified himself as a police officer or was in a situation where he could reasonably have expected that fact to be assumed. Three: that he believed the person to be arrested would cause death to himself or another.

Hill stood quietly in the center of the courtroom, next to a display pad on which she'd written all three points, and studied the twelve faces before her.

"I submit to you that . . . you never have to get to [issue] two or three because [McGowen] fails on issue one," she said resolutely. "If you look at the testimony of Jean

Spradling-Hughes, you look at the testimony of Jim Mount, you know that McGowen set about to go down to the district attorney's office and get a warrant for a woman who made a complaint against him. . . . he called the district attorney's office and he lied."

With that, Hill listed McGowen's "lies" for the jurors, everything from claiming to be on a special task force to telling Spradling-Hughes that Susan White told Jeannie Jaques, "I'm Susan White and I'm going to kill Michael Shaffer, the informant, and he will be dead by the end of the day."

Therefore, she said, McGowen knew the warrant wasn't valid, that it had been signed under false pretenses. But even if they chose to believe McGowen on the first point—and Hill reminded them that seven of his fellow officers said they should be careful when believing the defendant, that McGowen was a well-known liar—if they judged the warrant was valid, McGowen, she said, failed again on point three. When he confronted Susan White in her bedroom, she didn't open fire. Kent McGowen had the opportunity to withdraw into the house and call for help.

"Folks," Hill concluded, "at first blush, the easy thing for all of us to do is say, well, he's a police officer, he went there with a warrant. He said she had a gun . . . a gun was found there, so this must be a justifiable shooting. . . . You hear people say things are not always what they appear . . . to acquit him on self-defense, you have to believe what he's telling you. You have to be willing to trust what he's telling you. And I think, if you search your hearts, folks, you know how you feel. You cannot trust him. You cannot believe him."

Next, Brian Benken claimed the courtroom floor. Representing the defense, he laid out the case as he and Greenwood saw it, charging the sheriff's department with a sloppy job of investigating the scene. Much of the testimony had proved contradictory and inconsistent. One of the few uncontested facts, he ventured, was that Kent McGowen had fired the shots that killed Susan White. It was, he argued, not murder, but a police officer protecting his own life. Benken attacked the witnesses and the prosecutor. Hadn't Edward Porter attempted to downplay Susan White's problem with drugs? What about the ballistics expert, C.E. Anderson? His testimony had changed so frequently, he didn't know if White had worn her bathrobe inside out that night. "Discrepancies in testimony," Benken labeled them, and there were many.

"Jason was not the same clean-cut kid that you saw in court," argued Benken. "He hung around with a bad crowd, kind of had a fetish for guns. When Michael Shaffer was called upon to see if he could buy some stolen guns, who did he go to? He went to Jason, because he knew Jason's friends would have a source. Pointed a gun at a bus driver one time. You heard Deputy Lasky testify that Susan White was very protective of Jason."

This overprotectiveness of her son, Benken continued, ultimately led to her death. She became angry at Mc-Gowen, angry and upset. She threatened him at the scene of the sting. "If Deputy McGowen wanted to arrest her, get her for anything, he could have done it right then," Benken said, pausing for emphasis. "But he didn't.

"These deputies had a right to kick the door in at the time they entered. They had the right to have their weapons drawn. They . . . had the right to serve this warrant any time of the day or night."

The real blame for the tragedy, said Benken, rested on Susan White's shoulders. If she had just opened the door that night, allowed the deputies to arrest her, she would still be alive.

* * *

In criminal cases in Texas, the state, because it has the burden of proof, has the option of splitting its time alloted for closing in two parts, one half before and the other half after the defense attorney's summation. That's what prosecutors chose to do in the McGowen case. As Brian Benken left the podium, Edward Porter stood before the jurors, his half glasses tilted on his nose.

"Apparently, part of the defense in this case is that there is a conspiracy in the district attorney's office to get a police officer," he said with a slight smile. "A strong law enforcement district attorney in that office is bent on getting a police officer? Or is that office intent on enforcing the law fairly, evenly? No favorites."

If police were the first line of defense in the enforcement of laws, he reasoned, were they not also in the primary position to abuse those laws? Did they not have a responsibility to use their authority and knowledge of the law to protect citizens, all citizens? "Regardless of Susan White's behavior, odd, strange, not taking care of Jason, not controlling Jason, she's still entitled to that protection."

Porter then painted a picture of Susan's life for the jury. Yes, Jason had wandered into dangerous territory; he deserved no excuses. He was out of control, as was Susan's life; she'd had a messy divorce and been hospitalized. "Is there any wonder she's acting odd?" asked Porter.

McGowen said they had no relationship, that she had no reason to fear him. But Porter listed those who'd testified she did fear him: C.J. Harper, Lieutenant Coons, even Al Kelly, who'd only with great pain been able to break the unwritten code that barred one officer from testifying against another. Yet none of the officers she'd complained to had done anything to help her. Even in the 911 tape, White was voicing her fears of McGowen and calling out to Coons for help.

"Doesn't speak well of the sheriff's department, does it?" asked Porter.

McGowen's motive? Porter assessed it was anger and fear that Susan White's complaints could cost him his job. And he needed that job, said Porter, reminding the jury of McGowen's dismal employment record. "What better way to discredit a person who is filing a complaint on you than to arrest them and try to subject them to a criminal record?" he asked.

After listing the "lies" he charged McGowen had manufactured to convince Spradling-Hughes and Mount to authorize and sign the warrant, Porter suggested that inconsistencies in testimony could be settled simply by looking at actions as well as words. Michael Shaffer didn't hide from Susan White; he talked to her on the street, parked his car in open view blocks from her house. Jeannie Jaques never drove to Houston to retrieve her son and hide him.

"Only two people know what happened in that room. One of them is Susan White and she's dead," said Porter. "The other one is Deputy McGowen. Just because he's telling you his side of it doesn't mean it's true."

Porter went on to review the six and a half seconds of house alarm on the 911 tape, the physical evidence including the trajectory of the bullets, and Jeff Cope-land's testimony on the order of the shots—all evidence, Porter suggested, which proved that Susan White was not pointing a gun at Kent McGowen but cowering on the bed.

"Folks," Porter concluded, taking a sweeping look at the jury, "Deputy McGowen couldn't tell you the truth if his life depended on it. Susan White's freedom and her life depended on it. You know the results. I'm asking y'all to return a verdict of guilty as charged in this indictment."

*   *   *

The jurors sternly filed in a military-straight line through a door leading to the jury room to begin their deliberations. The spectators tarried, reluctant to leave, instead clustering together in murmuring factions throughout the courtroom. An hour passed, then another. No word. Finally, at 5:20, the jury relayed a note to the judge, asking to recess until the following morning. He granted their request.

As spectators cleared the courtroom, Porter sat, arms crossed, behind the prosecution table, mulling over his closing statement. He'd left something out, a small but vital bit of evidence: that Susan White was left-handed contradicted McGowen's assertion that she had held the gun in her right hand. *Would they remember?* he wondered. *Who would they believe?*

36

The atmosphere in Azios' courtroom crackled with tension between the two families as deliberations continued the following morning. Kent McGowen's parents and sister congregated with church friends in the hallway, sang hymns, and prayed for the jury to find him innocent. Meanwhile, Susan White's family, fighting to keep their anxiety at bay, observed as Azios dispensed with the mundane daily housekeeping of his courtroom, ruling on his overflowing calendar of plea-bargained drug cases and low-grade felonies.

The hours inched past. Finally, at two that afternoon, a buzzer sounded from the jury room.

Word spread through the courtroom and hallways like smoke from a fire: The McGowen jury had reached a verdict.

All other business cleared the courtroom, and the two families clustered in their separate cliques as the jurors solemnly reentered the courtroom. Not one looked in Kent McGowen's direction. Gloria wrapped her arm protectively over her mother's shoulders as Sandra grasped her father's aged hand.

The bailiff read the verdict: guilty.

Kent McGowen, who'd appeared sometimes angry but otherwise unemotional throughout the ordeal of the trial, glared at the eleven men and one woman who'd just convicted him of murder. Then, his head on the table, he sobbed. His mother and father cleaved together, as if hoping for the strength to endure a devastating physical blow. Even McGowen's flinty attorney, Clint Greenwood, bowed his head and cried.

Amid the emotionally charged, chaotic courtroom, Azios called a brief recess. When they reconvened, the jury would take up the next matter under their jurisdiction: sentencing Kent McGowen for the murder of Susan White.

After the jurors cleared the courtroom, McGowen and his family embraced, as did Susan White's. Gloria took her mother's hands in her own and smiled.

"We got him," she whispered. "They said he murdered Susie."

O.L. looked timidly at her oldest daughter. "You think Susie knows?" she asked.

"Yes, Momma," said Gloria. "She knows."

It was moments later when a shaken W.A. returned from the rest room to tell of a chance encounter with the man just convicted of his daughter's murder.

"Know what that man said to me?" he asked. "He told me, 'I didn't murder your daughter.' "

"What'd you tell him, Daddy?" asked Kay.

"Said, 'Seems to me the jury just said you did.' "

At 3:00, the court reconvened to decide on the sentence, which under Texas law comprised a wide range of options on a scale from probation to life in prison.

Edward Porter called Gloria to the stand.

Susie's death had affected the family greatly, she said.

"Susie was like all of us, she had some faults, but we loved her dearly," she testified, wiping away tears. "She was the center of our lives in lots of ways. She was a fun person. We're a real close family and we had get-togethers, Easter, Christmas, all the holidays. This last year and a half has been tough on us. I would ask for everyone's prayers for Jason because I don't know how Jason has dealt with this."

Porter then made a judgment call. He and Hill agreed that if the jurors found McGowen guilty, they would come down hard on him. Rather than call other witnesses to the stand, he rested.

To plead for leniency, Clint Greenwood recalled Kent McGowen. In questions and answers, McGowen said he respected the jury's verdict, but didn't agree with it. "I never went there to kill Susan White," he said. Both men were still shaken and crying. From the gallery, McGowen's parents could be heard sobbing. While he'd chastised Susan's family earlier, ordering them not to show emotion, Judge Azios said nothing as the McGowens' wails filled the courtroom.

"Do you have any dependents, Mr. McGowen?" Greenwood asked.

"Yes, I do. My three children. A girl, five, and two sons, eight and nine."

On cross-examination, Porter asked if he now realized it had been within his power to stop at any time the chain of events that led to Susan's death.

"It was my job to enforce the law," McGowen hissed back. "I was protecting my informant."

In closing arguments, Porter asked the jury to come down hard on this unrepentant deputy, saying that his actions struck at "the heart and soul of the criminal justice system." Brian Benken asked for the opposite, that they assess probation with community service, suggesting that in their hearts they knew "he didn't plan a con-spiracy to kill Susan White."

Azios ordered the jurors to their deliberation room. Hours passed quietly but not quickly, everyone realizing a decision could come down at any moment.

In the hallway, McGowen's sister, Melissa, ap-proached Kay, her eyes flashing. "Your family's going to hell for this," she shouted.

"I know where my family's going and it's not hell," Kay shot back. "If I were you, I'd be worried about where *your* family will end up."

Seething, Melissa appeared to want to slap her, but Carolyn McGowen grabbed her daughter by the arm and hurried her away.

"Did you hear that?" Kay asked.

"Consider the source," said Gloria. "Just consider the source."

At 4:30, the jury left for the day, only to return the fol-lowing morning. The hours dragged on, until finally, that afternoon, the buzzer again sounded. The attorneys were called and Judge Azios ordered the jurors brought into the courtroom.

With everyone convened, the bailiff read the sentence: fifteen years.

O.L. Harrison put her hand to her heart. They'd hoped for more, much more.

"Momma," said Gloria, wrapping her arm around her mother. "It's all right. He's going to jail. They sent him to jail."

But even Gloria wasn't prepared for what happened next. Before the clamor in the courtroom had cleared, Brian Benken tendered a written appeal, arguing that the defense had been unfairly prevented from giving an opening statement. He requested his client be released on bond while the appeal made its way through the higher courts.

A murmur rippled through the courtroom. McGowen had just been convicted of murder, sentenced to fifteen years. How, the Harrisons wondered, could his attorney now be asking that he be released? They were soon to learn the jury's sentence had actually ensured that McGowen go free, at least temporarily. Under Texas law, a defendant convicted and sentenced to fifteen years and one day for a crime was sent directly to jail. But anyone sentenced to even a day less became automatically entitled to be free on bond while an appeal of the case inched its way through the system.

Judge Azios agreed to Benken's request. A grinning Kent McGowen shuffled from the courtroom, handcuffed and accompanied by two uniformed deputies. Although he'd just been convicted of murder, once his paperwork was processed, he'd be released, able to roam the streets of Houston as if nothing had ever happened.

From the courtroom, Susan's shaken family trailed Edward Porter to the district attorney's building and upstairs to the Civil Rights Division. Don Smyth passed them in the hallway.

"I'm sorry," he said. "I know this is tough to understand."

In a conference room, Porter's secretary served soft drinks in cans as he attempted to explain what had just happened.

"Didn't that jury just say that man killed Susie?" asked W.A.

"Yes," said Porter.

"Then how come he's not going to jail?"

Edward Porter recited the law that allowed McGowen to at least temporarily postpone serving his sentence. Otherwise, he had few words. "We told you this was a tough case, but we won it. Once we did, we really thought the jury would come down hard on a cop who committed murder."

The Harrisons said little. They were grateful to Porter for the guilty verdict, but too stunned to absorb what had just happened.

"How long?" asked Gloria.

"How long, what?" replied Porter.

"How long before he goes to jail?"

Porter shrugged. "I don't know." What he didn't have the heart to tell them was that it could be years.

Epilogue

At the trial, I'd been a constant presence, notebook in hand, jotting down quotes and evidence. Possibly that's why, in her disappointment, O.L. Harrison viewed me as an interpreter of the chaos of the courtroom. After the verdict and McGowen's release, she sometimes telephoned, usually late at night, her aged voice cracked with sorrow. She hoped for reassurance that what she viewed as a great wrong would soon be righted. But, like Edward Porter, I knew enough about the court system to understand I couldn't tell her what she wanted to hear.

On May 3, 1994, two months after the trial began, many of us met in Judge Azios' courtroom again, this time for the judge to rule on Kent McGowen's motion for a new trial. By then Belinda Hill wasn't arguing that prosecutors hadn't erred in objecting to the defense team's opening statement. She admitted they had. She did, however, brand it a harmless error, insufficient to reverse the verdict. She based her argument on law that stipulated that the words of the attorneys were not evidence.

"I don't know how it can be considered to be harmful error when the jurors are told they're not to consider it [when making their decision]," argued Hill.

A perturbed Azios rejected the defense motion to set the verdict aside, allowing the appeal to begin its long process through the court system.

"What do you think?" I asked Porter outside the courtroom.

"Have to wait and see," he said, plainly disturbed by the trial's possibly fatal flaw.

Wait and see, we did, through that summer and into the fall. I continued to investigate the case. My one big hole: Although I'd made repeated requests, neither Kent McGowen nor his family agreed to formal interviews.

Much had changed for Bill and Carolyn McGowen since those heady days in the zenith of the Texas oil patch. In December 1993, almost three months before their son's trial, they'd declared bankruptcy. When I drove to their ranch, it was up for sale. They'd long since moved, and a couple living on the property refused to give me their phone number.

I had better luck with their son. One day, months later, a source slipped me Kent's pager number. I punched in my phone number and he called. When I identified myself, he claimed that he'd been the victim of a vast conspiracy in the district attorney's office, at H.P.D., and in the sheriff's department. But again he refused to meet with me.

As would happen repeatedly, I then received a telephone call a few days later from yet another source.

"Kent's telling everyone he talked to you," the woman said. "He says you're going to pay him thousands of dollars for an interview and write the book *for* him, all about how he's been framed."

I had no intention of paying Kent anything, I replied,

adding that I worked independently, not writing for either side.

Stories about McGowen filtered their way to me that year and into the next—that he had one job, then another; that he continued to insinuate himself into his ex-wife's life, sometimes following her home from her waitress job, bumping her car from behind as she drove.

Unexpectedly, in late February of the following year, 1995, the telephone rang one afternoon in my office.

"This is Kent McGowen," he said. "I just wanted to tell you a few things." With that, McGowen began a diatribe on the unfairness of his trial, attacking everyone involved, most notably Susan White. He claimed many things: that he'd had no relationship with White; that she'd had an incestuous relationship with Jason; that she was a known drug dealer.

"Number one," he said, rattling the words off as if he couldn't release them quickly enough, "she was forty-two. I was twenty-seven. Why would I have interest in an anorexic, bleached-blond drug dealer? I mean, I have a genius IQ . . . a bleached-blond drug dealer whose son is a well-known perp. It doesn't make sense."

He lambasted the prosecutors, falsely claiming he'd been cleared by everyone connected with the case, not only Internal Affairs, Homicide, and the FBI, but the U.S. Treasury Department. Bemoaning the cost of the trial, both emotional and financial, he claimed his father had lost out on a big oil deal with old friends, including ex-President George Bush. But when I asked about Bush, his voice hushed. "I shouldn't have said that," he whispered.

As the conversation continued, McGowen complained of being broke yet bragged he'd been contacted by movie producers and book publishers eager to pay a fortune to tell the story of his persecution. He boasted that two state senators would soon champion his cause, appalled at such a flagrant miscarriage of justice.

He spared no words when it came to the press, which had treated him unfairly, he claimed. "All I want is a fair shake," he said, gloating that he could have brought hundreds of character witnesses to the stand to rebuff the testimony of the deputies who called him a liar. "I have been getting beat down . . . I am sick of everyone jumping on the bandwagon."

I asked for sources, friends or family willing to be interviewed. The following day, he faxed me a hand-written list of fourteen friends he said would vouch for his character. I called all fourteen. Ten hung up on me or failed to return my calls. Only four agreed to be interviewed. One, his supervisor at the jail, maintained that Kent had been a good employee, a fair jailer. During a telephone interview, another, a fellow deputy, insisted Kent was innocent. "I wouldn't let him around my wife if I didn't believe that," he said. But as we talked on, he described Kent as seething the night before Susan's killing, when Lieutenant Coons had told him of her allegations against him.

The third, another deputy, agreed to lunch at a Chinese restaurant. Although I waited more than an hour, he never arrived. From that day on, he didn't respond to my pages.

The fourth met with me in person, a deputy from another county who'd been a friend of McGowen's since high school. In his apartment early one evening, we had a long talk. He said Kent was working for him at a side business he'd begun with a friend, a wash-and-detail service for eighteen-wheelers. In charge of sales, Kent was trustworthy; his friend had never known him to lie. But just a few weeks later, the deputy wanted to talk again. By then the business deal had soured. McGowen, he said, had promised business that never materialized. Then he'd filed a complaint with the state employment commission, claiming unpaid back wages.

"He's using the system against me," said the irate

friend. "Now I can see how he could have done that to that woman, you know, manipulated the system to get to her."

The following week, Kent convinced one last person to talk to me: his father.

In a bustling noon-hour restaurant crowd, Bill Mc-Gowen fidgeted in his chair and bemoaned the persecution he claimed his family had endured since the night of the killing. "The D.A.'s office has ruined us," he lamented.

I asked about Kent's claims of a multimillion-dollar trust fund. Did it exist? "No," he said, describing it as nothing more than money he'd salted away for Kent's college, money he'd been forced to tap into during hard times.

Soon, he assured me, the family's luck would turn, repeating his son's claim that two state senators were looking into this "grave miscarriage of justice." Placing his battered brown briefcase on the table, he patted it.

"I've got a list in here of people who believe Kent's innocent," he declared.

A short time later, it was raining as we stood to leave. Bill McGowen opened that same briefcase to pull out his umbrella. I glanced inside and saw only a blank yellow legal pad, a pen, and a pencil.

In the days that followed, I investigated the allegations McGowen had made against White in his telephone call to me, most notably that his defense team had documentation of an incestuous relationship between White and her son.

"No," scoffed my source. "There were never allegations of that type of misconduct."

Meanwhile, Kent continued to make the news. In 1995, Michelle, his ex-wife, charged him with misdemeanor assault, breaking through the door to her rented home and attacking her with a telephone as she attempted to call police. Kent spent two weeks in jail while he gathered the money for bail. As was characteristic of their relationship and the love-hate swings common in such marriages, months later, before the assault case went to trial, Michelle wanted the charges dropped. The D.A.'s office refused. Kent eventually pleaded no contest and was sentenced to time already served. Since then, Kent and Michelle have reunited, and she's given birth to a fourth child, a daughter.

At the same time, Susan White's family pursued a federal civil rights lawsuit against both McGowen and Harris County. During the October 1996 civil trial, their attorneys argued that the county was negligent for hiring McGowen, that there was ample evidence available that he was a bad cop. Jurors agreed and awarded $5.3 million in damages. A federal appellate court later reversed the decision, dismissing the county from the lawsuit and awarding McGowen a new trial, ruling that attorneys representing Susan's family, including Jason, had failed to prove that the county knew or should have known that McGowen was likely to use aggressive force.

The criminal verdict faced a similar fate. To the chagrin of Edward Porter and many at the district attorney's office, in April 1997, the Fourteenth Court of Criminal Appeals reversed McGowen's murder conviction based on the sustained objection that prevented the defense team from offering an opening statement. The D.A.'s office has filed additional appeals, hoping to salvage McGowen's conviction. What will happen? "I've given up second-guessing judges," said the assistant D.A. in charge of appeals. One thing he felt reasonably sure of: The case of Kent McGowen would enter the new millennium without closure.

Much has changed in the years since Susan White's killing. In July 1994, four months after McGowen's trial ended, Ron Acreman, his former roommate, the muscular deputy who called himself The Ultimate Police Machine, was convicted of raping a woman he met at a nightclub and sentenced to seventeen years in prison.

In the sheriff's department, Lieutenant Jay Coons, who ignored White's entreaties for help, has been promoted. He's a captain now, working in the jail.

At H.C.S.D. there's been only one unofficial concession made since that August night in 1992. "Deputies aren't allowed to serve warrants on civilians who've complained about them," says a deputy. "We call it the McGowen Rule."

In 1997, Belinda Hill, who argued before jurors that Kent McGowen had no more right in Susan White's house than a burglar, left the district attorney's office when she was appointed to a Criminal State District Court judgeship by Governor George W. Bush. She won election to that same seat in 1998. Of the original prosecution team, only Edward Porter remains, waiting and watching patiently for that final court decision, the one that will put Kent McGowen either behind bars or before a jury in a new trial.

"I'll be there," says Porter. "I'm ready."

Still, second trials can be tricky. Memories fade and witnesses disappear. Will he be able to again piece together the fragments of evidence and convince a jury to look beyond the signed warrant Kent McGowen brought to Susan White's door that night? Will twelve more of McGowen's peers agree that when he squeezed the trigger in August 1992, he committed murder? There are, of course, no guarantees.

At Resa's, too, time has brought change. The Kellys divorced and Jim no longer lumbers through the place, telling backslapping jokes. It has a new name: Resa's Prime Steakhouse and Piano Bar. These days, the bar pulsates with energy. Two piano players, their long hair secured in ponytails, rotate nights, crying out decades-old songs, from Frank Sinatra to Eric Clapton, to an often overflowing audience.

Susan's friends no longer number among the throng.

Ray Valentine, Helen Bazata, Jean Morris, Alan Jefferies—they've all moved on, to other clubs in other towns, or simply to other parts of Houston. Rarely is Susan's name mentioned. No one muses about what has happened to that former deputy sheriff, the one who shot and killed the slender blond woman with the sad stories, the one who sat alone at the piano bar and requested a James Taylor song.

As the nineties drew to a close, even Susan's mother stopped her late-night phone calls. Perhaps she'd given up her search for justice. Perhaps she'd grown to fear that if Kent McGowen was ever punished for her daughter's killing, it would be many years in the future, long after she and her husband were dead.

"Didn't that jury say that deputy murdered my Susie?" she'd whispered.

Compelling True Crime Thrillers

PERFECT MURDER, PERFECT TOWN
THE UNCENSORED STORY OF THE JONBENET MURDER
AND THE GRAND JURY'S SEARCH FOR THE TRUTH
by Lawrence Schiller
0-06-109696-2/ $7.99 US/ $10.99 Can

A CALL FOR JUSTICE
A NEW ENGLAND TOWN'S FIGHT
TO KEEP A STONE COLD KILLER IN JAIL
by Denise Lang
0-380-78077-1/ $6.50 US/ $8.99 Can

SECRETS NEVER LIE
THE DEATH OF SARA TOKARS-
A SOUTHERN TRAGEDY OF MONEY, MURDER,
AND INNOCENCE BETRAYED
by Robin McDonald
0-380-77752-5/ $6.99 US/ $8.99 Can

THE GOODFELLA TAPES
by George Anastasia
0-380-79637-6/ $5.99 US/ $7.99 Can

THE SUMMER WIND
THOMAS CAPANO AND THE MURDER
OF ANNE MARIE FAHEY
by George Anastasia
0-06-103100-3/ $6.99 US/ $9.99 Can

A WARRANT TO KILL
A TRUE STORY OF OBSESSION,
LIES AND A KILLER COP
by Kathryn Casey
0-380-78041-0/ $6.99 US/ $9.99 Can
